"O" Level Law

Other M & E books of interest:

"O" Level Law

PETER SHEARS, BA, LLB
Senior Lecturer in Law at Plymouth Polytechnic

ADVISORY EDITOR
PAULENE COLLINS, LLB, LLM
Barrister, Head of the Department of Law at North Staffordshire Polytechnic, Formerly Chief Examiner in General Principles of English Law at Ordinary Level at the Associated Examining Board

MACDONALD AND EVANS

Macdonald & Evans Ltd
Estover Road Plymouth PL6 7PZ

First edition 1984

Macdonald & Evans Ltd 1984

British Library Cataloguing in Publication Data

Shears, Peter
 "O" level law.
 1. Law——England
 I. Title   II. Collins, Paulene
 344.2   KD661

 ISBN 0-7121-1542-0

Printed in Great Britain by Hollen Street Press,
Slough, Berks.

Preface

An increasing number of students are now taking "O" level law as part of their curriculum in schools and colleges of further education. It has been found to be a useful, interesting and informative subject for sixteen year olds and mature students alike whether studied full-time or part-time.

A new syllabus and examination, "General Principles of English Law", was introduced in 1983 by the Associated Examining Board, one of the major examining bodies, and this book has been written to meet the requirements of that syllabus at an appropriate level. However, it also covers the syllabuses at "O" level set by the Oxford and Welsh Examination Boards and much of the main content of the book is common to other general introductory courses in English law provided in polytechnics and colleges. It is also intended to be of interest to the general reader as a readable introduction to the workings of the English legal system and the basic principles of law.

Throughout the book every effort has been made to present the complexities of the law in as straightforward a manner as possible while giving sufficient detail to enable the student to answer examination questions satisfactorily. The early chapters of the book provide a broad introduction to the nature of the English legal system—the nature of law itself, how it is made, by whom, and how and where it is administered. Several chapters are set aside to consider the ways and means by which the rights and duties of individuals under the law are enforced while the rest of the book highlights individual areas of substantive law. Throughout continued reference to relevant case law and the latest statutory provisions illustrate the workings of the law and the legal system.

A bibliography of suggestions for further reading has been included for the assiduous student and the general reader wishing to increase his knowledge. In each case only the most recent edition should be obtained. A special feature of the book of help to both full-time and part-time students is the appendix on examination technique. This relates the types of mistakes commonly made by students and how they can be avoided, and gives hints and suggestions on various aspects such as how to plan for the examination day and how to approach essay and problem questions. A final appendix contains a selection of questions from previous "O" level examinations.

It is customary to acknowledge the help and advice of others and I would simply like to state that without the hard work of Paulene Collins this book would not have been published. Although I wrote the text in Cornwall I was working in America when the time came to read proofs and the Editor shouldered much of the hard work for me. Further thanks are also due to Carolyn Welch who conjured the typescript from my dreadful handwriting, and finally I would like to record my appreciation of the kindness of the University of Oxford Delegacy of Local Examinations and the Associated Examining Board for allowing me to reproduce questions from past papers.

I am, of course, responsible for any errors which remain. I have stated the law as I believe it to be on 1st January 1984.

Saltash, Cornwall,   PS
1984

Contents

Table of Cases

Table of Statutes

TABLE OF STATUTES xix

Chapter 1

What is Law?

DEFINING THE LAW

It's a bit like defining an elephant. You may have trouble constructing an acceptable definition of law, but you would recognise a law if you saw one.

The law is a civilising influence within a society. Some writers have argued that the progress of a society towards civilisation can be measured by the sophistication of its legal systems. As the society becomes more complex then the system of rules develops, along with the machinery for enforcing those rules effectively.

This is not to say that the rules necessarily reflect the developed wisdom or morality within society. There may emerge a congruence, but there is no necessary or precise link. Obviously, if there were little or no reflection of the popular view within the law, then respect for the law would be lost, but the great moral debates within a society do not necessarily result in legal reform.

At present one such issue centres on the "sanctity of life". This is reflected in debates on capital punishment and abortion, on suicide, euthanasia, on so-called mercy killings and particularly on nuclear arms. Another emphasis lies on the "quality of life", in discussions about family relationships, the ease and availability of divorce, adultery, "latch-key" children, pornography, and the spread of vile video cassettes, and so on.

Whilst a single debate might stimulate a reform of the law, the dynamic of discussion and debate within a society, continually developing, and re-evaluating moral standpoints, has no essential link with law and law reform. A definition of law ought to assist understanding of law. It ought to be an aid to elucidation. But there is no generally accepted definition. It could be described as a set of rules we live by that prescribes rights and duties, responsibilities and obligations for every member of the society we live in. These rules not only provide limits to what we can and cannot do, but they also prescribe the manner in which various ends can be achieved, for example, making a will.

Tighter definitions abound. Each reflects the attitude of its author towards the function of the law. As examples—"a coercive order of human behaviour" (Kelsen), "a body of principles" (Salmond), "rules of action" (Blackstone), "prophesies of what the courts will do" (Holmes), "what officials do about disputes" (Llewellyn).

The law must have something to do with rules and their enforcement. Some of these rules rely for their effectiveness upon the individual involved. For instance, if a toaster does not work properly the buyer should assert his rights within the contract by means of which he acquired it. Thus if the person trying to make toast for breakfast was the recipient of the toaster as a birthday present the buyer should complain. Only the parties to a contract can enforce it. Other rules will be enforced no matter what the individual wants. The victim of incest will not have the final say as to whether the offender is prosecuted. The client after a successful, hygienic, but unlawful abortion may be the last person to wish the offender punished—but the decision rests elsewhere. These differing aspects of the nature and purpose of the law must each be appreciated clearly.

This book is about English law. The Scots are a law unto themselves, and the Scottish legal system is also different. So too, although to a lesser extent, is the legal system in Northern Ireland. There are considerable and increasing overlaps between these legal systems within the United Kingdom as a whole. But this book is about English law and no rule should be assumed to extend beyond England and Wales.

CLASSIFYING THE LAW

For the purposes of understanding how the legal system fits together, it may be useful to examine a variety of ways in which it can be taken apart and each part examined. That is, there are several possible ways to classify the law.

Civil and Criminal law

This is the most basic of classifications. Very broadly, criminal law is concerned with the general well being and civil law with individual rights and duties. It might be wrong, however, to classify an individual act as being either a civil or a criminal wrong. Many acts are both. For example, if you take your coat to be cleaned and the cleaner steals it then, clearly, the crime of theft has been committed. Furthermore there is a breach of the contract to clean and a tort of conversion (denial of your right to your property) has also been committed. It is not in the act itself that the distinction lies, but in the consequences which may follow from it. After you have been run over in a road accident the driver could be arrested and charged with the crime of reckless driving and he could be sued by you, the victim, in the tort of negligence. The act of driving so as to injure you was therefore a criminal offence and a civil wrong. This is sometimes called "dual liability".

There have been attempts made at defining crime generally, but the criminal law really comprises nothing more than the total of those activities which those responsible for creating and developing the criminal law have seen fit to include. Lord Atkin said (in *Proprietary Articles* v. *Attorney-General for Canada* (1931)):

> The domain of criminal jurisprudence can only be ascertained by examining what acts at any particular period are declared by the State to be crimes and the only common nature they will be found to possess is that they are prohibited by the State and that those who commit them are punished.

The nature of criminal liability will be considered in more detail later (Chapter 14), but the activities embraced by the criminal law extend from treason, murder and rape at one end to exporting antiques without a licence, flying a kite near an airfield, "feeding" parking meters, failing to sign your driving licence, sounding the car horn while the car is at rest and conversing with a bus driver at the other.

Similarly, various aspects of civil law will be drawn out in more detail in subsequent chapters, but it should be understood that while the criminal law comprises most of what the average citizen imagines as the law (at least at first), the civil law is a vast thing—a thousand years old and still growing! The more important areas within its scope include contract law, which in its applied aspects includes the sale of goods and services, credit, hire-purchase, agency, contracts of employment and landlord and tenant agreements—to name but a few. The civil law also includes the law of tort—an umbrella term for actions in negligence, nuisance, defamation, trespass and others. Further, it includes property law, the law of succession, most of family law and the law of trusts.

Later (Chapters 6 and 7) attention will be drawn to the nature of proceedings in civil and criminal law. They are easily distinguished. The procedure is different. The point of the proceedings is different. The outcome is different. These distinctions are marked with differences in the terminology used. It is an elementary error to confuse the terminology and say, for example, "trespassers will be prosecuted" for they cannot be (except in rare instances such as squatting or where byelaws have made trespass criminal, e.g. on the railways). Trespass is (generally) a tort. Tort is civil law. In civil proceedings the plaintiff *sues* the defendant. If he succeeds he obtains judgment in his favour and he will be awarded a remedy, the point of which is to compensate him for the civil wrong which the defendant has been shown on a balance of probabilities to have done him. This remedy may take the form of an order that the defendant pay the plaintiff money (damages) or perform a contractual obligation (decree of specific performance) or desist from infringing the plaintiff's civil law rights (injunction) or transfer property to him. There are other civil remedies too.

Criminal proceedings, on the other hand, involve the prosecutor prosecuting the accused (or the defendant) so as to prove him guilty beyond reasonable doubt (so that the bench of magistrates or the jury, if there is one, are sure) and thus secure a conviction and a sentence, the point of which is to punish the convicted person and to deter him and others from such activity as gives rise to criminal proceedings. The range of punishment is wide. It extends from conditional discharges and even absolute discharges at the one end to life imprisonment at the other. The power of the court varies from offence to offence and indeed from court to court within the hierarchy of the court system. This range of possible sentences will be examined more closely later (Chapter 7).

Private and Public law

Civil law is sometimes called private law for the obvious reason of its content. It is the law concerned with private individuals and their rights and duties, voluntarily assumed or otherwise, towards other private individuals. In contrast is sometimes taken public law. This is a wider concept than criminal law, but it includes criminal law. Also included are constitutional, administrative and social welfare law. Together these four elements comprise that law which has a public, overall, character.

Constitutional law

Constitutional law, the law of the British constitution, is often said to be unwritten in the sense that there is no single document in Britain called "The Constitution". However every British protectorate and colony has one, and so does nearly every country in the world. The reasons for this state of affairs are historical. There has been no fresh start after a revolution or other landmark in our history, unlike in the United States or Malaysia. Nevertheless, there are many documents from which the British constitutional law can be collected. There are

Acts of Parliament, like the Bill of Rights 1689, the Act of Settlement 1701, the Act of Union with Scotland 1707 and the European Communities Act of 1972, all of which contain major rules of constitutional law. Rules of more detailed importance are to be found in such statutes as the Representation of the People Act 1983, the Peerage Act 1963 and the Parliament Acts of 1911 and 1949, amongst many others. It seems that every year statutes are made which add to the constitutional law.

Further to this the law is found in common law rules such as that fundamental rule which pronounces that Parliament is sovereign; a rule now effected by the European Communities Act 1972. Furthermore there is a collection of conventions which applies to the constitution and there are the residual powers within the Royal Prerogative. Finally there exists the law and custom of Parliament itself, concerning its functions, procedures, privileges and immunities. This, then, is the subject matter of constitutional law.

Administrative law

Administrative law is concerned with public authorities. It comprises the law relating to the formation, powers and duties of such authorities and the procedures involved when they are formed or where their powers are exercised, or duties fulfilled. It is also concerned with the relationships between such public authorities, between the authorities and their employers and between them and the public at large.

Administrative law can be seen as a network of controls over the use of public powers, but it also provides the means by which the workload of public authorities can be successfully achieved. It provides the means for getting things done.

The public authorities in question extend from the Crown through the nationalised industries, the Commission for Racial Equality, ACAS (the Advisory, Conciliation and Arbitration service), the BBC and Independent Broadcasting Authority, local government, the water boards, and many others, including the maze of administrative tribunals set up, amongst other things, to settle disputes about the use of public power.

Social welfare law

Social welfare law is a relatively recent arrival on the scene of public law. Lord Scarman has written:

> Social security is now the subject of rights and duties. Inevitably, therefore, it is a legal subject.

In 1942 the famous Beveridge Report on social insurance and allied
services was published. It described the aims of the social security
system as the fulfilment of need and the purpose of payments made
within its stunningly detailed rules and regulations as being:

> ... to abolish want by ensuring that every citizen willing to serve
> according to his powers has at all times an income sufficient to
> meet his responsibilities.

The McCarthy Report in 1972 in New Zealand stated a slightly
different aim for their social welfare law:

> ... to ensure that everyone is able to enjoy a standard of living
> much like that of the rest of the community, and thus is able to feel
> a sense of participation in and belonging to the community.

Whatever the aims, and whether or not it is successful as a means of
achieving them, social welfare law is concerned with the nature of
contributory and non-contributory benefits (i.e. whether or not the
claimant is paid according to a record of input into the system),
unemployment benefit and benefits for sickness, disability, invalidity, maternity, children, and death. It covers compensation for
industrial injuries, pensions on retirement and for war service.
Finally, it is concerned, increasingly these days, with the "topping up"
of income by means of supplementary benefit for those out of work,
and family income supplement for those working for very low pay.

Municipal and public international law

Another way of classifying the law is to split it between municipal and
public international law. Municipal law is the law of one state—in
our case the United Kingdom. Thus municipal law for this purpose
would comprise the law of England and Wales taken together with
that of Scotland and that of Northern Ireland. The distinction is
drawn between this, the law of a single state, and public international
law which regulates dealings between different states and which is
largely made up of treaties, conventions and international agreements.

COMMON LAW AND STATUTES

The whole of the law of England and Wales can be split according to
where it arose, that is, classified by source. The law is either made by
the judges—developing principles case by case, by analogy with
earlier cases, along fairly settled lines, as will be examined later

(Chapter 3) or it is made in a broad sweep by Parliament by means of statutes (Acts of Parliament). There is, as will be seen (Chapter 3) a prescribed method for the creation of a statute.

Judge-made law is called common law. In theory it is comprised of rules which already exist and simply require pronouncement by the judge. In fact, of course, judicial creativity does exist, although it varies between judges. Acts of Parliament (statutes) sometimes enable others (e.g. ministers, local authorities) to make law on a very restricted basis. These laws appear as "rules" or "regulations" or "byelaws" and whilst they are made by others they possess the delegated authority of Parliament. All this law made by or on behalf of Parliament, taken together, is called legislation. Contract law and the law of tort are almost entirely common law. Company law and the law of employment have been created almost entirely by means of legislation.

COMMON LAW AND EQUITY

"Common law" is a slippery phrase. It is used to distinguish judge-made law from law made by Parliament. It is also used to distinguish that law originating from the English system as exported to other nations and law made along the lines of Roman law, called civil or civilian law. It is essential to be careful with terminology, not just with the terms used but also with their context. This classification takes the phrase "common law" yet again and uses it to distinguish the law developed by the judges (as opposed to legislation) and to pick out the law which dates back across the centuries to the old common law courts and that law which (although developed by the judges) dates back to the Court of Chancery (the court from which the modern Chancery Division was developed: *see* Chapters 2 and 4). This is a body of law called "equity". It is important to be able to spot equitable laws and principles and to be able to distinguish them from common law rules and principles. To do this requires some grasp of the history which gave rise to these two systems or strains of law within the English law taken as a whole. This brief look at English legal history will be taken next.

Chapter 2

How the Law has Grown

LAW BEFORE THE NORMAN CONQUEST

English law in any overall sense dates back to the Norman Conquest. Before then no unified system of law existed over the country. Indeed the country itself was unrecognisable as the unified whole, with a central government, as is so familiar today.

The picture before the Conquest was one of a country split into shires. The shires were split into hundreds and the hundreds into vills or townships. Life was local. Law was local. It was based on local custom. It was administered in local courts. These were at the hundred level and at the shire level. There were also at about this time courts organised by the local landowners called manorial or seignorial courts.

There were broad laws initiated by the Anglo-Saxon Kings. They were called dooms, but they were not often made. There was a council of advisers around the king, called the Witan but in as much as it had any judicial function it served only to settle disputes between the larger landowners. It was a political forum for the few.

LAW AFTER THE CONQUEST

Some of the effects of the Norman Conquest were to centralise the focus of the legal system, to unify the disparate local customs into one law common to the whole country (common law), and to create the basic structure of the court system which lasted until the late nineteenth century and beyond—but all that took hundreds of years.

It would have been impossible, for example, for the Norman king to abolish the local courts run by the lords of the manor and assume their jurisdiction. There was no legal obstacle, but these courts were an important source of income to the lords and no diminution escaped resistance from them. The central system of courts gradually took over and the manorial courts wasted away—over about 300 years.

An interesting factor in this fading away was the Statute of Gloucester 1278, which provided that no personal action for less than £2 could be commenced in the royal courts. This was an attempt to maintain the jurisdiction and existence of the local courts. However, the common law judges in the royal courts took it to mean that no action for more than £2 could be dealt with by the local courts. So, with the fall in the value of money which seems inevitable over time, the jurisdiction wasted away.

Another important factor in the centralisation of judicial activity was the emergence and evolution of the writ system.

THE WRIT SYSTEM

A writ was the document necessary to start an action in a royal court. It was a sealed letter, sent in the name of the king, containing instructions for the recipient. For example, if the plaintiff, the complaining party, wanted to obtain redress for injuries to himself or his property, he would pay for the issue of a writ of trespass. The letter was addressed to the sheriff of the county where the cause of action arose. It commanded the officer to see to it that the defendant, the person alleged to have wronged the plaintiff, be brought before the royal justices to answer for his actions.

Writs were obtained from the Chancery Writ Office, a department of state. If there was no writ on the register of writs (in stock, as it were) to cover the particular claim the plaintiff wished to bring, then, for an extra fee, the clerks would produce one to fit. However, this rather haphazard manner of law making was largely brought to an end in the thirteenth century. The combined effect of the Provisions of Oxford 1258 and the Statute of Westminster II 1285 was to allow the creation of new writs only where they were very similar to existing ones. Nevertheless, this gradual method of development did provide the basis of much of the common law we have today. Much of the development was based upon the old writ of trespass.

THE CURIA REGIS

In as much as the Anglo-Saxon kings had gathered around their close advisers and friends (the Witan), the Norman kings had a far more formal institution called the Curia Regis or "King's Court". The Curia formed the central administration. It comprised the king and his most powerful underlings, the great land barons, and a host of lesser members who gradually became specialised in various areas of administration. The full Curia met several times each year, a scene of great pomp and ceremony, but the administrators met more often.

Parliament can be traced back to the larger meetings, the court system to the lesser.

THE ROYAL COURTS AND JUDGES; THE EMERGENCE OF THE COMMON LAW

The royal courts, before which the parties named in the various writs were ordered to appear, were presided over by officials sent from the Curia called itinerant justices. They acquired this name because their journeys were regular and fairly predictable. Unless they were killed by dissatisfied litigants (far from unknown), they would follow the circuits traced most clearly under the reign of Henry II (1159-1189), to whom we owe a great debt for the structure of the legal system. Indeed the circuits survive today, and were in regular use until the early 1970s.

Royal officials had visited locally and extensively for the first time in 1085 and 1086 during the compilation of the "Doomsday Book"—an amazing achievement, without parallel in European history, and only possible in a conquered country. It shows the activity of William I as an administrator and systematiser rather than as a legislator. The original two volumes, and the chest constructed for their preservation, are still to be found in London. In the Middle Ages it was so respected that it was referred to simply as "The Record". Every county, every village is described; all the owners and servants were noted; even the livestock was counted. The objects were to establish the rights of the Crown, owner of everything by conquest, and, more importantly, to establish the potential for taxation. The reverence for "The Record" is thought to underlie the respect still paid to official records kept by the administration and by the courts. Indeed it is not too much of a leap in imagination to see these royal officials, representatives of the king, the apex of the feudal structure of the country, becoming judicial officials, royal justices. They called on a regular basis for administrative and, later, judicial purposes.

The idea of a judge on circuit is very familiar. Even in the worst "western" films an accused is thrown into jail until the judge visits town. It was much the same with the itinerant justices. Whilst it was a reliable and attractive, although expensive, proposition to have a dispute settled in the royal courts at Westminster, it was a more realistic proposition to have it settled locally and avoid the bother, expense and danger of travel. Thus the royal courts sitting locally became increasingly popular.

The law applied in these local courts was, obviously, the local customary law. Gradually, however, by a process of sifting and choosing between varying local customs found whilst on circuit, the justices, when meeting together at Westminster (where they were based), gently moulded together the common law, the law common to the whole country.

The process was neither simple nor swift, but it seems largely to have been completed by about 1250 when Henry of Bratton, or Bracton as he is commonly called, the first great writer of English law wrote his *Treatise on the Law of England*. This very important work created the impression of English law as a whole body of connected principles. He cites more than 500 cases of the king's judges. He was a judge himself, working mostly in Devonshire. From his work it is clear to see the emergence of the use of past cases as authority for the result of the case in hand. This is broadly called the doctrine of precedent. It is vital to the development of our law today. By this time the king's courts were the arenas for most cases of importance (except those involving ecclesiastical disputes). There were few statutes to hamper the judges. There was little of the pressure of Parliament (so familiar today) against the orderly development of the law. There are few local customs which deviate from the common law. As the royal courts supplanted the local courts so the common law replaced local customs. Their procedure was better. Trial by jury was developed.

There are few landmark dates, but 1215 is one: the Lateran Council then forbade the involvement of the clergy in the awful trials by ordeal. Since no representative of the Almighty to whom the settlement of the question had been submitted was available, trial by ordeal vanished, to be replaced with trial by jury. The importance of the local courts was further eroded.

The central royal courts at Westminster developed gradually from the administrative functions of the Curia Regis. The first was the Court of Exchequer, which emerged from the tax department of the Curia as the arena for the settlement of revenue disputes although this jurisdiction was widened by various methods. For example, the court obtained jurisdiction to try cases brought over debts by use of a trick (properly called a legal fiction) called *quominus*. It worked like this: A cannot pay money he owes the Exchequer because he has none. However, B owes A money and it is for this reason that A is less able to pay (*quominus* means "by which the less"). Therefore if the court were to reconcile the dispute over the debt it would be able to enforce the issue of revenue collection, its proper function. The jurisdictional distinctions between the common law courts grew very cloudy.

The next to appear was the Court of Common Pleas, which was basically a court for the adjudication of civil disputes between individuals. This was created by Henry II in answer to a promise in Magna Carta (1215) to have a fixed place for the settlement of "common pleas".

The third court was called the Court of King's Bench. It developed from hearings of both civil and criminal matters within the Curia at meetings "coram rege" ("in the presence of the king"). Apart from civil and criminal work the Court of King's Bench, presumably because of its royal origin, possessed a supervisory jurisdiction over the procedures used (although not strictly the decisions taken) in the other courts.

THE DEVELOPMENT OF EQUITY

By the thirteenth century there were problems in these common law courts. The judges were professional lawyers, whereas before they had been clerics. As lawyers they seemed more devoted to procedural matters than the development of the law and its use to achieve justice in individual cases. So much so that litigants who made procedural errors had their cases dismissed—whatever the depth of injustice they had suffered.

More specifically, many potential litigants were unable to bring actions before the courts because there was no writ on the Register of Writs to match the claim they wished to bring. The creation of entirely new writs had been stopped, so novel actions went unheard. Obviously, to bring an action on the writ closest to the claim amounted to a procedural error, and a waste of time and, importantly, money. Furthermore, even if a suitable writ could be found the only remedy available to the successful plaintiff was damages. The basic common law remedy was, and is, damages. There were plaintiffs for whom damages, a financial award, were inadequate or unsuitable. The plaintiff wanted his property back, not its monetary value. He wanted a persistent infringement of his legal rights stopped, not an award of money to compensate for the interference. So for these procedural and substantive reasons there grew a need for an alternative approach.

In a feudal system with a strong centralised administration, the logical avenue of complaint at the shortcomings of the mechanisms provided is towards the centre, to the king. Dissatisfied claimants petitioned the king in person. At first these petitions were dealt with individually by the king and justice was administered by him as the "fountain of justice", despite the rules and procedures of the courts. Naturally the pressures grew. Equally naturally the work was delegated.

A central figure in the administration, the Curia Regis, was the Chancellor. He was responsible for the chancery where his clerks issued writs to prospective litigants. He was the logical choice of official to deal with petitions about injustice on behalf of the king.

At first these were dealt with at formal meetings within the Curia. By the mid-fourteenth century petitions were addressed to the Chancellor alone rather than to the king or the Curia. In 1474 there is recorded the first case where the Chancellor issued a decree in his own name rather than in the name of the king. The Court of Chancery had emerged.

Over the years a body of principles developed within this court. This became known as Equity. It was (and is) not a systematic body of law. It was never intended to be so. It was only developed as and when the procedure or the substance or the remedy offered within the common law courts was seen to be inadequate.

As Lord Cowper explained (in *Dudley* v. *Dudley* (1705)):

> Now equity is no part of the law, but a moral virtue, which qualifies, moderates, and reforms the rigour, hardness, and edge of the law, and is a universal truth; it does also assist the law where it is defective and weak in the constitution (which is the life of the law) and defends the law from crafty evasions, delusions, and new subtleties, invented and contrived to evade and delude the common law, whereby such as have undoubted right are made remediless; and this is the office of equity, to support and protect the common law from shifts and crafty contrivances against the justice of the law. Equity therefore does not destroy the law, nor create it, but assist it.

So it is today. There is a supplementary system of law called equity. The most important part of it is the law of trusts. It is no longer necessary to go to a different kind of court to bring an action on, for example, a trust. The court system was radically restructured by the Judicature Acts of 1873-1875. It is true that the work of the courts is split amongst them for administrative convenience, but the necessity to go to court twice for, say, damages as compensation for an infringement of legal rights in the past (common law court) and then an injunction to prevent repetition in the future (court of equity) has gone. The administration of the two systems—the mainstream common law and the supplementary tributary equity—has been merged, although the systems themselves remain separate.

It follows that if a plaintiff is seeking a remedy which lies in the traditional jurisdiction of equity—say an injunction to prevent unlawful behaviour in future, or a decree of specific performance whereby the court will instruct an unco-operative party to a contract to perform his side of the bargain—then that plaintiff must satisfy the same standards which were required by the Chancellor back in the fourteenth century. The award of an equitable remedy lies in the discretion of the court. On the other hand the award of damages in an action based on principles of common law is automatic. The successful plaintiff must get damages if he proves his case (although the amount of money, called the "quantum" is for the court to decide).

These standards required by the Chancellor included, for example, that the petitioner must have come "with clean hands". This means that a petition based on unfairness and injustice by the defendant could not be brought by a plaintiff who himself had acted unfairly or unjustly. Consider, for example, the plaintiff in the case *Overton* v. *Bannister* (1844). Here a minor was entitled to benefit from a trust on attaining full age. She masqueraded herself as having done so, and the trustees paid up. Later when she really did come of age she sued them, asking to be paid again. She could prove her real age. The strict construction of the trust documents might have indicated that she had a right to be paid. However the case concerned the law of trusts, a part of the law of equity developed by the Court of Chancery over the centuries on the basis of justice, fairness and good conscience. Naturally the plaintiff lost.

Another centrally important feature, or maxim, of equity is "delay defeats equity". The complaint is of unfairness and injustice and the petition is for a remedy. It is not surprising, then, that the court would (and will) refuse to award an equitable remedy if the plaintiff has delayed making his application. As Lord Camden said (in *Smith* v. *Clay* (1767)):

> A court of equity has always refused its aid to stale demands when a party has slept upon his rights and acquiesced for a great length of time. Nothing can call forth this court into activity but conscience, good faith and reasonable diligence.

In the early days the Court of Chancery acted in inconsistent ways, case by case, each on its merits. Indeed the Chancellor's judgment of fairness and justice varied as between successive holders of the office. So much so that one of the greatest English historical scholars, John Selden (who lived from 1584 to 1654), wrote:

> Equity is a roguish thing, for it varies with the length of the Chancellor's foot.

It would be a mistake to regard equity today as being anything haphazard. It is rooted in a sense of natural justice, but it is staked and fixed by the doctrine of precedent and by the laws of evidence and procedure to the same extent as the common law. It is, however, still true to say that whereas the occasion upon which an equitable remedy can be sought is settled, its actual award is still at the discretion of the court.

Chapter 3

How the Law is Made: the Sources of Law

"When I use a word", Humpty Dumpty said in a rather scornful tone, "it means just what I choose it to mean—neither more nor less" (Lewis Carroll).

HISTORICAL SOURCES

Looking back over English legal history (as we did a little in Chapter 2) it is plain to see that the old local customs found in England at and around the time of the Norman Conquest are the historical source of our common law. They were moulded together, over a period of many years, by the itinerant justices so as to form a recognisable body of law common to the whole country. We also saw (in Chapter 2) that the methods and rulings of the old Court of Chancery can be regarded as the historical source of the supplementary system of law which is called Equity. One of the difficulties in discussing "sources" of law is that much depends on what you mean by "sources"—and it is here that Humpty Dumpty's remark comes to the fore.

These are broad, long-range ideas of historical sources of law. Views can be shorter and more specific. For example, the Supply of Goods and Services Act 1982 was based upon two reports: one from the Law Commission (No. 94) and the other from the National Consumer Council (*Service Please*, October 1981). So it could be said that these reports are the historical sources of the 1982 Act.

LITERARY SOURCES

These are sometimes called information sources. The literary source of any law is where we go to find it written down. It might be within an Act of Parliament. Old Acts are published in the Statutes of the Realm (1235-1713), the Statutes Revised (1235-1948) and in other works. New statutes are published by Her Majesty's Stationery Office (HMSO) as and when they are passed. It is important to look over a few Acts, to become familiar with the layout and (sometimes strange) terminology which is used.

If the law is not within an Act, then it might be traceable to the judgment in a particular case. It will be necessary to look up the decision in the law reports. There are a number of such reports published. The most authoritative are those produced under the auspices of the Incorporated Council of Law Reporting, called the "Law Reports", and the "Weekly Law Reports", although there are also many reliable reports published by others. The best known are the "All England Law Reports". Law reports are a record of what the judge actually said in the case. They make interesting reading.

LEGAL SOURCES

The phrase "legal sources of law" seems a little circular. The legal source of law is that characteristic of it which makes it more than just a rule which can be followed or not. It is the source which gives the law its legal validity and quality. It makes the rule binding as law.

There are only three methods by which a rule can be made valid as a law and unless one of them is used precisely then the rule is not a law. These methods establish the legal sources.

LEGISLATION

Legislation comprises Acts of Parliament, often called statutes together with various rules, regulations and byelaws which are made by others with the authority of Parliament delegated to them by Act of Parliament. Collectively, this law is called delegated legislation.

An Act of Parliament always begins with the same words:

> Be it enacted by the Queen's most Excellent Majesty, by and with the advice and consent of the Lords Spiritual and Temporal, and Commons, in this present Parliament assembled, and by the authority of the same, as follows:

What follows is law.

The Act might have been created for any of several purposes. Some Acts openly create new law. For example, the Transport Act 1981 lowered the maximum engine size which a provisional licence holding motor cyclist can ride to 125 cc from 250 cc. It also introduced the compulsory wearing of seat belts in cars. Incidentally, these changes were brought about by this 1981 Act amending an earlier Act, the Road Traffic Act 1972, which contains most of the law about road traffic matters. It is common for statutes to contain sections which have this amending effect on earlier Acts.

If the Act was not designed to create new law, it might be a repealing measure. For example, the Trade Union and Labour Relations Act 1974 was designed, amongst other things, to repeal the controversial Industrial Relations Act 1971.

Alternatively the Act might be a measure designed to tidy up the law, such as a consolidating statute, which draws together existing statute law on one subject under one heading; one example of this is the Sale of Goods Act 1979 which gathered together the old Sale of Goods Act 1893 and the four intervening amending statutes. In a sense, then, the 1979 Act is a republication of the 1893 Act in its current form. Another tidying up measure is a codifying Act. This gathers together all the existing law on a given topic—statutes, cases, regulations and all. The old Sale of Goods Act 1893 was a good example of such a measure. Sir Mackenzie Chalmers drew together all the existing laws, from all sources, into a codified whole.

Taking the sale of goods legislation in its present form, then, we have a consolidated code! (The code in 1893, amended by subsequent Acts which were gathered together in 1979.)

Once a statute is made it must be repealed for it to lose its validity as law. It does not fade away like old soldiers—although many statutes do become obsolete. We have the Law Commission now, to spot them and recommend their repeal. Parliament can make or unmake any law it chooses. This is called parliamentary sovereignty. It was lucidly defined in 1885 by A. V. Dicey, one of our greatest writers on constitutional law.

> The principle of parliamentary sovereignty means neither more nor less than this, namely, that Parliament thus defined has, under the English constitution, the right to make or unmake any law whatever; and, further, that no person or body is recognised by the law of England as having a right to override or set aside the legislation of Parliament.

It has been argued, however, that since the Treaty of Accession was signed on 22nd January 1972, we have parted with a little of this sovereignty in joining the European Communities. Not that the treaty is law here, but the statute implementing it is—as Lord Denning said (in *Blackburn* v. *Attorney-General* (1971)):

> It is elementary that these courts take no notice of treaties until they are embodied in laws enacted by Parliament, and then only to the extent that Parliament tells us.

We will return to check the extent to which the European

Communities can make law for us, but first it is important to see just how Parliament creates a statute. It is the most powerful form of law. Law can be made in the form of regulations, and so on, by those delegated sufficient authority by Parliament; it can be made, or at least developed, by judges in individual cases but Parliament can sweep away acres of case law, custom, rules and regulations and earlier statutes too, by a single Act. We must see how it is done.

Creating a statute

A government with a working majority will dominate law-making by Parliament. Manifesto promises appear as discussion documents (called green or white papers) and later as debating documents for the Houses of Parliament called Bills. It would be wrong, however, to assume that all government backed Bills are the result of manifesto promises. Of the bills introduced by the 1970-74 Conservative Government only 8 per cent. were attributable to their election manifesto. The 1974-79 Labour Government figure was 13 per cent. Some 81 per cent. and 75 per cent. respectively of the Bills introduced originated in government departments. The rest were emergency measures (e.g. the Drought Act 1976). Parliament also debated private members' Bills.

It is possible for any of the 650 members of the House of Commons to introduce a private member's Bill. Unless the government supports the idea (whether actively or passively by not opposing it) then the Bill has little chance of enactment. Each year there is a ballot of those members who wish to introduce Bills privately. The top 20 names are guaranteed time to introduce a Bill. There are ten Fridays, from 9.30 am to 2.30 pm set aside. The top six in the ballot generally have a good chance of success. Pressure groups like the Consumers' Association, Justice, the Howard League for Penal Reform and many others hang like wasps round a jam jar, awaiting the result of the ballot, prepared to bombard the successful few with many new ideas.

It is also possible for a private member to introduce a bill under the "ten minute rules" (S.O. 13). If given prior leave, a member may speak in favour of the introduction of a Bill for ten minutes after Question Time on Tuesdays and Wednesdays. This timing ensures publicity, and this is the general idea. Very few such speeches result in statutes, although the Murder (Abolition of the Death Penalty) Act 1965 started in this way.

The central point of government power lies within the Cabinet. This is a committee of about 20 members, personally selected by the Prime Minister. Within the Cabinet there are many sub-groups called

Cabinet committees. One such group is chaired by the Leader of the House of Commons. It is responsible for considering proposals for new legislation brought by government departments. It is also responsible for the preparation of the Queen's Speech. This is read by the monarch at the beginning of each session of Parliament (which runs from November to October) and lays out the proposals for legislation that year. There is a second Cabinet committee called the Legislation Committee. It is chaired by the Lord Chancellor, and it is responsible for the implementation of the timetabled programme. The Bills, the debating documents, are drafted by specialists called parliamentary counsel. The most important Bills are public bills, designed to change the general law throughout England and Wales. If Scotland is to be included it must be expressly included, and sometimes a parallel Bill for Scottish Law will be enacted.

Parliament also debates private Bills. These are sponsored by local authorities, public corporations and a few by large public companies. Obviously, they are designed to affect only the legal position of the private sponsor.

Bills can be presented in either of the Houses of Parliament, but they must pass through both. As a general rule, the less controversial Bills (e.g. consolidation measures) are introduced into the Lords first and the ones likely to cause more fuss are read first in the Commons.

The enactment of a bill

There are a number of formal stages through which a Bill must pass before it becomes an Act and therefore law. Each is a kind of hurdle. There is debate and discussion at all but the initial stage. The process enables government back-benchers to participate, and it also gives the opposition a chance to impress the electorate. Furthermore, it provides a number of occasions upon which the government can reconsider its proposals and perhaps modify them, if necessary. There is, therefore, a tangled web of politics woven into what might otherwise appear to be a rather dry procedure for lawmaking.

We will consider the enactment of a public Bill which is introduced first in the House of Commons. The vast majority of such introductions are made by written notice (S. O. 37 (1)). Every day in Parliament there is an order paper, a kind of agenda for the meeting. On the order paper for the chosen day there appears the title of the Bill and the names of those promoting it. At the beginning of public business the Speaker (the chairman) calls upon the member who formally hands a document made to look like a Bill to the clerk. If the introduction is made by a minister then a short speech will be made to move the presentation of the bill. The clerk will then read out the title of the bill. No questions are put. This is called the first reading. A day is chosen for the second reading and an order is made for the Bill to be copied and distributed.

When the day for the second reading arrives there are two possible methods of handling it. If the Bill is not very controversial then it can be referred to a second reading committee which reports back to the House and recommends a formal acceptance of the Bill without debate. This saves the time of the rest of the House. However, if 20 members object then this cannot be done so there does not have to be much controversy amongst the 650 members to mean that a second reading debate must take place. This debate is, in theory, as Erskine May (a famous writer about parliamentary procedures) puts it:

> the most important stage through which the Bill is required to pass; for its whole principle is then at issue, and is affirmed or denied by a vote of the House.

In fact, with a working majority for the government, the result is not in doubt and the debate (on the outlines and principles of the Bill rather than the fine details) loses its edge. If the Bill would require expenditure then the House must pass a financial resolution at this stage. This has the effect of limiting the possibilities of expansion, and increased expenditure, in later stages.

The first reading was very brief and formal; the second a debate only in outline. It is the next stage at which the details of the Bill are examined: this is the committee stage.

Most Bills are dealt with by standing committees of between about 15 and 50 MPs. There are usually about ten working on Bills at any one time. This obviously saves time on the floor of the House, although where a Bill is particularly important (e.g. the bill for the European Communities Act 1972), then this stage is taken on the floor in committee of the whole House. The members of these committees are chosen for their qualifications and interests and the party balance generally reflects that in the House. Therefore if the government has a large majority there it will control the committees too, and it is likely that the Bill going into committee will emerge with very few changes, apart, perhaps from those inserted by the appropriate minister, reflecting his second thoughts.

It is possible to refer the bill to either a select committee of one House or a joint committee of both. Such committees can take evidence from interested bodies, but these powers are little used. There has been an interesting experiment recently with special standing committees. Such a committee considered the Bill for the Mental Health (Amendment) Act 1982. Such committees are able to meet on up to three occasions as if they were select committees, receiving evidence. Thereafter they proceed clause by clause as usual. It seems a good idea for the future.

Once the committee has finished with the Bill it goes back to the House for the report stage at which the committee chairman produces the refined product for the scrutiny of the House. Amendments can be made (or unmade if the government was defeated in committee). This is the symbolic gesture of the whole House assuming responsibility for the Bill. Even if no amendment has been made, the Bill must be reported. Only if the Bill has been considered by committee of the whole House is this stage dispensed with.

The last stage in the Commons is the third reading. It usually follows immediately on the report stage and is taken without debate unless six or more members object. Where the Bill is debated here only verbal changes can be made. The principles of the Bill are now settled. This is the last opportunity for the House to reject the Bill before it passes on to the Lords for their consideration. If the vote is carried the Bill is said to have "passed through the House".

In the Lords the bill goes through substantially the same stages again. Often the committee stage of the Bill is taken by the whole House rather than by a small group of members as happens in the House of Commons. The atmosphere is more informal. The vitriolic exchanges in the other House are rarely heard.

When the Bill emerges from the Lords it may well have been altered. Sometimes this is a reflection of the inbuilt Conservative majority there. The Bill now returns to the Commons for reconsideration in its amended form. If the changes are not acceptable they are unmade and the Bill is sent back to the Lords. Usually a compromise is reached. If it cannot be, then the Commons have the last word.

The Parliament Acts 1911 and 1949 have curtailed the power of the Lords to use their power to delay. This allows them to hold up a money bill (certified as such by the Speaker) for a month and any other Bill for a year. The Lords can no longer stop a Bill becoming law if the elected chamber wishes it to be enacted. The Welsh Church Act 1914, the Government of Ireland Act 1914 and the Parliament Act 1949 were passed without the Lords' assent. The procedure was threatened in the Trade Union and Labour Relations (Amendment) Bills 1975, 1976 and the Aircraft and Shipbuilding Industries Bills in 1976 and 1977—but a compromise was reached in these instances.

The final stage of enactment is the royal assent. A pure formality today, it was last refused in 1707. It may be given by the sovereign in person. This was last done in 1854. It may be signified on her behalf by specially appointed officers called commissioners. The usual procedure (under the Royal Assent Act 1967) is that the chairman in each House (the Speaker and the Lord Chancellor) simply notifies the assent to both House. The words of the royal assent are "la reyne le veult" for public Bills and "la reyne remercie ses bons sujets, accepte leur benevolence et ainsi le veult" for financial Bills.

Once the assent has been given, personally, by the commissioners or (as is usual) by notification the Bill becomes law. It has been enacted.

Delegated legislation

Not all our law is made by our Parliament. Some is made by others who are authorised to do so by Parliament. These laws are just as effective as sources of rights and duties as are Acts of Parliament. The law made by means of delegated authority is called delegated legislation. This lawmaking power is always delegated within very strict limits. It is not a new idea, nor a reflection of the march of technological progress, although this has had an effect on the amount of rules, regulations, orders and so on, which are now made in this way. The practice of delegating authority was seen in 1832, in the Cholera Prevention Act (2 & 3 Will. 4, c. 10 the way statutes used to be named), which was designed to resist the spread of the dreadful disease of cholera. See how the power is delegated so that urgent requirements can be met without constant referral to Parliament. This is one of the main reasons for Parliament delegating authority.

> Whereas it has pleased Almighty God to visit the United Kingdom with the disease called the cholera . . . and whereas with a view to prevent as far as may be possible, by the Divine Blessing the spreading of the said disease, it may be necessary that rules and regulations may from time to time be established within cities, towns or districts affected with or which may be threatened by the said disease, but it may be impossible to establish such rules and regulations by the authority of Parliament with sufficient promptitude to meet the exigency of any such case as may occur.

More recently, the Consumer Safety Act 1978 was designed to prevent the spread of dangerous goods. The precise content of the necessary controls may be beyond the expertise of Parliament, and would certainly take up a lot of valuable time. So the authority to make the necessary regulations has been delegated:

> 1(1) The Secretary of State may make regulations containing such provision . . . as the Secretary of State thinks appropriate for the

purpose of securing that goods are safe or that appropriate information is provided and inappropriate information is not provided in respect of goods.

The laws which are made using authority delegated by such statutes appear in one of three main forms.

The first, and most dignified, is the Order in Council. These are used to implement matters of major importance. For example, during the Second World War the government acted by Order in Council in the exercise of powers delegated by the Emergency Powers (Defence) Acts 1939 and 1940. These orders are drafted by the appropriate government department and rubber stamped by the Queen in Council—an echo of the Queen and her court of advisers.

The second form is the byelaw. These are rules made by an authority subordinate to Parliament (e.g. local authorities and the British Railways Board) for the regulation, administration or management of their district or property or undertaking. In the Local Government Act 1972, for example, it says:

235 (1) The council of a district and the council of a London borough may make byelaws for the good rule and government of the whole or any part of the district or borough, as the case may be, and for the prevention and suppression of nuisances therein.

It is usual to find posters containing the local byelaws on signs at the corners of commons or on lamp posts.

The third form that delegated legislation takes is the detailed variety of regulations, orders, rules, schemes, warrants and directions and so on, whatever the term used in the enabling Act.

There is substantial criticism of the increased delegation of lawmaking power. It is said to be given to those who are not answerable at the ballot box, since, in reality, the instrument containing the law is drafted by the civil service, not the minister. Furthermore it is said that the old maxim *ignorantia juris non excusat* (ignorance of the law is no excuse) can hardly be accurate these days when there are more than 2,000 statutory instruments made each year—over, 5,000 pages of them. (In 1974 there were 8,669 pages!) It is added that Parliament does not scrutinise the exercise of its delegated power sufficiently. There is often some distance between the grant and use of such power; the Emergency Powers (Defence) Act 1939, for example, conferred power to make regulations, orders under the regulations, directions under the orders and licences under the directions.

To answer these criticisms there must be convincing reasons for delegating authority. Obviously, a great deal of parliamentary time is saved. Only about 100 working days of each parliamentary session are used for the legislative programme, and the government simply could not keep to its timetable without delegating the detailed lawmaking to others. Secondly, there may be emergencies to be met. There is a need for the power to make law quickly. Parliament is not always sitting, and rarely acts quickly even when it is. Thirdly, the increased technicality of life requires increasingly technical law, beyond the expertise of most members of Parliament. Ministers are given power and the duty to consult experts while using it. Similarly, local knowledge is required to make useful byelaws for any particular district. It is obviously necessary to delegate power to the locally elected representatives.

These are the reasons for delegating power. It is argued that adequate controls do exist over its use. Parliament can revoke the grant of power. It retains the right to legislate in the same areas. There is a Joint Scrutiny Committee which has responsibility for keeping an eye on the use of the delegated authority, and drawing the attention of Parliament to any controversial measures. Sometimes (rarely) the enabling Act requires that Parliament itself must approve an instrument. The courts can be asked to examine whether an instrument has been drafted outside the limits of the delegated power (*ultra vires*). Parliament itself calls to account the responsible minister at Question Time. It is a sound quality control where the minister must answer for his department's activities.

LAW FROM THE EUROPEAN COMMUNITIES

Since the United Kingdom agreed to join the European Communities in 1972 there has been a new source of law. The Treaty of Accession was implemented by the European Communities Act 1972. Under this Act the institutions of the communities have legislative power over the UK:

2 (1) All such rights, powers, liabilities, obligations and restrictions from time to time created or arising by or under the Treaties, and all such remedies and procedures from time to time provided for by or under the Treaties are without further enactment to be given legal effect or used in the United Kingdom shall be recognised and available in law, and be enforced, allowed and followed accordingly.

The importance of Community law cannot be overstated. Lord Denning said (in *Bulmer* v. *Bollinger* (1974)):

> ... when we come to matters with a European element the Treaty
> is like an incoming tide. It flows into the estuaries and up the
> rivers. It cannot be held back.

On the other hand, community law does not affect the whole of our
law. When it exists it is so important as to outweigh our law, but it is
only found in such areas as agriculture, the free movement of
workers, social security, competition and some aspects of company
law.

The foundation stones of community law are the treaties. These are
the Treaty of Paris (1951) which established the European Coal and
Steel Community and the two Treaties of Rome (1957) which
established the European Atomic Energy Community and the
European Economic Community.

The basic policies embraced by these treaties are implemented and
developed by means of various instruments which are usually drawn
up by the European Commission and sent for agreement to the
Council of Ministers. The Commission works closely with the
governments and civil servants of member states. Indeed, it has been
argued that the United Kingdom government is now free to act (if
other member states agree) as a legislative authority, avoiding the
scrutiny and control of Parliament, by initiating changes in
community law which then have direct effects on English law. The
European Commission is a committee of 14: there are two
commissioners each from France, Italy, Germany and the United
Kingdom, and one from each of the other member states. This
Commission is supposed to have a European point of view and in
some areas, such as the fine details of law about agriculture, it has
legislative power itself, delegated to it by the Council of Ministers.
The Council, which is composed of a senior minister from each of the
ten member states, is overtly nationalist in viewpoint. Each member
speaks for his own state. There is also a European Assembly which
has 434 directly elected members and little practical power, although
its opinion is usually sought about legislative proposals. It has the
power to remove the Commission from office if it can muster a two-
thirds majority to do so.

The instruments which implement community law and which
emanate from these institutions appear in various forms. Regulations
are made, directives issued, decisions made, recommendations made
and opinions delivered. Of these, recommendations and opinions
have no binding force upon those towards whom they are directed
and so are not strictly part of community legislation, although they
are technically part of the "instruments" referred to in the 1972 Act
(above) and could therefore be the basis of rule-making in the United

Kingdom. Regulations, directives and decisions comprise community legislation. Of these regulations are the most important. They are binding and directly applicable in all member states. They confer rights and duties which must be recognised by the national courts within member states. They pass straight into our law, with no need for parliamentary approval. Directives are not generally self-executing but instructions to make law rather than law in themselves. So member states are given a period of time, perhaps two years, within which certain prescribed laws must be made within each state, in accordance with the directive, and using the State's own legislative machinery. Interestingly, the European Court has sometimes been prepared to overlook this distinction and hold that a directive is capable of providing legal rights for an individual despite the fact that the member state has not implemented it fully (e.g. *van Duyn* v. *Home Office* (1975), *Becker* v. *Finanzamt Munster-Innenstadt* (1982)).

Finally, decisions; under Article 189 of the EEC Treaty a decision is "binding in its entirety upon those to whom it is addressed". So a member state might be bound, or just a single company within a state. They are usually administrative decisions implementing community law, like granting authorisations or exceptions.

There is a select committee in each of our Houses of Parliament which scrutinises community policies and legislative proposals, so that our Parliament is kept aware of what is happening in the area of community law.

STATUTORY INTERPRETATION

Acts of Parliament lay down general rules. Sooner or later an individual will be charged that he has infringed such a rule. So a court will be called upon to decide whether a general rule has been broken in a particular case. Usually there is little trouble with the words of the rule, used in the Act. The meaning is usually clear, but sometimes it is not and the court, still required to decide, must interpret the words.

There has been developed over the years a clumsy collection of so-called "rules" of statutory interpretation.

The first, and perhaps most obvious approach is known as the "literal rule". It reflects the traditionally narrow view which the courts have taken of statutory interpretation. The words in the Act are applied strictly and literally. The ordinary and natural meaning of the words used is regarded as being the meaning intended by Parliament. Lord Reid said (in *Black-Clawson* v. *Papierwerke* (1975)):

> We often say that we are looking for the intention of Parliament, but that is not quite accurate. We are seeking the meaning of the

words which Parliament used. We are seeking not what Parliament meant but the true meaning of what they said. In the comparatively few cases where the words of a statutory provision are only capable of having one meaning, that is the end of the matter and no further enquiry is permissible.

This rule was employed in *Whitely* v. *Chappell* (1868) where the statute in question made it a criminal offence to pretend to be "any person entitled to vote" at an election. The accused had masqueraded himself as someone whose name was still on the list but who had died. The "literal rule" applied here disclosed no offence, because the dead person was no longer "entitled to vote"!

Glanville Williams wrote:

> The literal rule is a rule against using intelligence in understanding language. Anyone who in ordinary life interpreted words literally, being indifferent to what the speaker or writer meant, would be regarded as a pedant, a mischief-maker or an idiot.

The Law Commission published a report in 1969 suggesting legislation to reform statutory interpretation. They too were not enamoured of the literal rule:

> ... to place undue emphasis on the literal meaning of the words of a provision is to assume an unattainable perfection in drafts-manship.

Incidentally, Lord Scarman has tried to introduce a bill to enact their proposals, but with little success. Where the literal rule in action leads to arrant nonsense (rather than a result which is clearly not what Parliament intended) then modification of approach is permitted.

We also have the "golden rule". Parke B said (in *Becke* v. *Smith* (1836)):

> It is a very useful rule in the construction of a statute to adhere to the ordinary meaning of the words used, and to the grammatical construction, unless that is at variance with the intention of the legislative to be collected from the statute itself, or leads to any manifest absurdity or repugnance, in which case the language may be varied or modified so as to avoid such inconvenience, but no further.

So it was that when in *R.* v. *Allen* (1872) the accused was charged with bigamy, contrary to the Offences against the Person Act 1861:

Section (57). Whosoever, being married, shall marry any other person during the life of the former husband or wife, whether the second marriage shall have taken place in England, or Ireland or elsewhere... shall be liable to (imprisonment) for any term not exceeding seven years.

In the case the point was made that, marriage being a change of legal status, a person cannot "marry" whilst married because he is already married, the court felt able to interpret the phrase "shall marry" in the Act as meaning "go through a ceremony of marriage"; the accused was convicted. The "golden rule" had been applied.

There is a third rule—quite inconsistent with the other two, called the "mischief rule", or the rule in *Heydon's Case* (1584). In that case the use of the rule was explained:

Four things are to be discussed and considered: (i) What was the common law before the making of the Act? (ii) What was the mischief and defect for which the common law did not provide? (iii) What remedy hath Parliament resolved and appointed to cure the disease of the commonwealth? (iv) What is the true reason for the remedy? Judges shall make such construction as shall suppress the mischief and advance the remedy.

So when the mischief rule is used, the courts seek out what Parliament intended to stop and they see to it that it gets stopped—whatever the words might, taken literally, mean.

The case *Smith* v. *Hughes* (1960) concerned the interpretation of a section of the Street Offences Act 1959. This Act makes it a criminal offence for a common prostitute to loiter or solicit in a street or public place for her professional purposes. The lady accused here had been attracting customers by tapping on the glass upstairs at a first floor window. Obviously, she was not "in the street", as the Act said it required, yet Parker CJ said:

Everybody knows that this was an Act intended to clean up the streets, to enable people to walk along the streets without being molested or solicited by common prostitutes. Viewed in that way, it can matter little whether the prostitute is soliciting while in the street or is standing in a doorway or on a balcony, or at a window, or whether the window is shut or open or half open. In each case her solicitation is projected to and addressed to somebody walking in the street.

The 1969 Law Commission Report recommended a move away

from the "literal rule" towards the "mischief" approach. It must be admitted that there is a danger in allowing the judges too much freedom to elaborate the expressed wishes of Parliament. It could tempt people towards litigation where they "gamble" on the outcome of a case. Nevertheless a move away from the bald "literal" interpretation of statutes must be welcome.

Apart from, and in addition to, these three rules there are other approaches, rules, guidelines and presumptions which the courts use when interpreting statutes:

(a) *Ut res magis valeat quam pereat*—let the thing stand rather than fall. Assume that the draftsman is not repeating himself.

(b) *Expressio unius, exclusio alterius*—what is included excludes that which is not. So that if particular words like "house" and "office" are not followed by general words like "other buildings", then the generalities are excluded.

(c) *Ejusdem generis*—of the same kind. So, if general words do follow particular ones, they must be interpreted so as to include only things "of the same kind". For example, "dogs, cats (particular) and other animals (general)" would exclude lions, tigers and camels but it might include budgies and ornamental fish.

(d) Presume that unless the Act specifically states that it does so, it does not oust the jurisdiction of the courts, alter the settled common law, infringe international obligations, repeal earlier Acts, deprive an owner of his property, extend its effect beyond the United Kingdom, nor create "strict liability" offences (i.e. those for which no intention need be proved, like parking on a double yellow line and other more serious offences—*see* Chapter 14).

Further to these rules and presumptions, statutes usually contain interpretation sections (e.g. the Sale of Goods Act 1979, s. 61) which define words used in the Act. There is also the Interpretation Act 1978 which assists in an overall way (e.g. singular includes plural, masculine includes feminine). The judges also take into account the long title of an Act but not the margin notes. However, external documents like discussion papers and (especially) Hansard are not used. Nevertheless, if an Act followed on a particular formal report then it seems to have been established in *Black-Clawson* v. *Papierwerke* (1975) that reference can be made to it whilst identifying the mischief the Act sought to correct.

CASE LAW

Having considered legislation and its related topics, we now need to observe the other main source of law in action—case law—or law from decided cases, developed over the years by the judges, case by case, by analogy with earlier cases. The idea is simple. If the facts of a case are similar to an earlier one, particularly one decided by a superior court, then the rule laid down then ought to be followed.

Of course, the consistency of decision-making extends back for centuries across English legal history, but the formal structure of binding authority which exists today required two foundations. First a clear hierarchy within the court system—developed rather haphazardly over the years. This was achieved by the Judicature Acts 1873-1875. They created the framework of courts we have today, although some details have been modified. Second, a reliable system of law reports was required. If the court is to follow an earlier decision, then the report of that earlier case must be authoritative. This was finally achieved in 1865 when the General Council of Law Reporting was established: it was incorporated in 1870. The Law Reports and Weekly Law Reports are published under the auspices of the Incorporated Council. They are of great authority. They are checked by the judges before publication. There are still private reports published, as there have been over the centuries. Probably the most famous are the All England Law Reports.

So the formal rule whereby one court is bound to follow the decision of another court taken earlier in a similar case is only about 100 years old.

This formality is sometimes called the doctrine of precedent or *stare decisis*. Case law is the source of law. The doctrine of precedent is the mechanism by which it develops.

The doctrine of precedent: who binds whom?

The binding nature of a decision works down the court system:

The Court of the European Communities
Where the case turns upon a point of community law then the European Court has the last word. The European Communities Act 1972 says:

> 3 (1) For the purposes of all legal proceedings any question as to the meaning or effect of any of the treaties, or as to the validity, meaning or effect of any community instrument, shall be treated as a question of law and, if not referred to the European Court, be for determination as such in accordance with the principles laid down by and any relevant decision of the European Court.

So the court in Luxembourg has the last word on matters of community law. Under the EEC Treaty the English courts obtain rulings on points of community law (which commonly take a year to obtain) which they then apply to the case at hand. It is a method of centralising and stabilising the interpretation of community law.

The House of Lords

Apart from matters of community law, the House of Lords is the final court of appeal within the English legal system. Its decisions on civil and criminal matters bind all inferior courts. Until 1966 it even bound itself! On 26th July 1966 the then Lord Chancellor, Lord Gardiner, issued the famous Practice Statement. It has been regarded as binding, although it was not made as part of the judgment in a case:

> Their Lordships regard the use of precedent as an indispensable foundation upon which to decide what is the law and its application to individual cases. It provides at least some degree of certainty upon which individuals can rely in the conduct of their affairs, as well as a basis for orderly development of legal rules. Their Lordships nevertheless recognise that too rigid adherence to precedent may lead to injustice in a particular case and also unduly restrict the proper development of the law. They propose therefore to modify their present practice and, while treating former decisions of this House as normally binding, to depart from a previous decision when it appears right to do so. In this connection they will bear in mind the danger of disturbing retrospectively the basis on which contracts, settlements of property and fiscal arrangements have been entered into and also the especial need for certainty as to the criminal law. This announcement is not intended to affect the use of precedent elsewhere than in this House.

This is a lucid explanation of the present position in the House. The power to over-rule has been used only very sparingly since 1966. Indeed, if one party to a case wishes to ask the House to exercise this power it must state so clearly in the documents of the case (*Practice Direction* (1971)).

The Court of Appeal

In simple terms, this court is always bound by decisions of the House of Lords and it is generally bound by its own decisions. The court is split into a civil and criminal division.

The civil division can only depart from its own decisions in the three instances set out in 1944 by the then Master of the Rolls, Lord Greene (in *Young* v. *Bristol Aeroplane Co. Ltd.* (1944)), who said that:

(a) the court is entitled and bound to decide which of two conflicting decisions of its own it will follow;

(b) the court is bound to refuse to follow a decision of its own which conflicts with a House of Lords decision;

(c) the court is not bound to follow a decision which was taken *per incuriam* (i.e. in ignorance of a relevant authority such as an Act or previous decision).

Further to these, it was held in *Boys* v. *Chaplin* (1968) that interlocutory (i.e. preliminary to actually dealing with the case) decisions are not binding.

In the criminal division it is thought that since the liberty of the individual concerned may be at stake then an approach more closely attached to each case and slightly less to the benefit of general rules is appropriate. *R.* v. *Gould* (1968) is a notable example, where the earlier decision in *R.* v. *Wheat and Stocks* (1921) was expressly over-ruled. The cases concern whether a reasonable belief that a previous marriage has been dissolved is a defence to a bigamy charge. From the later case it appears that it is.

The High Court

Where civil cases are tried at first instance the decisions do not bind other High Court judges. The divisional courts do follow their own rulings, except occasionally in the Queen's Bench Division. Otherwise the High Court is bound by the Court of Appeal and the House of Lords.

The Crown Court and the courts of inferior jurisdiction

No precedents are set by the decisions of these courts (which include county courts and magistrates' courts) and all the courts above bind. When a High Court judge sits in the Crown Court, however, it seems probable that the usual High Court position would apply, although this is, as yet, unclear.

To what extent are the decisions binding?

The court bound by settled authority is bound by the essence of the earlier case, the precedent.

The judgment of a court can be divided into two. Each part has a Latin name: the *ratio decidendi* and the *obiter dicta*.

The ratio decidendi

This translates as "the reason for the decision", but the meaning is less clear. No judge actually says "now, this is the reason for my decision"; the *ratio* of any case has to be divined from the words of the judgment. Methods vary. Thus definitions of precisely what the *ratio decidendi* of any case is also vary.

Professor Cross:

> Any rule of law treated by the judge as a necessary step in reaching his conclusion.

Professor Goodhart:

> The *ratio decidendi* of a case can be defined as the material facts of the case plus the decision thereon.

Professor Wambaugh:

> When a case turns on only one point, the proposition of the case, the reason of the decision, the *ratio decidendi*, must be a general rule without which the case must have been decided otherwise.

The obiter dicta

The *ratio* is the essence of the case. Everything else belongs to the *obiter dicta* (which translates as "words spoken by the way"). Whilst it may be a matter of conjecture what precisely constitutes the *ratio*, it is agreed that everything which does not is *obiter*.

Only the *ratio* of a case is binding. *Obiter dicta* may be persuasive, particularly where, for example, a judge has explained hypothetical situations and stated what the law would be and one of these sets of circumstances actually appears. For the doctrine of precedent to work it is not necessary to await the recurrence of precisely the same facts; only the essential relationships need reappear.

Consider these two cases which concern the tort of negligence.

Donoghue v. *Stevenson* (1932). Here the plaintiff suffered through finding the remnants of a decomposed snail in ginger beer which she was drinking. She sued the manufacturer. It was held that he owed his consumers a duty to take care since he and they were "neighbours" in law. Lord Atkin said:

> You must take reasonable care to avoid acts or omissions which you can reasonably foresee would be likely to injure your neighbour. Who then, it law, is my neighbour? The answer seems to be persons who are so closely and directly affected by my act that I ought reasonably to have them in contemplation as being so affected when I am directing my mind to the acts or omissions which are called in question.

Ross v. *Caunters* (1979). A solicitor drew up a will. There was a gift in it to the wife of one of the witnesses. The Wills Act 1837, s.15, prevented her taking it simply because she was his wife and such people cannot benefit in this way. She sued the solicitor for negligence. It was argued that there could be no negligence because the solicitor owed the plaintiff no duty of care.They were not "neighbours" in law. Sir Robery Megarry V-C said:

> The solicitors owed a duty of care to the plaintiff since she was someone within their direct contemplation as a person so closely and directly affected by their acts and omissions in carrying out their client's instructions to provide her with a share of his residue that they could reasonably foresee that she would be likely to be injured by those acts or omissions... a direct application of the principle of *Donoghue* v. *Stevenson*.

These two cases may appear quite different. However, they are close enough for the first to be a binding authority on the second. The essence is the same, even though the circumstances are radically different.

The advantages and disadvantages of having a doctrine such as this are set out neatly in the Practice Statement quoted earlier but in list form the advantages are said to be:

(*a*) certainty, in that where a point has been settled then lawyers are enabled to advise their clients accordingly;

(*b*) the possibility of growth, which is provided by the system having been, as it were, opened at the apex in 1966;

(*c*) the wealth of detailed rules which has been assembled over many years of steady growth and the practical nature of the law thus developed, since it is based upon cases that actually happened rather than the hypothetical situations envisaged by statutes.

The disadvantages are said to be:

(*a*) the rigidity which is inevitable within a system which is open only at the apex; a bad decision taken at a high level could remain for many years until a litigant has the time and the money and a closely similar case comes along;

(*b*) the practice of distinguishing where some judges avoid the binding nature of precedents by seizing upon some artificial distinction between the case before them and the precedent and thereby creating illogicality;

(*c*) the wealth of detail brings with it enormous bulk and complexity, making the law difficult and expensive to discover; and

(*d*) the system itself is an unsatisfactory way of developing the law in that it relies upon suitable cases coming up (the "accidents of litigation"). It is said that the advantages outweigh the disadvantages.

CUSTOM

If the legal system is traced back far enough it will lead to ancient local customs. Today local customs are not very important as a source of law, but they are occasionally recognised as having binding force. Such a local custom is described as being a usage or rule which has gathered the force of law and is binding within a defined area upon the persons affected by it. It is for the person who alleges that the custom exists to prove that it does. This is often the resort of those about to be affected by, for example, a building project. In order to obtain judicial recognition there are various hurdles to leap.

(*a*) The custom must be reasonable. In *Wolstanton* v. *Newcastle-under-Lyme Corporation* (1940) it was alleged that the descendant of the lord of the manor had inherited the right to undermine land without having to compensate for subsidence thereby caused. This was unreasonable.

(*b*) It must be certain as to the subject matter of the persons benefiting and of the locality. In *Wilson* v. *Willes* (1806) the tenants of a manor claimed the right to cut turf for their lawns. This was too uncertain.

(*c*) The locality must be recognisable, e.g. a manor or a parish or a field. In *Mercer* v. *Denne* (1905) the right alleged was to dry fishing nets upon a particular stretch of beach. This was upheld.

(*d*) The custom must be, apparently, ancient. That means that it must have existed as Sir Edward Coke wrote:

since a time when the memory of man runneth not to the contrary.

A date of 1189 has been set, but in practice the oldest local people testify, and then those opposing the right are put to it to show that at some time between the earliest date established by this testimony and 1189 the right did not exist. In *Simpson* v. *Wells* (1872) the right alleged was to obstruct the footway with a refreshment stall on "fair days". Sadly the fair in that place dated only from 1327.

The right must have been continuously available since "time immemorial". It need not have actually been used continuously. This was recently confirmed in *New Windsor Corporation* v. *Mellor* (1975), where the right of the local people to "indulge in sports and pastimes" upon the village green, called Bachelors' Acre, was upheld.

(*e*) The alleged right must have been peaceably used, *nec per vim, nec clam, nec precario* (neither through force, nor stealth, or the need to obtain permission).

(*f*) Fairly obviously, it must not be contrary to any statute, since these local customs are only recognised as exceptions to common law.

(g) It must be consistent with other recognised customs in that area. Sir William Blackstone wrote:

> If one man prescribed that by custom he has a right to have windows looking into another's garden, the other cannot claim a right by custom to stop up or obstruct those windows; for those contradictory customs cannot both be good, nor both stand together.

MINOR SOURCES

It is worth considering briefly a collection of other sources and influences which have helped to shape the law despite being of lesser importance.

The Law Merchant

Lex mercatoria, as it is sometimes known, was the body of customary rules drawn from the practices of merchants, partly based in international law, and dating back to the Middle Ages. The merchants had their own courts called "pie poudre" and "staple", using swift and simple procedures and using their own rules.

The debts we owe to the law merchant include the concept of negotiability (which allows a document containing an order to pay money to be transferred from one person to another), and thus bills of exchange, and many aspects of the law of partnerships, agency and insurance. In addition, much of maritime law stems from this source. Mercantile and maritime law have always been close relatives.

Canon law

Church law developed apart from the common law, and was administered in separate ecclesiastical courts. The debts owed here are of two kinds. First there are rules of canon law which passed into the general areas, such as most of family law and probate together with particular offences, like blasphemy and blasphemous libel. It is interesting that these offences are preserved whereas others, like adultery and usury, were never generally adopted. The second debt is more one of general approach. This is clearly seen in the doctrines and practices of equity (considered in Chapter 2). This is so because the early Lord Chancellors were churchmen.

Roman law

This is the whole basis of most continental legal systems, but it has had very little effect in English law. This effect itself is only indirect.

Canon law is based to some extent on Roman law (the clerics were highly trained in it) and canon law has influenced English law. Further to this, there is an international aspect to mercantile and maritime law which is Roman in origin.

Textbooks

Before law reports became as totally reliable as they are today, that is, before 1865, textbooks were often cited as authority for law. Nowadays they are used when there is little or nothing in the way of precedents from which the court can take guidance.

LAW REFORM

The law, through the operation of the doctrine of judicial precedent, may become out of date and in need of reform. Or there may be a need for a more general reform of a complete area of law. In 1965 the Law Commissions Act created a committee of five full-time lawyers, "to take and keep under review all the law . . . with a view to its systematic development and reform, including in particular the codification of such law, elimination of anomolies, the repeal of obsolete and unnecessary enactments, the reduction of the number of separate enactments and generally the simplification and modernisation of the law". There is a separate Commission for Scotland. The Law Commissioners produce reports, recommendations and draft bills, the majority of which are adopted and become law.

If a branch of the law has evolved piecemeal then a "consolidating" statute may be passed which brings together all the existing statute law in a consolidated form with the aim of clarifying the law. A "codifying" statute differs from consolidation in that it brings together the existing statute and common law in a given area again to clarify and simplify the law. Examples of codifying statutes are the Offences against the Person Act 1861 and the Sale of Goods Act 1893, (now repealed and replaced by the Sale of Goods Act 1979). In all cases one of the main problems is in finding the necessary parliamentary time for such legislation since it often lacks popular appeal and is unlikely to win votes from the electorate.

There is also the Criminal Law Revision Committee which keeps under review areas of the criminal law which need reform.

If there is a question of considerable public importance which requires investigation and a report then a Royal Commission may be established; for example the Royal Commission on Legal Services which reported in 1979. It looked into the structure, organisation, training and entry into the legal profession, and their effect on the provision of legal services to the public. A number of recommendations were made relating to law centres, tribunal proceedings, criminal legal aid and other matters.

Chapter 4

Where the Law is Administered

The law is administered where anyone makes a judicial decision. So courts are, obviously, included. So too are tribunals. Policemen and ministers of the crown too administer the law. In this chapter we will examine the court system of England and Wales and then take a look at tribunals at work.

CLASSIFYING THE COURTS

The court system today reflects the massive reorganisation carried out by the Judicature Acts 1873-5. Before that there was a mild form of chaos both within the courts and between them. The Judicature Acts set up the Supreme Court of Judicature. There is no such place: the term is a collective one for the Court of Appeal, the High Court and the Crown Court. Interestingly, the House of Lords is not part of the Supreme Court, despite being the final court of appeal in most matters. This reflects a political accident. The Liberal government, with Lord Selbourne, drafted and passed the 1873 Act which, inter alia, abolished the House of Lords as a final court of appeal (not as the second chamber of Parliament) in line with their policy against inherited power. The Act did not come into force until 1875. Meanwhile the Conservatives took power under Disraeli in February 1874. They reinstated the House in its judicial capacity, but neglected to place it within the Supreme Court.

There are various ways in which the present courts could be classified. Each has its uses for the purpose of elucidation, but none is altogether satisfactory. First, courts might be "inferior" or "superior". This shows how some are limited both in the cases they can try and the geographical area over which they have jurisdiction, whereas others have no such limits placed upon them.

Secondly, courts might be "first instance" or "appeal" courts. A court of first instance is a court which tries cases for the first time, e.g. the county court in a civil dispute, or the magistrates' court in a criminal action. Because courts can make mistakes when arriving at decisions, opportunities exist for having the mistakes rectified. Hence there is an appeal procedure, whereby the aggrieved party can take his case to a higher court and have the matter reviewed. In such cases, the matter will come before an appeal court, e.g. the Court of Appeal which, if it finds that the decision of the lower court was wrong, will reverse it and substitute its own decision.

Thirdly, courts might be "courts of record" or not. A court of record keeps its records on a permanent basis and has the power to fine and imprison for contempt of its authority and orders.

Fourthly, courts might be "civil" or "criminal" according to the nature of the matters dealt with. This, with only a couple of exceptions, is not a clear line since many courts deal with both.

The civil/criminal classification is the one most used, and is perhaps the easiest to represent diagrammatically (*see* Figs. 1 and 2). However, the fact that it is neither clear nor particularly logical should be noted.

CIVIL COURTS

Whilst the major courts dealing with civil cases are shown in Fig. 1 it is important to realise that there are others which do not fit easily into

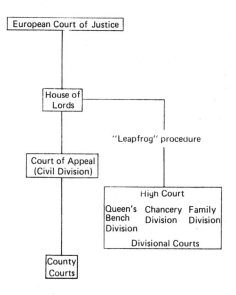

Fig. 1 *Courts which deal with civil cases.*

this representation of the overall structure. After all, the system is not designed for diagrams! It is important to understand at least broadly how the courts fit together. The structure is, of course, largely designed for appeal routes. It is also important to know a little of the work of each court which deals with civil cases.

The Court of Justice of the European Communities

This is not strictly an English court. It sits in Luxembourg. It does, however, have a certain authority within the English legal system. Where a point in any case concerns the interpretation of community law, any court may, and the final court of appeal in a member state must (under art. 177 of the EEC Treaty), refer the case to the European Court for a ruling. This is binding authority on the point of law. This ruling usually takes between six months and a year to obtain. The national court must then decide the case in the light of the interpretation dictated to it. Naturally, the court has jurisdiction within the community to deal with community disputes.

There are eleven judges in the European Court. They are appointed for six years and they can be reappointed; most have been, some three times. They appoint a president from amongst their number, who serves for three years at a time. The UK Judge at present is Alexander John Mackenzie Stuart, a judge from the Supreme Court of Session in Scotland. The court is assisted by five Advocates-General. They are independent advisers. There is one assigned to each case by the President of the Court. It is provided by the EEC Treaty, art. 166:

> It shall be the duty of the Advocate-General, acting with complete impartiality and independence, to make, in open court, reasoned submissions on cases brought before the Court of Justice, in order to assist the Court.

This is done by giving an "opinion" about a case after it has been heard and before the court gives judgment. The Advocate-General sits on the bench, but not with the judges. It is a very important job. Judges have transferred to it. No transfer the other way has yet been seen.

The European Court gives a single judgment. No reference is made to dissenting opinions. The judgment is enforced through the national courts of member states.

The House of Lords

For most cases this is the final court of appeal within the English court system. It may no longer have the last word in community law, but otherwise, and in both civil and criminal cases, there is nowhere else to go to have a decision reversed. The law as settled in the case can be changed by legislation, or even (in rare circumstances, as has been noted above in Chapter 3) over-ruled in a later, similar case by the court itself. Otherwise, this is where the last cards are played.

The Law Lords usually sit in threes or fives, but sometimes in sevens. They do so unrobed in the Palace at Westminster, in a committee room. The court sat for the first time as a committee on 26th May 1948. Before then, the hearings were regarded as ordinary sittings of the House of Lords as the second Chamber of Parliament. This committee procedure was intended as a temporary measure. The House of Commons Chamber had been destroyed by enemy action on 10th May 1941. The Commons moved into the Lords' Chamber. The Lords moved into the King's Robing Room in the Royal Gallery. When rebuilding was in progress in 1945 the builders installed a heating system below the Robing Room. It was impossible to hear what was being said. The pile-drivers downstairs drowned even the loudest of advocates. So the Law Lords moved to a committee room. They have yet to emerge.

The Law Lords themselves are the senior members of the English judiciary. They are, in practice, appointed from the Court of Appeal from time to time as the need arises. In theory they could come from the High Court or even directly from the practising Bar. There are between seven and eleven judges. Usually two are Scottish and often one is Irish. This reflects the fact that the House serves as final court of appeal for the Court of Session in Scotland and the Court of Appeal in Northern Ireland. The House is not the final appeal court for Scottish Criminal cases.

The Lord Chancellor (a government appointment) is responsible for the work of the court, and sometimes presides in person. On the rare occasions when the Appellate Committee sits in the Lords' Chamber he usually presides, robed and bewigged.

The jurisdiction is virtually entirely appellate. The court hears appeals from the Court of Appeal (and its equivalent in Scotland and Northern Ireland). There is no right to appeal. Permission must be granted, either from the Court of Appeal or the House itself. The case must be one of public importance. In criminal cases the issues must be based on a point of law. In practice virtually all final appeals are on such points and 90 per cent. of them are on the interpretation of statutes.

The House also entertains appeals direct from the High Court in civil cases according to the "leap-frog" procedure provided by the Administration of Justice Act 1969. Here, the trial judge must issue a certificate that the case is one of public importance and either that it concerns statutory interpretation or that the outcome is bound by a previous decision of the House itself (which would, obviously, also bind the Court of Appeal). Further to this certificate, the House itself must give leave to appeal. In this way the case "leap-frogs" the Court of Appeal. (An interesting illustration here is *Vestey* v. *Inland Revenue Commissioners* (1979), which is a case showing both the "leap-frog" procedure and the House using its power to overrule its own previous decisions, assumed in the Practice Statement in 1966, which was noted in Chapter 3.)

As will be noted below, the Queen's Bench Division of the High Court has a certain criminal jurisdiction. Appeals lie directly to the House in such cases, again with leave and only in really important cases. This is provided by the Administration of Justice Act 1960. The House also hears cases from the Courts-Martial Appeal Court.

The Court of Appeal (Civil Division)

The Judicature Acts 1873-75 created the Court of Appeal, although its present form dates only from 1966. On 1st October of that year the Criminal Appeal Act 1966 came into force; it split the court into two divisions, civil and criminal. The civil division deals with cases from the High Court, the county courts, the Restrictive Practices Court and also from various tribunals such as the Employment Appeal Tribunal and the Lands Tribunal.

The court consists of between eight and eighteen Lords Justices of Appeal. In rare cases a sole judge may sit to hear an appeal but the usual number is three or five. They are generally appointed from the High Court, although it is possible for a practising barrister to be appointed. The Master of the Rolls presides in the civil division. Further to these the Lord Chancellor, former Lord Chancellors, the Law Lords and the President of the Family Division of the High Court all have the right to sit, but very rarely do. More often, and particularly in the criminal division, High Court judges sit with the Lords Justices of Appeal.

The Court has the power to uphold or reverse the decision of the lower court. It can, but very rarely does, order a new trial. This might happen, for example, where new evidence has come to light which could, had it been available at the time the case was tried, have affected the lower court's decision.

The High Court of Justice

The High Court was created by the Judicature Act 1873-75, but in its present form it dates only from 1971, when the Administration of Justice Act 1970 was implemented. The court generally sits in the

Royal Courts of Justice, an elegant building at the Aldwych end of the Strand in London. The building was designed in a thirteenth century style in 1874 by G. E. Street. It also houses the Court of Appeal, but, unlike that court, the High Court also sits at other centres around the country. Indeed, wherever a High Court judge (called a "puisne" judge, pronounced "puny") sits, there sits the High Court. The Lord Chancellor bears the ultimate responsibility for such matters. Puisne judges must be barristers of at least ten years' standing and are usually appointed from Queen's Counsel. In theory circuit judges can be promoted, but this is not common.

The High Court is split up into three basic divisions, each of which is further divided. In theory, any puisne judge can deal with any High Court matter; in practice they specialise. Often this specialisation reflects their professional expertise when they were barristers. This is especially true in the Chancery Division. There is no jurisdictional limit to the High Court's civil work, although the smaller cases are dealt with by the county courts (*see* below). Each of the three divisions has an appellate jurisdiction. This work is mostly done in separate courts, confusingly called divisional courts.

The Chancery Division

Here the first-instance jurisdiction covers the administration of the estates of the dead, trusts, mortgages, rectification of deeds, partnerships, the winding-up of companies, bankruptcy, revenue, planning and landlord and tenant disputes. Sometimes these and other cases are dealt with within the Division by particular courts. There are, for example, the Companies Court, the Bankruptcy Court, the Patents Court and the Court of Protection which deals with managing the affairs of mental patients.

The appellate jurisdiction covers appeals from decisions of the Inland Revenue Commissioners, and appeals on bankruptcy and land registration cases from county courts. This Division is presided over by the Lord Chancellor in theory and the Vice-Chancellor in practice.

The Family Division

This division was created by the Administration of Justice Act 1970. There used to be a division called Probate, Divorce and Admiralty—a strange mixture, once called by Sir Alan Herbert, whose entertaining writings are highly recommended, the Division of "Wills, Wives and Wrecks". The Family Division took over the wives, the wrecks went to the Queen's Bench Division, and the Family and Chancery Divisions divided the wills: the contentious cases go to Chancery.

Obviously, the first-instance jurisdiction covers family matters, such as all cases concerning marriage including its validity and termination (except undefended divorces, which are county court material), legitimacy, wardship, adoption, guardianship, domestic violence and disputes over family property.

The appellate jurisdiction reflects the fact that minor domestic matters can be dealt with at first instance elsewhere, and the appropriate appeal route would lie here. Thus, cases from the county, magistrates' and Crown Courts in such matters are dealt with by a divisional court of two or three puisne judges. This division is presided over by the President of the Family Division.

The Queen's Bench Division

This is the largest and the most over-worked of the three. It is presided over by the Lord Chief Justice.

The first-instance jurisdiction covers mainly contract and tort actions. These are cases involving claims for huge awards of damages, (lesser matters are dealt with by county courts).

The division also includes the Admiralty Court, which deals with such matters as claims for injury or loss through collisions at sea, the ownership and loss of and from ships, towage and salvage. It is common to find experienced laymen (called lay assessors) who assist the judge in the Admiralty Court.

Also included here is the Commercial Court which provides, in addition to open-court hearings of commercial claims, an arbitration service for businessmen. These claims might include insurance, banking, agency, negotiable instruments.

The appellate jurisdiction is complicated. A single judge can hear appeals from certain tribunals (e.g. the Pensions Appeals Tribunal) and from commercial arbitrations, particularly on points of law (under the Arbitration Acts 1950 and 1979). The divisional court, of two or (usually) three judges has a certain civil appeal function, for example, from the Solicitors' Disciplinary Tribunal.

However, the divisional court has two other important functions. First it hears the appeals from magistrates' courts and the Crown Court (where the case has been tried in a magistrates' court and has been to the Crown Court for appeal or sentence) by way of "case stated". This strange phrase means simply an appeal on the basis, not that the facts found were wrong, but that either the decision as to the law relating to those facts was wrong or that the decision-makers were acting beyond their jurisdiction.

Second, it exercises the supervisory jurisdiction which this division has inherited from the ancient Court of King's Bench, at which the monarch himself originally presided. This power is one to scrutinise the activities of all the inferior courts, tribunals and other arenas in which decisions affecting the rights of individuals are made (including decisions by ministers) and to see that these decisions are taken in a proper manner. The court does not usurp the decision-making power itself; it merely checks the manner of its exercise. The court has four main weapons. They are three prerogative orders and one prerogative writ (these very names indicate their royal ancestry).

The first order is caled mandamus ("we order"). It is used to compel the execution of a legal duty. It must be a duty and not a discretionary power. Thus in *R*. v. *Bedwelty UDC* (1934), mandamus was issued at the request of a ratepayer who insisted that the local authority should allow an examination of its accounts, whereas in *Re Fletcher's Application* (1970) the order was refused to an applicant who insisted that the Parliamentary Commissioner (the Ombudsman) should investigate his complaint. This was because the relevant statute provides that he "may" investigate. He has a discretion. It is not a legal duty.

The second order is prohibition; the third is called certiorari. Lord Atkin explained (in *R*. v. *Electricity Commissioners* (1924)):

> Both writs are of great antiquity, forming part of the process by which the King's Courts restrained courts of inferior jurisdiction from exceeding their powers. Prohibition restrains the tribunal from proceeding further in excess of jurisdiction; certiorari requires the record or the order of the court to be sent up to the King's Bench Division, to have its legality inquired into, and, if necessary, to have the order quashed ... Doubtless in their origin (they) dealt almost exclusively with the jurisdiction of what is described in ordinary parlance as a court of justice. But (their) operation has extended to control the proceedings of bodies which do not claim to be, and would not be recognised as, courts of justice. Wherever any body of persons having legal authority to determine questions affecting the rights of subjects, and having the duty to act judicially, act in excess of their legal authority they are subject to the controlling jurisdiction of the King's Bench Division.

Prohibition, then, is available to prevent such a body as Lord Atkin was referring to from acting without jurisdiction or contrary to the rules of natural justice. It is applicable before the event.

After the decision has been taken, certiorari may be appropriate. This order lies to correct the decision taken without jurisdiction, or contrary to natural justice or where there is an error of law actually in the written record of the case. The phrase "natural justice" is used here. Maugham J explained (in *Maclean* v. *Workers' Union* (1929)):

> The phrase is, of course, used only in a popular sense and must not
> be taken to mean that there is any justice natural among men.
> Amongst most savages there is no such thing as justice in the
> modern sense. The phrase "the principles of natural justice" can
> only mean, in this connection, the principles of fair play so deeply
> rooted in the minds of modern Englishmen that a provision for an
> inquiry necessarily imparts that the accused should be given his
> chance of defence and explanation.

This requirement of "fair play" is usually explained by means of
two rules with latin names. The first is *audi alteram partem*, which
means "let the other side be heard". Allegations that this rule has been
broken usually involve lack of time allowed to prepare a defence or
indeed lack of notice of the hearing itself, whether an oral hearing is
necessary, whether the right to cross examine witnesses exists, the
right to be represented by a lawyer, and so on. The other rule is *nemo
judex in causa sua*, which means "no-one should be a judge in his own
cause". It is sometimes called the rule against bias. A very famous
instance of this rule being broken concerned a Lord Chancellor, Lord
Cottenham, who had decided a case in favour of a canal company in
which he held shares, although it is said that he had forgotten about
them. The case is called *Dimes* v. *Grand Junction Canal Proprietors*
(1852). Lord Campbell said:

> No-one can suppose that Lord Cottenham could be, in the
> remotest degree, influenced by the interest that he had in this
> concern; but, my Lords, it is of the last importance that the maxim
> that no man is to be a judge in his own cause be held sacred. And
> that is not to be confined to a cause in which he is a party but
> applies to a cause in which he has an interest... This will be a
> lesson to all inferior tribunals to take care not only that in their
> decrees they are not influenced by their personal interest but to
> avoid the appearance of labouring under such an influence.

There are two other orders available from the divisional court, the
injunction and the declaration. Often an injunction is applied for via
the office of the Attorney-General in a relator action. This means, in
theory, that the Attorney-General, on behalf of the public, seeks to
have an activity stopped. This is commonly done to stop the activity
pending a full hearing by a court. The declaration is not so much a
remedy as a means of clarifying what the law is. Once the position has
been made clear, the parties abide by it. Thus it may have the same
effect as a remedy.

As a point of procedure the applicant is now able to apply for judicial review rather than ask for any one order. This new procedure follows the recommendations of the Law Commission in their 1976 Report No. 73.

Finally on the divisional court, a brief glance at habeas corpus. When somebody is imprisoned or restrained illegally, no matter by whom, his release can be obtained by means of this writ. The court will require the imprisoner to justify the restraint. If he cannot, the individual is freed. There are few modern instances. These tend to come from those in detention awaiting extradition or deportation or where an immigrant has been refused entry and is awaiting his return. The writ has, however, a long and valiant history. It dates at least from Magna Carta (signed on 15th June 1215) ("To no one will we sell, to none will we deny, to none will we delay, right or justice"). It was on an application for habeas corpus that slavery was declared illegal in England (*Sommersett* v. *Stewart* (1772)) when a negro was released even though slavery was legal in his home territory.

County Courts

The county courts were established in 1846 by the County Courts Act 1846 to provide quick and inexpensive relief in the case of small civil disputes. The Courts Act 1971 provided that they should be staffed by a circuit judge, appointed on the advice of the Lord Chancellor. The court hears disputes relating to its own district. There are approximately 300 districts throughout England and Wales. The judge normally sits alone, though on very rare occasions trial may be by a jury of eight persons (e.g. in cases of fraud). In addition to there being a judge, each court has a registrar, who is an assistant judge. There is also a permanent official called the chief clerk who runs the office and is in charge of the office staff. The registrar is empowered to try cases where the amount of money involved does not exceed £500. If both parties agree, however, the jurisdiction of the registrar extends to any matter within the jurisdiction of the court. About 90 per cent. of all civil cases are brought in county courts. The vast majority are for small (e.g. up to £500) money debts.

Cases are normally brought within the district where the defendant lives or carries on business, or if land is involved, where the land is situated. Appeals from the county court generally lie to the Court of Appeal (Civil Division). The jurisdiction of the county courts is very wide. It covers:

(*a*) actions in contract and tort, where the sum involved does not exceed £5,000; in the case of certain torts (e.g. defamation) the court has no jurisdiction unless both parties agree;

(*b*) equity matters, such as trusts, mortgages and dissolution of partnerships;

(*c*) actions involving title to land, where the rateable value does not exceed £1,000;

(*d*) actions concerning probate and letters of administration, where the value of the property does not exceed £30,000;

(*e*) winding-up of companies where capital does not exceed £120,000;

(*f*) matrimonial causes. Under the Matrimonial Causes Act 1967 a county court may be designated a divorce county court, and has jurisdiction in the case of undefended divorces. In fact, all matrimonial causes (e.g. a divorce and nullity) must begin in a divorce court, though defended cases will be transferred to the High Court. All county courts are able to hear applications brought under the Domestic Violence and Matrimonial Proceedings Act 1976;

(*g*) adoption of children;

(*h*) landlord and tenant disputes;

(*i*) race-relations;

(*j*) consumer credit;

(*k*) admiralty matters not exceeding £5,000, except in salvage cases where the amount is limited to £15,000;

(*l*) arbitration.

This last point—arbitration—is of great and increasing importance within the county courts. Since the Administration of Justice Act 1973 virtually any county court matter can be dealt with in a relatively informal way. The judge (often the registrar) sits unrobed. The strict rules of evidence do not necessarily apply. The proceedings are heard in private. Arbitration can be requested by either party. Since the revision of the County Court Rules in 1981, if a case concerns a claim of up to £500 then arbitration is automatic unless the circumstances are exceptional (e.g. an allegation of fraud). So it is that small claims, particularly consumer disputes, are usually handled this way.

Typical examples are:

(*a*) claims arising out of the purchase, hire or repair of consumer goods;

(*b*) claims against persons providing consumer services, e.g. garages, plumbers, electrical appliance repairs;

(*c*) claims for arrears of rent;

(*d*) claims arising out of negligence, e.g. a road accident. Normally this is covered by insurance, but if the amount claimed is less than the excess on the policy, or if the driver wants to retain his no claims bonus, the injured driver or pedestrian can sue the driver who was negligent.

Small claims are normally initiated and dealt with by the plaintiff acting on his own behalf. Indeed the cost of employing a solicitor to speak for the plaintiff is not recoverable even if the action succeeds. An action is started by filling in a "request" form and a "particulars of claim" form. These are available at the office in the local county court. If the plaintiff succeeds he will be entitled to recover some of the expenses incurred in bringing the claim. These include:

(a) costs of bringing the action. (This is roughly 10 per cent. of the size of the claim, with a minimum fee of £5. It is paid by the plaintiff when the forms are completed and handed in at the court);

(b) out of pocket expenses (e.g. police reports, company searches);

(c) witnesses' expenses.

Magistrates' Courts

The jurisdiction of the magistrates' court is predominantly criminal but it does have some civil jurisdiction. The civil jurisdiction of the magistrates includes the following:

(a) affiliation orders;

(b) matrimonial relief (e.g. protection against violence, maintenance orders);

(c) custody and adoption of children;

(d) orders committing children to the care of the local authority.

(e) granting and renewing for licensed premises;

(f) enforcement of rate demands, taxes and certain debts owed to the gas, electricity and water undertakings and local authorities;

(g) granting and renewing licences under the betting and gaming legislation.

When dealing with family law matters such as (a)-(c) above the magistrates are specially trained and at least one woman justice must sit. The bench is sometimes called a "domestic court". The public are excluded and the press restricted. Appeals lie to the Family Division of the High Court in groups (a) to (d).

CRIMINAL COURTS

The major courts dealing with criminal cases are represented by the diagram given in Fig. 2.

The Court of Justice of the European Communities/the House of Lords

We saw these in the last section. The vast majority of their work lies in

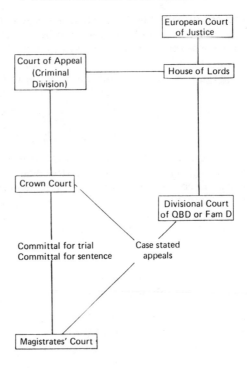

Fig. 2   *Courts which deal with criminal cases.*

civil and administrative matters, but they do handle criminal cases too.

The Court of Appeal (Criminal Division)

We saw the broad composition of the Court of Appeal in the last section. The Criminal Division was created by the Criminal Appeal Act of 1966. The division replaced the Court of Criminal Appeal (which had itself replaced the Court for Crown Cases Reserved under the Criminal Appeal Act 1907) and is presided over by the Lord Chief Justice.

This division deals with appeals from the Crown Court against conviction or sentence. The Attorney-General can refer cases to the court (under the Criminal Justice Act 1972, s.36(1)) for consideration of points of law after an acquittal. The court's judgment will not affect the acquitted person, but it may affect future cases. Under the

Criminal Appeal Act 1968, the Home Secretary is able to refer a case in whole or in part to the court for its consideration. This may happen even if there has already been an unsuccessful appeal.

The Crown Court

The Crown Court was created by means of the Courts Act 1971, implementing the Beeching Commission Report. Three main kinds of judges preside, depending upon the seriousness of the case; High Court judges, circuit judges and part-time judges called recorders.

The sittings of the court are held in first- and second- and third-tier centres, based on six circuits in England and Wales. The first-tier courts are the most important, and deal with the most serious cases. The circuits are the Northern, the North-Eastern, the Midland and Oxford, the Wales and Chester, the Western and the South-Eastern. Each has a Circuit Administrator. They are based in Manchester, Leeds, Birmingham, Cardiff, Bristol and London, and are managerial rather than judicial officers. Each circuit has a presiding judge to carry the judicial responsibility (there are three in the South-Eastern Circuit, including the Lord Chief Justice).

The Crown Court has exclusive jurisdiction over all serious criminal trials, called trials on indictment (pronounced "inditement"). These are the cases too serious to be tried by magistrates, but they are not of equal seriousness. They are divided into four classes. The three types of judge are attached to the classification thus:

Class 1
These include any offences where the death penalty survives, plus murder, rape, genocide, offences under the Official Secrets Act 1911, s.1, plus incitement, conspiracy or attempts at any of these. Being the most serious offences, these cases are always tried by High Court judges.

Class 2
These include manslaughter, infanticide, child destruction, unlawful abortion, incest or intercourse with a girl under 13, sedition, mutiny, piracy, offences under the Geneva Conventions Act 1957, s.1, and incitement, conspiracy or attempts at these. Here, the judge is usually of the High Court rank, but if the presiding judge of the circuit so authorises, any such trial could be dealt with by a circuit judge or a recorder.

Class 3
This is the residual category: any offence triable solely on indictment

not classified elsewhere is a Class 3 offence. Any of the three types of judge can try them.

Class 4
These are triable by any of the judges, and mostly include the offences where the accused could have been tried by magistrates, but given the choice, elected to be tried by judge and jury in the Crown Court. In addition, causing death by reckless driving and burglary are included here.

The court also deals with appeals from magistrates' courts and juvenile courts and committals for sentence from magistrates' courts. On these occasions it is normal for two, three or four magistrates to sit with the judge, the decision being a majority one. Appeal cases involve a rehearing of the evidence when the appeal relates to disputed facts.

Divisional Court of QBD
We met this court in the last section. It was noted there that there lies an appeal from the magistrates' and crown court by way of case stated on the application of the law to decided facts.

Magistrates' Courts

Magistrates are also known as justices of the peace. This office is very ancient. It dates from the end of the twelfth century when, as "keepers" rather than "justices" of the peace, their task was administrative rather than juidicial. By the mid-fourteenth century the judicial aspect had developed. It was enacted in 1344:

> ... that two or three of the best people of each county should be assigned as guardians of the peace by the King's Commission (18 Edw. III stat. 2, 1344).

Their precise powers and duties varied from time to time, but by 1368 they were exercising judicial powers regularly and alone. The title of "justice of the peace" appeared officially for the first time in 1361. As Professor Plucknett wrote (in 1929):

> For the rest of the Middle Ages, and indeed ever since, hardly a Parliament passed without adding some new duty to the work of the justices of the peace.

Magistrates' courts are local. They have a geographical jurisdiction as well as a legal one. That is, they deal with particular matters that arise within their prescribed area. There are no juries in magistrates' courts. Justices are appointed to a particular commission area. Each county, all the London commission areas and the City of London have separate commissions. Justices are appointed by the Lord Chancellor on behalf of the Queen, although in the counties of Greater Manchester, Merseyside and Lancashire appointments are made on her behalf by the Chancellor of the Duchy of Lancaster. These appointments are made upon the recommendations of local and regional advisory committees. The precise membership of these committees varies from place to place although the members are usually all existing or retired magistrates. The secretary's name is available (he is often the clerk to the magistrates) and it is to him that completed application forms are sent by or on behalf of aspiring justices. There is no salary. Expenses are paid, and training courses are compulsory. There is no legal qualification required, but lay magistrates must live within 15 miles of their commission area. Magistrates no longer sit in court after age 70. There are over 20,000 lay magistrates.

Stipendiary magistrates are full-time salaried justices who are legally qualified (barristers or solicitors of at least seven years' experience) and who possess the full powers of a bench of lay magistrates (who most often sit in groups of three). They sit alone, usually in large cities and towns where the pressure of work is greatest. There are over 40 in London, where they are called "metropolitan stipendiary magistrates". There are about half as many again spread around the rest of the country.

There are also some ex-officio magistrates who hold the office because they hold or have held another office. For example, High Court judges and the Lord Mayor and aldermen of the City of London are ex-officio magistrates.

Each bench of magistrates is assisted by a legally qualified and specially trained justices' clerk. The clerk also runs the court, helps to train new magistrates and administers the legal aid system in his court. The clerks have assistants who are similarly legally qualified.

The magistrates have the jurisdiction to conduct summary trials and the responsibility to screen the evidence before committing an accused for trial at the Crown Court.

Summary trial
This is the trial of summary offences and of those more serious offences where the accused had the choice and chose summary trial. Summary offences are minor, often regulatory offences carrying up to the magistrates' limits as to punishment (generally 6 months and/or a £1,000 fine). The vast majority are motoring offences.

Under the Magistrates' Courts Act 1980 s.12, it is often possible to plead guilty by post to these offences. There are over 1,500,000 people convicted each year of summary offences in England and Wales.

The Magistrates' Courts Act 1980, ss.17 *et seq.*, detail the offences where the accused is able to choose the mode of trial: these offences are said to be triable either way. If the accused is to be given the choice, the clerk will always warn him that if he elects summary trial (which he usually does), the magistrates reserve the right to commit him to the Crown Court for sentence if they feel he deserves punishment beyond their powers. These powers, apart from fines and imprisonment, include the power to make compensation orders in favour of the victim of crime, restitution orders where appropriate, supervision orders and community service orders.

Committal proceedings

Where the alleged offence is too serious for summary trial it is called 'indictable' or 'triable on indictment only'. The indictment itself is the written accusation against the accused. Technically, the bench is one of examining magistrates here and not a court properly so called.

There are two types of committal proceedings. First, where the evidence is all produced and the accused is invited to make a statement. He is not asked to plead guilty or not guilty because this is not a trial; it is an assessment of the strength of the evidence. The magistrates must decide whether there is a prima facie case to answer. If so, the accused is committed for trial. There are severe press restrictions at such hearings. Only names and charges can be published, unless the restrictions are lifted by the request or with the consent of the defendant.

The second type is much more common, and far quicker. It is called a "new style" or "paper" committal. This is because it falls within the Magistrates' Courts Act 1980, s.6(2). Here none of the evidence is considered in detail. There are three requirements: all the evidence must be in writing, the accused must have a solicitor acting for him in the case, and his lawyer must not wish to enter a submission that there is no case to answer. The defence can require that the full examination take place.

Some magistrates are specially trained to sit in juvenile courts (which exist under the authority of the Children and Young Persons' Act 1933). There they try children (those between 10 and 14 years old) and young persons (those between 14 and 17). The basis of much of this work is the Children and Young Persons' Act 1969. Incidentally, criminal proceedings cannot be brought against a child under ten. The idea of the 1969 Act was to replace criminal proceedings with "care proceedings" under which the court can require parents to take proper care and control of a child, or issue supervision orders (where local authorities or the probation service are involved) or care orders (where the offender may be actually removed from his home and put into local authority premises) or hospital orders, or guardianship orders. The offender is thus dealt with as one needing help and guidance rather than corrective treatment. Compensation orders can be made, and the parent or guardian must normally be made to pay the offender's victim. The court must meet in a different room or at a different time from (at least one hour before or after) the adult hearings. The public are excluded, but not the press. However, there are press restrictions; for example, they are not allowed to publish the offender's name without specific authority from the court or the Home Secretary. There are three justices, including at least one man and one woman who hear the case and all must be under 65.

COURTS WITH SPECIAL JURISDICTIONS

Employment Appeal Tribunal

Sir John Donaldson, the Master of the Rolls, said:

> a superior court of record presided over by a judge of the Court of Appeal, the Court of Session or the High Court, is a court and not a tribunal, whatever it may be called. (*Law Society's Gazette*)

This court was created by the Employment Protection Act 1975 which has now been taken into the Employment Protection (Consolidation) Act 1978, but the provisions are the same:

> 135 (1) The Employment Appeal Tribunal established under section 87 of the Employment Protection Act 1975 shall continue in existence by that name for the purpose of hearing appeals under section 136.
> (2) The Employment Appeal Tribunal... shall consist of:
> (*a*) such number of judges as may be nominated from time to time by the Lord Chancellor from among the judges (other than the Lord Chancellor) of the High Court and the Court of Appeal;
> (*b*) at least one judge of the Court of Session nominated from time to time by the Lord President of that Court; and
> (*c*) such number of other members as may be appointed from time to time by Her Majesty on the joint recommendation of the Lord Chancellor and the Secretary of State.
> (3) The members of the Appeal Tribunal appointed under section (2)(*b*) shall be persons who appear to the Lord Chancellor

and the Secretary of State to have special knowledge or experience
of industrial relations, either as representatives of employers or as
representatives of workers...

136 (1) An appeal shall lie to the Appeal Tribunal on a question
of law arising from any decision of, or arising in any proceedings
before, an industrial tribunal under, or by virtue of, the following
Acts —

(*a*) the Equal Pay Act 1970;
(*b*) the Sex Discrimination Act 1975;
(*c*) the Employment Protection Act 1975;
(*d*) the Race Relations Act 1976;
(*e*) this Act.

The EAT also deals with appeals on law or fact from decisions of
the Certification Officer under various statutes. This officer decides,
for instance, whether a union is genuinely independent of an
employer's control for the purpose of genuine representative activity.

There is an appeal route from this court to the Court of Appeal, or
the Court of Session in Scotland. It has a central office in London,
but it can sit anywhere in the country. It is properly constituted with a
judge and two or four laymen, although one layman will do, if the
parties agree to this. If there is more than one layman they must
equally represent employers' and workers' points of view. Hearings
are public, except where national interests or important points, such
as vital trade secrets, are at stake. Legal aid is available. Witnesses can
be summoned, the production of documents can be ordered and all its
judgments can be enforced.

However, the procedure is relatively informal. Robes are not worn.
There is no bench or witness box. The court can be addressed without
standing up. Costs are not generally awarded against the losing party,
unless the proceedings are regarded as having been unnecessary
and/or vexatious.

Coroners' Courts
Coroners are appointed by the county councils from barristers,
solicitors or medical practitioners of at least five years' standing.
They can be dismissed by the Lord Chancellor for inability or
misconduct. The office of coroner dates from the twelfth century.
Today, the appointment and jurisdiction of coroners are governed by
the Coroners Acts 1884–1980.

This court has a geographical jurisdiction—like the magistrates'
and county courts. It is a local court. The main function of this court
is to inquire into deaths in its districts where there is reasonable cause
to suspect:

(*a*) that the deceased died a violent or unnatural death; or
(*b*) the death was sudden and the cause unknown; or
(*c*) the death occurred in prison.

If the coroner so decides, a jury of seven, nine or eleven may be appointed to assist in deciding the identity of the deceased, the cause of death and where the death took place. Majority verdicts of the jury are acceptable, provided that there are not more than two dissentients. The procedure is inquisitorial, the coroner himself questioning witnesses who can be compelled to attend. Other interested persons can be represented, and, with the coroner's permission, they can question the witnesses. There are no speeches to the coroner, nor to the jury.

The other area of coroners' jurisdiction concerns treasure trove, of which Sir William Blackstone wrote (in 1765):

Where any money or coin, gold, silver, plate or bullion, is found hidden in the earth, or other private place, the owner thereof being unknown... the treasure belongs to the King: but if he that hid it be known, or afterwards found out, the owner and not the King is entitled to it.

The coroner must decide whether the articles in question were hidden, in which case they go to the Exchequer (and as a matter of custom the owner of the land and especially the finder are compensated), as with the Roman silver found in Mildenhall, Suffolk in 1946 (now in the British Museum), or just lost, in which case the finder is allowed to keep them, unless the true owner can be traced.

Restrictive Practices Court

This court was set up originally by the Restrictive Trade Practices Act 1956 (now consolidated into the Restrictive Practices Court Act 1976 and the Restrictive Trade Practices Act 1976) to inspect agreements relating to the supply of goods and services to see that they are not contrary to statute nor unfair to consumers. The Fair Trading Act 1973 and the Resale Prices Act 1964 added to the workload. The Director General of Fair Trading makes most of the referrals to the court. The court is composed of five judges and ten laymen with appropriate experience appointed by the Lord Chancellor on behalf of the Queen. Three of the judges come from the High Court, one from the Court of Session in Scotland and one from the Supreme Court of Northern Ireland. Usually the court comprises one judge and two laymen, although if the matter is only one of law a judge may sit alone. In any case his is the only verdict on points of law. Appeals lie to the Court of Appeal, the Court of Session or the Court of Appeal of Northern Ireland.

Courts-martial

These are concerned only with the armed forces. They are governed by statute, mainly the Army and Air Force Acts 1955 and the Naval Discipline Act 1957. Minor disciplinary offences are dealt with by superior offices. Very serious cases, such as murder or rape, are handed over to the civilian courts. Otherwise, serious offences are dealt with by courts-martial.

The procedure in court-martial is similar to that of the civilian courts. The accused can be represented. The court has a legally qualified adviser on the relevant points of law. The decision is taken by three or five superior officers. There is a preliminary inquiry to see that there is a case to answer. There is no jury. An acquittal is final, but a finding of guilt is subject to confirmation by a superior officer. This is seen as a check against injustice.

There has been, since 1951, a Courts-Martial Appeal Court. This is now governed by the Courts-Martial (Appeals) Act 1968. It is very similar to the Court of Appeal (Criminal Division) both in procedure and in the fact that the Lords Justices of Appeal preside, with High Court judges and various others appointed by the Lord Chancellor.

Naval Courts

The Merchant Shipping Act 1894 provides that the commander of any of Her Majesty's ships while abroad can convene a Naval Court to deal with any matter of immediate importance, such as the wrecking, abandonment or loss of a ship. Naval officers preside. The procedure is formal. The powers are considerable (including fines and imprisonment). An appeal route lies to the divisional court of the Queen's Bench Division and thereafter to the Court of Appeal.

Ecclesiastical Courts

There is an ancient and complex hierarchy of courts within the Church of England. They no longer have jurisdiction over laymen.

Court of Chivalry

In *Manchester Corporation* v. *Manchester Palace of Varieties* (1955) this court was convened to decide whether a theatre could display the coat of arms of the City of Manchester. It had not been convened since 1737. Its jurisdiction is to adjudicate upon the right to use armorial bearings and ensigns. In theory it is presided over by the Earl Marshal. The Lord Chief Justice sat on his behalf in 1955. It seems to have no power to enforce its judgments.

Judicial Committee of the Privy Council

The Committee consists, in theory, of the Lord President of the Council, ex-Lords President, the Lord Chancellor, the Law Lords, the senior judges of the overseas jurisdictions (who sit on cases from their own countries from time to time), and other members of the Privy Council who hold or who have held high judicial office. In practice the Lord Chancellor and four of the Law Lords sit unrobed, using a procedure similar to that used in the House of Lords when sitting as a court.

The jurisdiction falls into five broad categories:

(*a*) final appeals from the Isle of Man, the Channel Islands, British Colonies and Protectorates and from those Commonwealth countries who have not decided to handle their final appeals internally;

(*b*) appeals from the Admiralty Court when sitting as a "prize court" (dealing with the ownership of ships and cargo in connection with capture by enemy warships), and from the Colonial Courts of Admiralty and the Court of Admiralty of the Cinque Ports;

(*c*) appeals from the ecclesiastical courts;

(*d*) medical appeals from those struck off by the Professional Conduct Committee of the General Medical Council (under the Medical Act 1978).

(*e*) Special references from the Sovereign concerning, for example, the powers of colonial judges and legislation in Jersey.

TRIBUNALS

In addition to the ordinary courts there has grown up in post-war years a network of administrative tribunals dealing with various aspects of welfare and employment law. These tribunals differ from the courts in that they are staffed by specialists in particular fields rather than by judges. For example, an industrial tribunal hearing an unfair dismissal case will be staffed by persons who have had considerable experience in industry, one from or representing an employers' organisation, the other representing a trade union or workers' organisation. Similarly, where a person applies for industrial injury benefit, his application will not be successful unless it can be shown that the injury or disease arose out of the employment; this matter will be decided by a medical appeal tribunal, consisting of two doctors and a lawyer.

The purpose of such tribunals is to provide cheap and quick justice. Procedure is informal with the members of the tribunal asking questions of appellant and respondent. The advantages of tribunals are said to be:

(a) specialist knowledge which can be brought to bear on particular issues;
(b) the procedure is informal and not accusatorial;
(c) there are no court fees and costs are not normally awarded;
(d) decisions are normally arrived at quickly;
(e) they reduce the pressure of work on the ordinary courts;
(f) they are not bound to follow their own previous decisions.

They thus have wide discretionary power.
On the other hand, the disadvantages are that:

(a) tribunal decisions are not so well publicised as court decisions;
(b) tribunal hearings are sometimes held in private and this can arouse public suspicion;
(c) reasons for decisions are not always given;
(d) lack of insistence on the strict rules of evidence can lead to injustice;
(e) representation is not always allowed, and legal representation is rare;
(f) technical expertise does not always provide judicial impartiality and tribunal chairmen are not always lawyers;
(g) rights of appeal are limited;
(h) wide discretionary power can lead to inconsistency and unpredictability.

These tribunals, although numerous, have very limited and specific jurisdiction, granted by statute. Their decisions often reflect policy as much as law. They have had fairly uniform standards imposed upon them by a statute of 1958, now consolidated into the Tribunals and Inquiries Act 1971. The 1958 Act implemented most of the recommendations of the Franks Committee, which reported in 1958. These standards include the giving of reasons for decisions, the appointing of chairmen by the Lord Chancellor, allowing clear appeal routes on points of law to the High Court and allowing representation (although this is not often by lawyers). There is a Council on Tribunals which meets once a month to scrutinise the workings of the major tribunals, and reports on them annually. It deals with complaints about tribunals from the public. There are very few of these; about 40 a year from the 200,000 cases heard. Presumably, either there is very little wrong with the tribunals—or very few people have heard of the Council.

Industrial Tribunals
The Royal Commission on Trade Unions and Employers' Associ-

ations described the purpose of industrial tribunals as being to provide:

an easily accessible, speedy, informal and inexpensive procedure for the settlement of disputes

between employers and workers. Professor Rideout describes them as

among the greatest and most successful inventions of administrative law.

They were first set up in 1964 under the Industrial Training Act to decide matters concerning levies which employers had to pay, for having their workforce trained, to industrial training boards. Since then their jusrisdiction has increased and extends to matters relating to:

(*a*) contracts of employment;
(*b*) unfair dismissal;
(*c*) health and safety at work;
(*d*) sex discrimination;
(*e*) equal pay;
(*f*) redundancy.

The chairman of each tribunal is a barrister or solicitor of at least seven years' standing and he sits with two lay members, one representing an employers' organisation or the self-employed, the other an employees' organisation. Tribunals sit at about 95 centres throughout the country. The decision is by majority and is normally given at the hearing, though in more difficult cases it will be sent to the parties at a later date. Hearings are normally in public but can be in private where an issue involving national security arises. Appeal lies to the Employment Appeal Tribunal on a question of law, except in the case of certain appeals concerning enforcement of health and safety at work procedures in which case appeal is to the High Court, Queen's Bench Division.

Supplementary Benefit Appeal Tribunals

The right to supplementary benefit for those whose requirements exceed their resources is now provided by the Supplementary Benefits Act 1976.

Disputes over entitlement used to be handled by the Supplementary Benefits Commission, but since the implementation of the Social Security Act 1980, they are now settled by a "benefit officer".

There is an appeal route from his decision to a Supplementary Benefit Appeal Tribunal. There are about 120 around the country. They are constituted of a chairman and two ordinary members. The chairman is (nowadays) often a lawyer, and with some years experience as an ordinary member. Special training for chairmen is being introduced. He is selected from a panel chosen by the Lord Chancellor. One ordinary member is selected, after interview, from those appearing, as the 1976 Act puts it:

> to have knowledge or experience of conditions in the area to which the panel relates and of the problems of people living on low incomes.

The other ordinary member is chosen from those, again in the words of the 1976 Act:

> appearing to the Secretary of State to represent work-people.

In practice, local trades council federations put candidates forward.

Each tribunal also has a clerk to keep notes of evidence and check points of law. Sometimes the clerk is accused of becoming too actively involved with the hearing. There are senior chairmen, who are appointed from lawyers of at least seven years' experience. Their function is to oversee the working of SBATs in their assigned areas. They also hear complaints about procedure and participate in the selection of chairmen.

At the hearing, the benefit officer's decision is put forward by a presenting officer, who specialises in tribunal work. Only about half the appellants turn up for the hearing. The tribunal can continue without them, or adjourn. The hearings are held in private. The procedure is relatively informal, and to an extent flexible at the discretion of the chairman, although in 1977 guidelines for procedure were published. There is an appeal route on points of law to the Social Security Commissioners. The Health and Social Services and Social Security Adjudications Act 1983 provides for the amalgamation of SBATs and the National Insurance Tribunals.

Domestic tribunals

These tribunals are rather different. They are concerned with the internal regulation of an organisation rather than with the implementation of broad governmental policy. They can be divided into two types. First, there are those based on contract, so that if you join an organisation you thereby subject yourself to the jurisdiction of its internal regulation. Trade unions, social clubs and some professional organisations have such tribunals. Second, there are those domestic tribunals created by statute such as the Professional Conduct Committee of the General Medical Council (Medical Act 1978) and the Solicitors' Disciplinary Tribunal (Solicitors Act 1974). Tribunals like these have appeal routes into the court system. Those which rest in contract law do not, although their procedures are under the supervision of the divisional court of the Queen's Bench Division.

INQUIRIES

These hearings are different from courts and from tribunals in that they tend to be set up to do a particular job rather than to perform a continuing function. There are several different kinds of inquiries:

(a) Tribunals of Inquiry which are set up, as and when needed, by Parliament in order to discover all the facts surrounding a particular event. The appropriate Secretary of State is responsible. Powers given are usually equivalent to those of the High Court to summon witnesses and order the production of documents. Such inquiries followed the Profumo scandal (1963), the Aberfan disaster (1966) and "Bloody Sunday" in Londonderry (1968).

(b) Inquiries into objections; for example, public local inquiries into the compulsory acquisition of land for hospitals, roads, new towns, or local inquiries into alternative proposals, for example, various routes for a new road.

(c) Inquiries into accidents, such as railway and aircraft crashes, to establish causes (rather than place the blame).

(d) Investigations of companies under the Companies Acts.

(e) Planning inquiries under the town and country planning legislation which are held in order to compile county "structure plans" and "local plans" regarding medium- and long-term developments of land use.

Local inspectors conduct inquiries and report to the appropriate minister. The minister makes the decision, and must answer for it in Parliament. Reasons must be given (since the passing of the Tribunals and Inquiries Act 1958), and despite the fairly common absence of an appeal route, the rules of natural justice must be observed.

The Council on Tribunals supervises inquiries as well. The Lord Chancellor can make procedural rules for inquires (under the Tribunals and Inquiries Act 1971), but only after consultation with the Council.

Chapter 5

The Personnel of the Law

THE LEGAL PROFESSION

The legal profession in England and Wales is divided into barristers, solicitors and legal executives. The general term lawyer can be taken to mean any of these or indeed just to indicate that someone knows some law! The main division, into barristers and solicitors, dates back to about 1340, although the title of "solicitor" only dates from the fifteenth century. Before then, their work was done by three groups—solicitors, attorneys and proctors. They fused in 1831 when the Law Society was created, and all the remaining distinctions were removed by the Judicature Act 1873. Legal executives, as a separate branch, date only from 1963 when their Institute was set up.

Barristers

"Barristers-at-Law" conduct cases in court. Their main role is one of advocacy. They have exclusive right to be heard in the House of Lords, the Judicial Committee of the Privy Council, the Court of Appeal, the three divisions of the High Court (except the Bankruptcy Court), the Crown Court (except where cases have come to it on appeal from the magistrates, or where the accused has been committed to the Crown Court for sentence) and the Employment Appeal Tribunal. (Both barristers and solicitors can appear in the county court and magistrates' courts.)

Barristers belong to one of the four Inns of Court, i.e. Lincoln's Inn, Gray's Inn, the Inner Temple and the Middle Temple. These Inns are unincorporated societies governed by the Masters of the Bench, who themselves are judges or senior barristers. A person wishing to become a barrister must apply first to become a student at one of the Inns. He must keep terms, i.e. dine at his Inn a certain number of times (usually 24). He must attend an approved practical training course and pass the necessary professional examinations before being called to the Bar. He must then become a pupil in chambers with a qualified barrister for one year. After six months he is allowed to present minor cases on his own in court. A barrister's work also consists of paper-work, e.g. advising solicitors on legal problems (called "giving counsel's opinion") and drafting pleadings for use in litigation.

The principal governing body of the Bar is the Senate of the Inns of Court and the Bar. This body lays down general policies and is concerned to promote and uphold the standards, honour and independence of the Bar. It has certain disciplinary powers. Training and education matters are shared between the Senate and the Inns of Court.

Barristers and their clients are not bound in contract. Your barrister cannot sue you for his fees. You cannot sue him for negligence in the conduct of your case, except for work done in chambers (his office).

This exception was seen in *Saif Ali* v. *Sydney Mitchell and Co* (1978), which was about a car crash. A barrister advised suing only one defendant. By the time his error was noticed it was too late to sue another one. (There is a statutory limitation period of three years during which personal injury claims must be brought.)

The barrister gets paid when your solicitor pays him on your behalf, and adds the fee to your bill. A barrister cannot in theory refuse to represent a client. The barrister has a duty to respect the confidence of his client. He cannot take instructions directly; you must brief him via your solicitor, although some barristers have special permission to work in law centres directly with the public. Your solicitor is likely to have chosen counsel for you. This is said to be a good quality control of the Bar, since without a good reputation, a barrister is unlikely to get much work. Barristers cannot advertise, form partnerships or share profits. They usually share chambers and the services of a clerk with whom solicitors usually negotiate fees, etc.

Barristers have a divided loyalty. They must do their best for their clients, but they owe duties to the court as well. The proper development of the law requires that all relevant material is drawn to the attention of the court in all cases. The barristers have a duty to do this, even if such materials may sometimes adversely affect their client's cause.

If a barrister is successful over a numbers of years he might apply to the Lord Chancellor to be appointed Queen's Counsel. Sometimes QCs are referred to as "silks" because the gowns they wear in court are made of silk whereas "junior" barristers' gowns are made of "stuff". Becoming a QC is often referred to as taking silk. Incidentally, a junior barrister is one in practice but not a QC. During the year of practical experience required before becoming a junior, barristers are "pupils".

Having risen to the dizzy heights of the rank of QC a barrister is less likely to do anything but appear as an advocate and give opinions, although changes in the relevant rules (31st May 1977) enable QCs to draft documents. The changes also removed the strictness of the old two counsel rule which meant that if one briefed (employed) a QC then a junior had to be employed too. Although the rule is no longer strict, QCs still commonly appear in court with juniors.

Solicitors

A "Solicitor of the Supreme Court" is a general practitioner in law. His main function is to advise clients on legal and financial matters. His work consists chiefly in conveying land and houses, checking title to land, drawing up wills, forming companies and advising on matrimonial matters and criminal law. Solicitors in larger firms tend to specialise, e.g. one may specialise in taxation, whilst another may specialise in company law. Neither solicitors nor barristers can form themselves into limited liability companies. Solicitors practise either alone or in partnership. Many solicitors are employed in industry and local government jobs.

As far as court work or litigation is concerned, the solicitor prepares the case and ascertains the facts. He also arranges for witnesses to be present and documents to be submitted. Unlike a barrister a solicitor has only a limited right of advocacy. He can appear in the county court and magistrates' court. He can also appear in the Crown Court on an appeal from the magistrates' court and where the accused has been sent by the magistrates for sentence to the Crown Court. In bankruptcy matters he can appear in the High Court. In addition, he may appear before an industrial tribunal.

In order to become a solicitor it is necessary to pass the appropriate professional examinations. The papers taken will vary with the applicant's initial qualifications. It is usual for an applicant to have a degree. Naturally, greater exemptions are available to those who have degrees in law. It is also necessary to serve a period of apprenticeship, called articles, working in a solicitor's office. The usual period is two years. Having qualified in this way the candidate has his name entered onto the Roll (by the Master of the Rolls). It is not possible for a newly admitted solicitor to practice alone straightaway since for his first three years he must have an experienced supervising solicitor to oversee and vouch for his accounts. As a result, three years are normally served working in another practice. In fact few solicitors in general practice do not work within partnerships. Sometimes such firms can become very large.

The governing body of solicitors is the Law Society. Eighty-five per cent of solicitors belong to it, but it has power, notably disciplinary, over all practising solicitors. It organises the admission, education and training of prospective solicitors. It represents solicitors in dealing with the public. It administers the Legal Aid and Advice Schemes. It maintains a Compensation Fund to which all solicitors contribute annually and from which clients can be repaid losses caused by the default or neglect of solicitors. Discipline is regulated by the Solicitors Disciplinary Tribunal which is an independent body containing laymen. It stands apart from the Law Society. In 1974 in response to complaints that claims against solicitors were dealt with by other solicitors this body took over the work earlier undertaken by a Disciplinary Committee which had been set up in 1919.

Solicitors are contractually bound to their clients. They can sue for their fees, and be sued for negligence. The relationship is basically one of principal and agent. Thus, the solicitor has the agent's right to indemnity for acts done and liabilities incurred within his authority as agent. Further to this, the relationship is regarded by equity as "fiduciary"; that is, both sides must show the utmost good faith. Each must disclose everything to do with the case: you must tell your solicitor everything, and he must respect your confidence. Indeed, he cannot be forced, even by court, to reveal what you have told him. This is called privilege. Much of the law relating to solicitors, their status, discipline, remuneration etc., is contained in the Solicitors Act 1974. With regard to remuneration, you can always have your bill checked by the Law Society if you regard it as excessive.

Using powers conferred by the 1974 Act, the Lord Chancellor appointed an officer called the Lay Observer whose duty it is to consider and report on complaints from the public about the manner in which complaints about solicitors have been handled by the Law Society.

Legal executives

The Institute of Legal Executives was established in 1963 in order to give professional status to those people who work in solicitors' offices but who, for one reason or another, have not been admitted as solicitors. There are examinations to pass and a period of apprenticeship to serve in order to become a legal executive. This period can be as long as eight years before Fellowship of the Institute can be granted. Legal executives perform a variety of functions side by side with solicitors. Obviously, if a solicitor must be employed for a particular task (e.g. conveyancing, advocacy in the lower courts) then legal executives are excluded, but otherwise they have wide areas of experience and knowledge. Some specialise and achieve high levels of expertise.

The Lord Chancellor, using a power conferred by the Administration of Justice Act 1977, has granted a limited right of audience to legal executives. Thus, since the County Courts (Right of Audience) Order 1978 came into force, legal executives have been able to speak in the county courts for unopposed adjournments and applications for judgement by consent. It was hoped that further rights might be recommended by the Royal Commission on Legal Services which was set up in 1976 and reported in 1979, but it was not to be.

THE JUDGES

Professor Griffith (in his book, *The Politics of the Judiciary*) has written:

> The most remarkable fact about the appointment of judges is that it is wholly in the hands of politicians. High Court and circuit judges, recorders, stipendiary and lay magistrates are appointed by or on the advice of the Lord Chancellor who is a member of the Cabinet. Appointments to the Court of Appeal, to the Judicial Committee of the House of Lords, and to the offices of Lord Chief Justice and President of the Family Division are made on the advice of the Prime Minister after consultation with the Lord Chancellor, who himself consults senior members of the judiciary before making his choice or consulting with the Prime Minister.

It is interesting that the power to choose is vested in the politicians, but it is also important to observe that there are minimum qualifications which must be possessed by those from whom such choices can be made.

Law Lords

Properly called Lords of Appeal in Ordinary or members of the Judicial Committee of the House of Lords, they are usually chosen from the judges in the Court of Appeal but the minimum qualification is that the candidate should have been qualified as a barrister for 15 years. On appointment they are created life peers. They also sit in the court called the Judicial Committee of the Privy Council (*see* Chapter 4).

Lords Justices of Appeal

They sit in the Court of Appeal, and are usually promoted from the High Court, although the minimum requirement is qualification as a barrister for 15 years.

High Court judges

Also called puisne judges, they are usually appointed direct from practising barristers, of at least ten years' standing. It is possible, but rarely done, for a circuit judge to be promoted to the High Court.

Circuit Judges

These are the judges who preside in county courts and the Crown Court and they are appointed from barristers of at least ten years' standing or from recorders of three years' experience.

Recorders

These are the part-time judges of the Crown Court and they are chosen from solicitors or barristers who have been professionally qualified for at least ten years and who are prepared to sit for at least one month each year. It is noteworthy that only here do solicitors qualify for consideration.

THE JUDICIAL OFFICERS

The Lord Chancellor

He is the head of the legal profession and judiciary and nominal head of the House of Lords sitting as a court. The office of Lord Chancellor involves a political as well as a legal appointment, in that he is a member of the government and Speaker of the House of Lords. Appointment is by the Prime Minister and the Lord Chancellor is a Cabinet Minister. In addition to being head of the judiciary, he is Chairman of the Judicial Committee of the Privy Council. He advises the Queen on the appointment of High Court and circuit judges, justices of the peace, stipendiary magistrates and recorders. He is the keeper of the Great Seal of the Realm—which is the signature of the Crown in its corporate capacity. The Lord Chancellor changes with a change of government. The Lord Chancellor is also actively concerned with law reform. The Law Commission, which was set up in 1965 to promote law reform, has its members appointed by the Lord Chancellor.

There is a theory called the separation of powers which holds it to be a sound organisation for a state where the judiciary, the legislature and the executive are kept apart. In Britain this is seen to some extent, but nothing like completely. Here, for instance, is the Lord Chancellor with a place in the judiciary (a judge), the legislature (a speaker in the House of Lords in Parliament) and the executive (a member of the Cabinet).

The Attorney-General

He is a legal adviser to the government. As such he is a practising barrister and head of the English Bar; points of professional etiquette are referred to him. He is also a Member of Parliament (usually in the House of Commons) and the appointment changes with change of government. His role in advocacy is to prosecute in important criminal cases and represent the Crown in civil matters. In addition he brings cases on behalf of the general public, e.g. cases of public nuisance.

The Solicitor-General

He is the deputy of the Attorney-General and assists him in his work. He is a practising barrister and normally a Member of Parliament. The appointment changes with a change of government. Both the Attorney-General and the Solicitor-General are called the Law Officers of the Crown and as such both are barred from private practice.

Director of Public Prosecutions

The Director of Public Prosecutions is a senior civil servant and therefore remains when governments depart. Appointment is by the Home Secretary and, in order to qualify, he must be a barrister or solicitor of at least ten years' standing. The DPP is only concerned with criminal matters and one of his functions is to advise the police on important prosecutions. Sometimes the DPP prosecutes through his own staff called Treasury counsel, in cases such as:

(*a*) serious crimes, like those connected with terrorism;
(*b*) crimes involving corruption and public mischief, e.g. councillors accepting bribes or cases where false information has been given to the police in order to mislead them or waste their time.

Sometimes the consent of the Attorney-General is necessary before prosecutions can be initiated by the DPP, e.g. under the Official Secrets Acts 1911 to 1939.

Masters

There are various matters which must be dealt with between the commencement of a legal action (the serving of documents etc.) and the actual hearing. They are sometimes called interlocutory matters, and include the production of documents and decisions on the best place and date for the hearing.

In the High Court there are Queen's Bench Masters (appointed from barristers of at least ten years' standing) and Chancery Masters (appointed from solicitors of at least ten years' standing). There are also officers called Taxing Masters who deal with the assessment of costs in court actions. They too are appointed from solicitors with at least ten years' standing.

The Official Solicitor

This is an officer of the court who appears on behalf of those unable to help themselves:

(*a*) the mentally ill;
(*b*) children being adopted;
(*c*) people in prison for contempt of court.

Official Referees

These are specialist circuit judges who deal with cases requiring detailed scrutiny of books and documentation, like alleged accounting frauds.

Circuit Administrators

When the circuit system was last considered, when the Crown Court network was devised in 1971, officers called circuit administrators were appointed to each of the six circuits (*see* Chapter 4). They deal with the efficient management of the circuit for which they are responsible. All administrative difficulties are referred to them.

On each circuit there are also presiding judges, of High Court rank, who are responsible for the efficient use and availability of judges. They liaise with the circuit administrator.

LAYMEN AMONGST THE PERSONNEL OF THE LAW

Lay magistrates

These were considered in the last chapter when we dealt with magistrates' courts. There are well over 20,000 lay justices—paid only expenses. About 98 per cent. of criminal trials are dealt with by them. The judicial system, at least at the petty end of criminal justice, could not be run without them.

Tribunal panel members

These too were considered in Chapter 4. The tribunal network is large and developing. The use of laymen in the administration of justice there is essential. Their expertise and practical experience is of central importance in the handling of the matters referred to tribunals.

Lay assessors

In the same way as lay panel members assist tribunals with expertise, lay assessors assist certain courts. They are professional or scientific experts who provide their knowledge and experience to assist the judge. They are most often found in the Admiralty Court, which is technically part of the Queens Bench Division of the High Court. Here they advise the judge in cases concerning collision at sea, poor seamanship, navigational error and so on. They can also be found in other courts within the QBD, when matters involving detailed scientific investigation are being dealt with.

Juries

Anyone between 18 and 65 years old can be summoned to sit as a juror, unless he is amongst those excluded—such as lawyers, judges, policemen, the mentally ill and certain convicted criminals. There is also a category of people who can be excused jury service—like MPs, medical practitioners and members of the armed forces. If a good enough reason can be given to the officer of the court who (representing the Lord Chancellor) summons a panel of jurors, then they might avoid serving. The most common excuse is a long-standing holiday booking. Individuals can be called to serve more than once. It is an offence not to attend. At the trial the jurors are sworn in. The defendant can challenge up to three without giving a reason, more if he can justify his challenge. The whole panel can be challenged (very rare), for example, on the basis that a proper selection has not been made from the electoral roll. This is called challenging the array. In the rare instance of insufficient jurors having been summoned, any eligible person passing by the court can be required to attend. Such activity is called praying the tales, and the unlucky stroller is called a talesman.

The function of a jury is to decide upon matters of fact. Juries are found every day in the Crown Court. They are also in coroners' courts. It is possible, but very rare to find them in county courts and the High Court (e.g. 1 per cent of QBD cases). Here, they deal with defamation, malicious prosecution, false imprisonment and some fraud cases.

Verdicts are usually unanimous. However, majority verdicts are acceptable to the judge after two hours and ten minutes of jury deliberation. The majority must be at least ten where the jury consists of twelve. Only 6 or 7 per cent of jury verdicts are by majority in criminal cases. There are more in civil cases, but civil juries are very rare. Most of the law about juries has been consolidated into the Juries Act 1974 and special recent provisions were made by the Coroners' Juries Act 1983. The crime of threatening or bribing jurors is called embracery.

Chapter 6

Bringing a Case in the Civil Courts

CIVIL ACTIONS

Where one party sues another for an alleged breach of the civil law then a civil action takes place. The parties are plaintiff and defendant. Should an appeal against the decision be lodged later, they would be called appellant and respondent. The parties might be individuals, or companies or partnership firms. The purpose of the action is to obtain a civil remedy. There is a variety of remedies, but the most common is damages—money—assessed as compensation.

AN ACTION IN THE HIGH COURT

The jurisdiction of the civil courts was considered in Chapter 4. Obviously, the case would be brought initially in a court of first instance. The best-known first instance civil courts are the county courts—which deal with small cases, and the High Court—which deals with larger ones. This is a very broad generalisation; for details *see* Chapter 4.

We will consider the procedures followed in the High Court. As an example we will follow an action for alleged negligence, resulting in serious personal injuries to the plaintiff. We will assume that the plaintiff can afford to bring the action—that he can pay his costs. If he wins he may recover them from the defendant. If he loses he may have to cover his and the defendant's costs. It is a risky and expensive business. Whether the plaintiff wins or loses his case he may still have to pay some of his own legal costs. If he has insufficient resources, but a good case, then he may qualify for legal aid. He will get "legal assistance" anyway. We will consider these topics later. Even if the plaintiff can afford to sue, he ought to do his best, through his solicitor if need be, to settle without litigation. If he cannot, and he can afford to sue, this is the usual procedure.

The plaintiff serves the writ

A writ is obtainable from the Central Office of the Supreme Court in

London or from the district registry. The plaintiff briefly outlines his claim in the writ (i.e. negligence) and the remedy sought (i.e. unliquidated damages). Next the writ is served on the defendant, i.e. he is given a sealed copy, or, alternatively (and more usually) his solicitor accepts service of the writ on his behalf.

The defendant acknowledges service of writ

Acknowledgment is made by the defendant returning an acknowledgment form to the court office from which the writ was issued.

Pleadings

Pleadings are then delivered by one party to another; this can take a very long time. Pleadings are drafted by counsel and cover all material facts. They consist of the following:

The statement of claim

This is sent by the plaintiff to the defendant and sets out his cause of action (e.g. negligence), losses incurred and injuries suffered. It is important that this be drafted with care, since at the trial the plaintiff will not be able to make any allegation of which the defendant has no knowledge. If the statement lacks detail the defendant can ask for "further and better particulars".

The defence

This is sent by the defendant to the plaintiff. In the defence the defendant's version of the events is set down and any specific denials of allegations made by the plaintiff. If the defendant does not specifically deny an allegation, he will be taken to have admitted it by the court. The plaintiff can require "further and better particulars" of the defence. If the defendant feels that he has an action against the plaintiff he can issue a counterclaim.

The reply

This is not always used but enables the plaintiff to answer any new point raised by the defendant in his defence document.

Preparing the evidence

Once the pleadings have been exchanged (often only a statement of claim and a defence will appear), the parties are in a position to build their cases. Evidence will be crucial. Any relevant documents held by either party must be disclosed to the opponent. It is called discovery of documents and it can be ordered by the court if necessary. The idea is to confine the trial, when it happens, to clearly disputed issues. Surprise documents are not encouraged.

If one side has knowledge which is essential evidence to the other then, and again in the interests of clarifying the issues, questions are formally asked (and replies can be ordered). Such questions are called interrogatories. A simpler exercise is the notice to admit. If our negligence action concerned a faulty repair on a vehicle, then the defendant might be required to admit that the signature on a repair bill was his. This reduces the mass of evidence which the plaintiff has to take into court to prove his case. If he intends to refer to a document which is in the possession of the defendant he might issue a notice to produce a document. This will put the defendant on notice to have the paper with him in court, where the plaintiff intends to refer to it in the contested evidence.

Once the "paper-chase" is complete, the case is "set down" for trial.

The trial

When the day of the trial arrives the parties may be kept waiting. A list of cases is prepared in advance and backlogs are common. This might provide a last chance to settle out of court.

When the case is eventually "called on" the plaintiff's counsel speaks first. The disputed issues are outlined to the judge (and in the rare event of one having been sworn in for a civil trial, the jury). Then the plaintiff's witnesses are called and examined, cross-examined (by the counsel acting for the defendant) and, if cross-examination has weakened any of the original answers, the witness is re-examined.

Incidentally, although witnesses usually attend willingly (their expenses are paid) if they are reluctant to do so they can be forced to by a "subpoena". Ignoring this amounts to contempt of court: a fine—or even imprisonment—could follow. The evidence is given on oath or affirmation. If a witness produces a story remarkably different from what the plaintiff expected, then the judge can give permission for him to be treated as a "hostile witness", and questions can be put to destroy the credibility of the evidence brought out by the party who called the witness. Naturally, cross-examination by the defence counsel is always designed to do this.

Once the plaintiff's counsel has finished presenting his case it is the turn of the defence to seek to refute it. If the case seems extremely thin, then the defence might submit that there "is no case to answer", and if the judge agrees, then the case is dismissed.

If the defence calls witnesses then the plaintiff's counsel will cross-examine, seeking to undermine the evidence they give. Once both sides have presented their evidence each will sum up to the judge. The defence, then the plaintiff. Naturally, the burden of proving the case usually lies on the party who brought it, the plaintiff. He must prove his case "on a balance of probabilities"—he must show that his evidence is more likely than not to be correct. In the rare event of a jury being present, the judge then sums up the factual evidence which has been presented, and directs the jury on the law and what each side has to establish to their satisfaction before their side of the case can be supported. Usually there is no jury. The judge will decide both matters of fact and of law and deliver his judgment. If he decides to take time to consider, and delivers it later, it is referred to as a "reserved" judgment. He always gives the legal reasoning behind his decision. This is called the *"ratio decidendi"* and it forms the essence of the case for the purpose of the doctrine of precedent (*see* Chapter 3).

The losing party may wish to appeal. If it is the defendant who has lost, an application for a "stay of execution" might be made to delay the implementation of the judgment pending the appeal.

The appeal route would, of course, be to the Court of Appeal (Civil Division). If there are grounds to appeal against the final decision (as opposed to a decision on an intermediate, perhaps procedural, matter) then there is generally a right to appeal. No leave to appeal need be sought. These grounds for appeal must be more than just disappointment at the result of the case. The loser might feel that the trial judge was mistaken in the view he took of the law in question, or in his understanding of the weight and nature of the evidence or in that he refused to admit admissible evidence or refused to exclude inadmissible evidence. If there was a jury, the ground for appeal might be that the judge misdirected them.

This action was brought in order to obtain monetary compensation for injuries caused by negligence—called damages. The idea of damages is to compensate the party who has suffered financial loss or physical injury. That is, to restore him financially to the position he would have been in were it not for the defendant's wrongful conduct. Damages can be general and special, liquidated and unliquidated.

Genaral and special damages

Suppose that David, whilst on his way to work, is knocked down by a bus driven negligently by Charlie, a bus driver employed by Greenminster County Council. If David can show that Charlie was negligent, David is entitled as of right to:

(*a*) general damages in respect of the injury (to cover pain and suffering); and
(*b*) special damages, to compensate him for loss of earnings, if the injury has prevented him from going to work.

Liquidated and unliquidated damages

Liquidated damages are ascertainable or fixed damages and are most common in the event of a breach of contract. Here both parties agree that, if a certain eventuality takes place or does not take place, one shall pay to the other an agreed sum of money, e.g. a builder might agree with a building owner that if a certain section of work is not handed over by a certain date, damages will become payable to reimburse the building owner for his loss. If the fixed sum is greatly in excess of the loss which was or might have been suffered as a result of the breach of contract, then it might be seen as a "penalty" clause. The court ignores penalty clauses and awards the loss sustained.

Unliquidated damages are damages whose amount is not agreed upon in advance, i.e. unquantified damages. This is the normal remedy in tort where the judge determines how much a defendant should pay to a plaintiff.

On very rare occasions a court might award "exemplary" damages, if they have been applied for, and if the wrong done to the plaintiff is sufficiently outrageous.

Enforcement

If the plaintiff is successful and is awarded damages he becomes a judgement creditor and the defendant a judgment debtor. If the money is not paid, then the judgment debtor must return to court to have the judgment enforced. The civil courts do not do so unless asked. The possible ways of enforcement include sending the bailiffs to take goods belonging to the judgment debtor, selling them at public auction and giving the amount due to the judgment creditor and any balance back to the judgment debtor. In the High Court this is done by means of a writ called *"fieri facias"*—commonly called "fi.fa." Another way is to have an "attachment of earnings order" made. Then the defendant's employers will deduct instalments at source. A "garnishee" order could be made, instructing someone who owes the judgment debtor money to pay it direct to the judgment creditor. A charging order could be made over the judgment debtor's property, which, if pressed, could result in it being sold. There are other possibilities too, but each has its limitations.

The initial step in civil litigation is for the prospective plaintiff to ask himself "if I win could he pay me"? If he could not it will be an elaborate waste of a lot of time. Such an impecunious defendant is called "a man of straw". Never sue a man of straw.

Apart from damages there are various other remedies available where appropriate from civil courts, such as injunctions and decrees of specific performance. They are considered elsewhere in this book—with discussions on equity (Chapter 2), tort (Chapter 12) and contract (Chapter 13).

Chapter 7

Bringing a Case in the Criminal Courts

CRIMINAL TRIALS

The parties to a criminal trial are usually the Queen and the individual accused. The prosecution is brought by the Crown on behalf of us all, so whereas a civil action would be named in reports after the parties involved (e.g. *Donoghue v. Stevenson*), most criminal cases are referred to like this: *R. v. accused*, where "R." stands for "Rex" if there is a king on the throne and "Regina" if we have a queen. So the case might be called *R. v. Jones*.

The prosecution is actually brought by a barrister in the Crown Court or a barrister or solicitor or the police in the magistrates' court. The police usually start the action but may employ a specialist to speak in court. It is possible, although rare, for a private individual to initiate criminal proceedings. In some particular areas of the criminal law, for example, the Trade Descriptions Act 1968, alternative agencies initiate prosecutions (in the case of the 1968 Act it will be the trading standards departments of local authorities). The Director of Public Prosecutions is often involved in the prosecution of really serious crimes (*see* Chapter 5).

The accused will attend the trial either because he has been summoned to attend by the court (if it is a relatively minor charge) or because he has been arrested (for a more serious matter) by the police and produced from custody for the trial.

All criminal cases are heard initially by magistrates. We considered in Chapter 4 how the court deals with the trial of summary offences and the preliminary inspection of the evidence to be brought in the trial of a more serious—indictable—offence.

It may well be that the accused has been committed for trial but released on bail to wait his turn in the overworked courts. The questions involved in the granting of bail will be examined later (Chapter 14). The place of trial will depend upon the seriousness of the charge. The accused is presumed innocent until the prosecution has established their case "beyond a reasonable doubt"—so that the magistrates or the jury, as the case may be—are sure of his guilt.

SUMMARY TRIAL PROCEDURE

This is the procedure used by the magistrates when dealing with the trial of summary offences and of those offences "triable either way" when summary trial has been selected. Incidentally, where a summary offence is alleged the prosecution must normally be brought within six months of the commission of the offence (unless a statute creating an offence states otherwise: Magistrates' Courts Act 1980 s.127).

Most summary trials are for motoring offences. These are mostly to be found in the Road Traffic Act 1972, s.179 of which provides that where an offence such as speeding, careless or reckless driving is alleged then the accused must be warned at the time of the offence that prosecution will be considered. If this is not done (unless the driver did not stop, or he or the registered keeper of the vehicle could not be traced in time), then the driver or keeper must be presented with a summons or a notice of intended prosecution within 14 days of the offence.

As to the procedure at the trial, the accused appears at court to answer the summons. The justices' clerk will read out the offence with which he is charged and ask if the defendant is pleading guilty or not guilty. For example it might be a charge of speeding, contrary to the Road Traffic Regulation Act 1967, s.78A. The prosecutor would then go on to outline the events to which the charge relates, summarising the events of the particular morning when the accused was observed to have driven too quickly along a certain street, and so on.

For charges like this, indeed for any offence which is triable only summarily and not punishable by more than three months' imprisonment, the accused will often be offered the opportunity to plead guilty by post, and therefore not have to turn up at court (Magistrates' Courts Act 1980, s.12). Our accused intends to plead not guilty, so he has to attend.

This offence is not "triable either way", so he will not be given the choice of jury trial in the Crown Court.

Since when the clerk asked him how he wishes to plead he replied "Not guilty", the policeman or the solicitor acting for the police as prosecutor now presents the case against the accused, calling witnesses as desired. Obviously the policeman who observed the events in question will be called. The accused's defence solicitor can cross-examine the witnesses after they have given their evidence for the prosecution.

If the evidence appears very thin, particularly after the cross-examination of the prosecution witnesses, then the defence may submit that there is no case to answer. If the magistrates agree, the case is dismissed.

Otherwise the defence then presents evidence and calls witnesses. It may be that the accused is the only one.

A speech can be made by or on behalf of the accused, before or after or instead of his sworn evidence. (The procedure of making an "unsworn statement from the dock", however, has been abolished.)

After both sides have presented their cases the magistrates deliver their verdict. They often retire to a nearby room to discuss it first. They can call on the clerk for advice on matters of law, but not about the facts.

Once the decision has been taken the court will pronounce sentence. The chairman of the bench does so. Usually the defence makes a speech in mitigation first. In our speeding case, for instance, it might be that the man was late for work, or that his wife was in labour. Both sides can address the court about his character. His previous convictions, if any, are brought to the court's attention. The sentence, if the man is convicted, in such a case as this, would probably be a fine and an endorsement of his driving licence with penalty points; for speeding cases it will be three points. Each year there are about 300,000 summary trials for speed limit offences. There are guilty verdicts in 98 per cent of them.

Apart from motoring offences, summary trial by magistrates could lead to any of a variety of sentences. The list includes absolute discharge, conditional discharge, binding over, fines, attendance centres, detention centres (males only), probation, community service orders, imprisonment (generally five days to six months for any single offence), suspended sentences of imprisonment, and others. Sentence can be deferred until a report on the convicted person's mental, physical, social or personal circumstances has been obtained. The sentence could also be increased to "take into consideration" other offences which have been admitted by the prisoner despite his not having been convicted of them.

The court could also order restitution (e.g. of stolen goods still in his possession) and/or compensation (up to £1,000 per offence) and/or any necessary revision of the required contribution towards legal aid, if he had been in receipt of it, and/or forfeiture of any property used for criminal purposes. There are certain limited circumstances where the prisoner could be committed to the Crown Court for sentence for a summary offence; for example where a fresh offence has been committed during the operational period of a suspended sentence imposed by the Crown Court. The sentence for this later offence can now be added to the punishment for the earlier offence (for which the sentence had been suspended).

There is an appeal route to the Crown Court against conviction or sentence on grounds relating to matters of fact and/or matters of law. The whole case is reviewed. There is also an appeal route to the Divisional Court of the Queen's Bench Division of the High Court by way of case stated (*see* Chapter 4).

PROCEDURE FOR TRIAL ON INDICTMENT

The trial of these more serious—indictable—offences, and of those offences triable either way where trial on indictment has been selected, takes place in the Crown Court before a judge and jury. The nature and structure of the Crown Court system was examined in Chapter 4. The jury as an institution involving laymen in the administration of justice was considered in Chapter 5. Before appearing in the Crown Court for trial, these cases would have been considered by a magistrates' court conducting "committal proceedings" (*see* Chapter 4). The accused may have been remanded in custody or (more likely) remanded on bail; the system of bail will be considered later (*see* Chapter 14).

An indictment is a formal document containing the accusation of crime which is read out to the accused in court. There will be a statement of the alleged offence and the particulars of where and when it is alleged to have been committed by the accused. This is the start of his trial. It is called the "arraignment". He will then be asked to plead guilty or not guilty. If he pleads guilty the evidence and the accused's background and previous convictions (if any) will be presented. Then he will be sentenced. If he pleads not guilty, or if he refuses to plead (which is taken as a not guilty plea), the trial proceeds. The jury is sworn in, each unchallenged (*see* Chapter 5) member saying:

> I swear by almighty God that I will faithfully try the several issues joined between our Sovereign Lady the Queen and the prisoner at the bar and give a true verdict according to the evidence.

Anyone who prefers not to take the oath (which has religious overtones) can affirm.

The prosecution barrister puts forward his case first. His is the burden of proof. He gives his opening speech to the jury. He tells them what to expect. Then he calls his witnesses and, on oath, each gives his "evidence in chief" in response to the questions put. "Leading questions"—putting words into the witness's mouth—should not be asked. Hearsay evidence is not usually allowed; the witness can only say what he saw or heard—first- not second-hand evidence is required. Then the accused's barrister can cross-examine the witness, obviously, to check the value of the evidence given, to expose any shortcomings or weaknesses of what has been said, or to cloud or weaken the evidence in the minds of the jury. The prosecution barrister can re-examine if he feels he can restore the quality of the evidence.

After all the prosecution witnesses have been examined, defence counsel opens his case. The accused can give evidence, if he wishes. He cannot be forced to. He can no longer make an unsworn statement from the dock. Then the defence witnesses are called, examined, cross-examined and re-examined as necessary.

Then prosecuting counsel sums up his case to the jury. Then defence counsel does likewise. Then the judge sums up the whole case—drawing the attention of the jury to the relevant points of law and the burden of proof, the value of corroboration, the dangers of evidence which is largely based on visual identification alone. The judge must do all he can to clarify the issues for the jury, but he must not assume the task of the jury himself.

The jury must be left to decide matters of fact in accordance with the judge's directions on matters of law. The jury will next retire and consider their verdict.

This usual procedure is varied sometimes, for example, where the jury is taken to the scene of the crime so as to better understand the evidence: if a view of this kind is arranged it comes as early in the trial as possible.

If the verdict is not guilty, the accused is freed. If guilty, he must be sentenced. The judge hears evidence of background and any previous convictions. The defence will usually make a plea in mitigation, stressing the essential good character and worthiness of the prisoner, the isolated nature of this criminal act, and so on. Reports on the prisoner's condition can be ordered. Other admitted offences can be taken into consideration.

The sentence will be taken from a list including death (only for treason and for piracy with violence), imprisonment (which may come fully into operation, or be fully or partly suspended), youth custody (for those between 15 and 21), fines, and a variety of non-punitive orders like hospitalisation, community service, probation, absolute or conditional discharge, binding over, deportation (for those with no right of abode), disqualification from driving, compensation, restitution, forfeiture and contribution towards costs.

The prisoner can appeal against conviction and§or sentence, on matters of fact and§or law to the Court of Appeal (Criminal Division). The appeal must usually be lodged within 28 days of conviction. If the appeal is only on a matter of law then it can be lodged as of right. On a matter of fact or mixed fact and law, leave to appeal must be given by the Court of Appeal or the trial judge. The most common basis for appeals is misdirection of the jury in the trial judge's summing up.

In rare cases, with leave of the Court of Appeal or the House of Lords, a further appeal can be made to the House of Lords. The case must be of general public importance.

Chapter 8

Legal Aid and Assistance

INTRODUCTION

Lord Denning summed up the impact of the various forms of financial assistance on the availability of legal advice when he said:

> I have often said that since the Second World War the greatest revolution in the law has been the system of legal aid. It means that in many cases the lawyers' fees and expenses are paid for by the State: and not by the party concerned.

The key to understanding here is to spot the different ways in which the poor and rather poor can get the help of a solicitor at a low price or at no cost at all namely:

(*a*) fixed fee interviews;
(*b*) Legal advice and assistance—the "Green Form" scheme;
(*c*) Legal advice and assistance—"assistance by way of representation";
(*d*) Legal aid for civil court proceedings;
(*e*) Legal aid for criminal court proceedings.

THE FIXED FEE INTERVIEW

Many solicitors are prepared to advise a client for half an hour for £5. Some charge less. Some may not charge at all. This service is not subject to a means test. No form needs to be filled in. No evaluation is made—it would take the half hour! The service is available to everyone. There is a reference book called the "Legal Aid Solicitors List" which is to be found at public libraries, town hall information offices, magistrates' courts, county courts, legal aid offices and Citizens' Advice Bureaux, amongst other places. The "£5 interview", as it is sometimes called, will not extend beyond advice. No action is likely to be taken on the client's behalf under this scheme, no telephone calls, letters, representation etc. It may be worth noting that free advice on legal problems is available at Citizens' Advice Bureaux (many have a rota of solicitors who give their time and effort free), neighbourhood law centres and similar places.

LEGAL ADVICE AND ASSISTANCE

The "Green Form" scheme

This scheme covers practical help from a solicitor: advice, writing letters, negotiating on a client's behalf, obtaining the specialist opinion of a barrister, preparing a case, for example, if his client has been called to an individual tribunal hearing where he claims to have been unfairly dismissed from his job. In fact this system provides full legal service up to, but not including representation in court or before a tribunal or arbitrator. Most problems can be solved without the need for representation: consumer grievances, landlord and tenant problems, divorce, maintenance, making a will, and so on. Under this scheme a client can obtain the services of a solicitor for nothing or for a contribution (explained below), if he satisfies the means test (below) up until the solicitor has performed work for which he would otherwise have charged £50. In the case of an undefended divorce or judicial separation the limit is £75. Note, however, that these figures are revised from time to time. They were accurate in early 1984.

In order for a potential client to avail himself of the benefit of this scheme he should patrol the high street until a solicitor's office is found that displays the legal aid sign. It is purple in colour and resembles two people playing chess. There the scheme is available.

Having made an appointment with the client the solicitor will conduct the means test and give an instant reply about whether the applicant qualifies under the scheme. (In practice he may have conducted a fixed fee interview first.) The method is to complete a green coloured application form (the solicitor will do this) and refer to a "key card" which contains details of how much the client must pay: this will depend on his assessed income (i.e. his total income minus various allowances). In order to qualify the client's savings and income must be below set limits which are frequently revised.

All savings count, both husband's and wife's—unless they live apart or the case concerns a conflict between them (e.g. a divorce). The house they live in, the furniture and effects and the tools of their trades are not included. Then deductions are made for dependants. Then the final figure is measured against the limit—under it and the client qualifies. In April 1983 the deduction for dependants were £200 for the first, £120 for the second and £60 each for any others. The limit for the final figure was £700.

The income is also taken into account. From the gross weekly income (including pay and child benefit, pension, etc.) is deducted tax and national insurance and (in April 1983) £29.55 for the spouse, and £13.13 for each dependant under 11 years old, £19.73 for those between 11 and 15, £23.69 for those aged 16 or 17 and £30.83 for those aged 18 and over.

Those who qualify for supplementary benefit or family income supplement enter the scheme free, as do those whose residuary income (i.e. the gross less the permitted deductions) is less than £47. If the figure is between £47 and £99 then a contribution of between £5 (£47-55) and £55 (£95-99) is the maximum that can be required. So the least benefited is for example, the client who is involved in a divorce case—who may be entitled to £75 worth of work for £55—because his income (even after all the deductions allowed) is still between £95 and £99 per week, and his savings (his "disposable capital") is less than £700. If the residuary capital exceeds £700, or if the residuary income exceeds £99, then the applicant does not qualify for legal advice and assistance under the Green Form scheme.

If the applicant qualifies he is told at once and the solicitor can start work for him immediately.

If money or property is recovered by the solicitor for his client there are circumstances under which part of it will be put towards paying the solicitor's bill (where it exceeds any contribution payable), but there are many instances where it will not be, e.g. where maintenance payments have been recovered, or where the issue concerned unpaid social security benefits of some kind.

The solicitor requires permission from the local Legal Aid Office before he can exceed the £50 (or £75) limit of work, or where the applicant has already been given assistance under this scheme, on the same matter, by another solicitor.

Assistance by way of representation

This is an extension of the Green Form scheme. The qualifying conditions and hurdles are the same. With the Green Form another is completed by the solicitor, and if the local Legal Aid Office feels that it would be reasonable for the client to get assistance by way of representatio then, within the same maximum contribution (if one is required), the solicitor is able to prepare the case and represent his client. In most civil cases, for example, this will be in the magistrates' court covering separation, maintenance, custody, affiliation, and defended adoption proceedings. It also covers representation before the Mental Health Review Tribunal.

LEGAL AID FOR CIVIL COURT PROCEEDINGS

Legal Aid, if you qualify covers work leading up to and including civil court proceedings and representation by a solicitor and/or a barrister, as necessary.

Legal Aid covers the House of Lords, Court of Appeal, High Court, county courts, magistrates' courts (in civil and domestic matters, but check the overlap with legal advice by way of representation already noted above), the Employment Appeal Tribunal, the Lands Tribunal, and others, but it does not cover coroners' courts, defamation actions or any other tribunal work (although legal advice and assistance, above, covers virtually everything, so some help may still be available).

It can take weeks to obtain a legal aid certificate. The solicitor cannot act until it is granted. It cannot be backdated. There is provision for emergency legal aid if the case is very urgent. It can be granted at once, but it lasts only until the full application for legal aid has been dealt with. The applicant must agree to co-operate fully with the DHSS assessment officer. Furthermore, the full cost of the case must be paid if it is found that the applicant does not qualify for free legal aid, or if an offer of legal aid with a contribution payable is turned down by the applicant.

The solicitor, in normal cases, fills in and sends off the application form. An assessment officer from the local DHSS usually interviews the applicant to assess financial resources—a means test.

The local Legal Aid Office assesses the chances of the case succeeding. Legal Aid will only be granted if it would be reasonable to do so i.e. the case has a reasonable chance of success. The financial and quality tests have both to be passed. The financial test involves the calculation of savings and income. Savings (disposable capital) are all added together. If the total is less than £2,500 the applicant qualifies. If it is between £2,500 and £4,000 a contribution is required—but it generally will not exceed the excess over £2,500. Over £4,000 and the anticipated costs have to be enormous before the applicant will qualify. Annual income is grossed up and deductions are made for (April 1983 figures) the spouse (£1,537) each dependant under 11 (£683), between 11 and 15 (£1,026), aged 16 or 17 (£1,232), 18 and over (£1,603).

If the residual income is less than £1,965 the applicant qualifies, and legal aid will be free (subject to satisfying the disposable capital rule!). If it is between £1,965 and £4,720 a contribution will be required. The maximum possible is a quarter of the excess over £1,965 and is usually payable over a year. If the figure exceeds £4,720 the applicant does not qualify. Once the applicant has satisfied the DHSS of his (lack of) means, and the Legal Aid Committee about the quality of his case, then if he is to be awarded free legal aid he is issued with a certificate to that effect. If he is to be expected to contribute towards the costs of his action, he is offered a certificate.

If the action proceeds and is successful then the property or money recovered can be affected by the controversial statutory charge under which the Legal Aid Office can deduct the costs of having aided the applicant. This would not happen if the losing party were ordered to pay both parties' costs.

It is argued that legal aid is not designed to provide a free legal service. It is one which reflects the same costs as a privately represented individual might expect—it is not connected with social security (welfare) benefits. If a privately represented person wins in a civil case the loser will only be bound to pay the successful party's reasonable costs—the bare essentials necessary to bring the case. The solicitor's bill may well exceed this. The successful party may well have to pay the balance himself.

LEGAL AID FOR CRIMINAL COURT PROCEEDINGS

The defendant in a criminal case may obtain legal guidance from a legal advice centre of some kind (e.g. a Citizens' Advice Bureau) or by means of a fixed fee interview with a solicitor or under the Green Form Scheme. Many magistrates' courts also have a system of duty solicitors who are able to take instructions from defendants who realise they need legal advice only after they arrive at court.

In any event, there is a special scheme for legal aid in criminal cases; it was significantly revised in early 1984 and may well be further amended during the following years—local magistrates' courts and the local Law Society may be considered to be useful sources of information about new developments.

A standard form for applications has been laid down: the details required include the defendant's financial circumstances (including full details of his own income and that of any members of his household), his dependants, and any outstanding payments such as hire-purchases and bank loans. The form is normally considered first by the Clerk to the Justices or one of his professionally qualified assistant clerks; if the application comes within the statutory financial limits (*see* below) and is one where the "Widgery criteria" would justify the grant of legal aid, the certificate will be granted by the Clerk.

The "Widgery criteria" are so named because Lord Chief Justice Widgery was a member of the committee which said in its report in

1966 that it was in the interests of justice that (subject to any requirements based on financial circumstances) legal aid should be granted in the following cases:

(*a*) where the charge is a grave one (e.g. involves serious damage to the defendant's reputation or might lead to him losing his liberty); or

(*b*) where the charge involves substantial questions of law; or

(*c*) where the defendant may not be able to follow the proceedings properly (e.g. where the defendant cannot speak English or he is disabled in some way); or

(*d*) where witnesses need to be traced or expert witnesses need to be cross-examined; or

(*e*) where legal representation is required for some other reason (e.g. it is most undesirable for the defendant to cross-examine a child witness in a case about sexual offences against the child).

The financial limits are now set out in the appropriate legal aid regulations. Once the amount of an applicant's income and capital have been assessed (using the details on the form) he will be required to pay a contribution towards the costs of the legal advice he gets. The money will be ordered to be paid into the court office in 26 weekly instalments. The amount to be paid is worked out on the basis of the income in the three months before the date when the form is completed. If the case ends before the 26-week period expires the justices have the power to remit any future payments (which means that there will be nothing more to pay) but they cannot waive any "arrears" of payments which should have been made. Payments made by defendants who are later acquitted may be ordered to be refunded (and this will normally be done).

Failure to pay the necessary contributions may lead to the Clerk revoking the legal aid certificate after he has given the defendant the opportunity to explain why the payments have not been made.

Examples may help to show the way the system works:

(1) The defendant is charged with a number of road traffic matters and intends to plead not guilty, but no questions of law appear to be involved and the facts seem to be straightforward: on the basis of the Widgery criteria the application may be expected to be refused by the Clerk. (This would be done regardless of the financial questions since they would need to be considered only if there was any need to decide how much ought to be paid by the defendant.)

(2) The defendant is charged with theft of goods from a shop and has no previous convictions; he intends to plead not guilty. The Widgery criteria apply (see type (*a*) above) and the financial assessment will need to be done. His "disposable income" is £45.50 per week but he has no "disposable capital". The regulations require a contribution of £1.00 per week to be paid by him for 26 weeks.

(3) The defendant is charged with selling an unroadworthy vehicle (a summary offence) and intends to plead not guilty; significant arguments about the law are expected. The Widgery criteria (item (b) above) apply and the financial assessment will need to be done. His "disposable income" need not even be considered because he is drawing supplementary benefit.

If a certificate is not granted by the Clerk there is power for the matter to be referred to other authorities to consider. If the case is about a summary offence the application is referred to the magistrates by the Clerk but the applicant and his solicitor are not (normally) invited to attend to make the application. If the refusal is made solely on the grounds of the applicant's means there is no appeal available. The new and special procedure is the creation of a right of appeal to the legal aid committee in cases involving indictable offences provided there are at least three weeks to go before the date fixed for the trial or committal of the case to the Crown Court. Notices of refusal of legal aid will advise the applicant what appeals may be available to him.

One of the constant problems about legal aid for a long time has been the different rates of grant/refusal which appear in the national statistics. The most serious difficulty about these figures, however, is that they do not contain an adequate assessment of the nature of the cases in which applications have been made, so it is impossible to decide how serious the situation really is. The 1981 refusal rate in Warrington was seven times as high as it was for the same period in Macclesfield. In 1982 the figures were even more emphatic: the refusal rate in Warrington was then 41 per cent but in Macclesfield it was only 3 per cent. But who can tell whether this was simply because the solicitors in the one area (and their clients) asked for legal aid in many cases where the Widgery criteria clearly excluded their cases?

Applications for legal aid to cover cases going on to the Crown Court may be heard and decided by magistrates' courts; the most common order, indeed, covers the proceedings at the magistrates' own court as well as at the Crown Court and financial contributions are collected in a similar way for these. It will be remembered that cases may go through to the Crown Court because (amongst other things) the defendant relies on his right to jury trial (if available) or because the magistrates consider that the defendant's record and general background make it necessary to impose a greater punishment than they have the power to order: legal aid for the further hearing may be (and usually is) ordered by the magistrates.

Chapter 9

Legal personality

NATURAL AND LEGAL PERSONS

The word person derives from latin: *per* (through) and *sonare* (to sound). It seems that the idea of a *persona* comes from the mask worn by an actor through which he spoke to the audience. A person in law does not need arms and legs. Obviously we are all persons in law, but so are entities like registered companies. Any entity which is capable of separate legal identity—as the possessor of legal rights, responsible for the performance of legal duties, is a person as far as the law is concerned. However, it is usual to speak of natural persons when dealing with humans and to speak of legal or juristic persons when dealing with separate entities like companies. Partnerships, clubs and trade unions are not legal persons. They have no legal existence apart from the people of whom they are composed. The identity of such legal persons as companies will be probed more deeply in the next chapter.

NATURAL PERSONS

Status and capacity

Status is like a badge. It denotes membership of a particular class or grouping of people. There is no problem about wearing several badges at once: Jenny is 20 years old and married, with two daughters. She was born in Plymouth. She has at least four statuses (badges): adult, married, British, parent. Each status carries with it certain rights and duties under the law. Each brings a capacity to do certain things—to make a will, vote and so on.

Status and capacity are closely interwoven—if Jenny were a barrister by profession then she would be unable to sit as a juror—despite being qualified to do so through her adult status.

This chapter briefly inspects a few tapestries of status and capacity.

Nationality

Nationality is the link between an individual and a state. A person may have dual or even triple nationality, derived from parents and place of birth, or none at all—stateless. Nationality is most important where the rules of public law (*see* Chapter 1) are concerned. For example, only a British citizen (or of the Republic of Ireland) can vote in British elections. Aliens need work permits if they are employed in Britain, and they can be deported. Lack of status means lack of capacity.

British citizenship is controlled by the highly complicated British Nationality Act 1981.

Under this Act a child born in the UK is British if either parent is British or settled in Britain. A new born baby found abandoned in the UK is deemed to be British unless the contrary is shown. If neither parent is British at the child's birth in the UK, but later becomes a British citizen, or settles in Britain, then the child can be registered as British. Even if this does not happen registration is an entitlement if the child lives in Britain until he is ten years old.

A child adopted by a British citizen becomes British too, from the date of the United Kingdom court order.

A child born abroad is British at birth if either parent is British (otherwise than by descent) or if either parent is abroad on Crown (or other designated) service. This means that a child born of British parents abroad is British but his own children will not automatically be British. This is said to maintain connections with the UK. Naturally, Crown servants working abroad are not affected by the limit on citizenship by descent to those born abroad. Similarly, a child born abroad can be registered as British within 12 months if he has a British parent (British by descent) where that parent had a parent who was British otherwise than by descent. This is allowed only if the child's British parent had spent at least three years in the UK at any time before the birth. If the registration is not made within the year, then it is possible later in the child's life if the child and both his parents subsequently live in the UK for three years. Again these regulations are designed to reflect connection with Britain.

British Dependent Territory citizens (e.g. those from the Cayman Islands, Hong Kong) and British Overseas citizens can register as British citizens after five years' residence in the UK.

British citizenship can also be acquired by naturalisation. This means that the applicant must satisfy the Home Secretary that he has resided in the UK or colonies or been abroad on Crown service for a sufficient length of time—usually four of the last seven years, including the one before the application. Further, he must show that he is of good character, and is competent in the English language (or

Welsh) and he intends (if allowed) to remain in the UK (or colony or on Crown service abroad). The naturalisation can be revoked (as can registration, if it had been obtained by fraud).

Domicile and residence

Most people live in the country of which they are citizens. Some do not. They decide, or their employers decide, that overseas there are better places to live. If a permanent home is set up there then whilst nationality may be British, domicile is not. A person's domicile is a matter of fact, although legal consequences follow. He is in a particular country, he intends to stay there (called *animus manendi*). It is his domicile. Everybody has a domicile. Nobody has more than one. It might be:

(*a*) a domicile of origin—a legitimate child has the father's domicile, an illegitimate one has the mother's, a foundling has the domicile of the place where he was found; or

(*b*) a domicile of choice. The domicile of origin is changed as the person chooses to be domiciled elsewhere. Anyone over 16 can make such a choice. A married woman at one time took her husband's domicile, but the Domicile and Matrimonial Proceedings Act 1973 provides the choice for her too, although on marriage her domicile will generally be that of her husband, at least to start with. If a married couple split up and a child goes or stays with the mother, then her domicile becomes the child's too. Sometimes this is called the domicile of dependent persons.

This idea of domicile is important. For example, if a person is domiciled abroad then the laws of that country apply to him. If legal formalities are undertaken there, in accordance with that law, for example, marriage or divorce or making a will, then despite the fact that the English law has not been followed (e.g. only one witness to a will required there, but two in England), the result of the operation of that law (divorce, marriage, distribution of property after death) will be recognised by the English courts as valid.

So a change of domicile means a change of rights, duties, obligations etc. in accordance with the legal system in the new homeland.

Residence is another matter of fact. A person's residence is a narrower concept than that of his domicile. It has nothing to do with his nationality. For example a man domiciled in England has his residence in Plymouth. He is subject to the general law of England, and in so far as that law has a more localised nature, his residence will be important; for example he will probably be on the electoral roll for the constituency in Plymouth in which he resides (perhaps Devonport), he will be subject to the localised jurisdiction of the

Plymouth County Court, and Plymouth Magistrates' Court. His taxes will be inspected and collected by those responsible for Plymouth, and so on. A lady living in Stoke-on-Trent would be subject to the same general law, but to different localised details.

Obviously, a person's residence is a very important factor in determining his domicile. Residence will not change where only temporary changes are made, e.g. for holidays.

Minors

The Family Law Reform Act 1969 set the age of majority at 18. The law protects young people. It also restricts their capacity in various ways:

(*a*) a minor cannot own land, but he can own personal property;

(*b*) before the age of 18 a minor cannot vote, make a will (with one exception, *see* Chapter 16), make a contract which binds him (with 2 exceptions, *see* Chapter 13), get married without someone else's consent (*see* Chapter 15), see an "18" rated film at a cinema (*see* Chapter 11), order alcoholic drinks on licensed premises, enter a betting shop, or a sex shop, be tattooed (except by a qualified medical practitioner) or (generally) work night shifts.

The legal capacity of children is measured by age. Under ten a child is incapable of crime (*doli incapax*) and will not be charged, although care proceedings could be brought if his parents cannot or will not control him. Under 12 he cannot be sold an animal as a pet. Under 13 he cannot generally be employed. Under 14 (but over 10) he is criminally responsible if he can be shown to have understood the wrongful nature of the action in question. Under 14 he cannot accept any article from a rag dealer. Under 14 a boy cannot be convicted of any offence involving sexual intercourse. Once a child is ten years of age he is criminally responsible and his fingerprints and palm prints can be taken by the police (on a magistrate's order). Under 15 a child cannot enter a knackers yard. Under 16 a child cannot buy liqueur chocolates or fireworks, education is compulsory (from five) and restricted part-time employment is allowed. Under 17 a child cannot hold a pedlar's licence, nor can he buy or hire any firearm.

There are progressive minimum ages for driving motor vehicles: 16 (moped, mowing machine, invalid carriage, small agricultural tractor), 17 (motor-cycle, small passenger and goods vehicles, some road rollers), 18 (medium sized goods vehicles) and 21 (other road vehicles, e.g. most heavy goods vehicles).

There are no age requirements for liability in tort, except when some intent is required and the child is too young to have formed such an intent.

Persons suffering from mental disorder

In the law of tort mentally disordered persons occupy much the same position as minors. There is generally no motive element in tortious activity and so the lack of mental capacity is not directly relevant. Obviously, in the exceptional cases where motive is necessary, and the incapacity precludes formation of intent, then no tortious liability arises.

There is protection in the law of contract. A contract is an exercise of free will, so if the person understood nothing of what was going on, and if the other party to the alleged contract was aware of his infirmity, then the contract can be made void (avoided or cancelled) at his option. This means that he can, if he wishes, choose to carry on with it. The contract is valid, but voidable. If he ratifies the contract when he knows what he is doing (during a lucid interval) then the contract is no longer voidable.

If the person in question is so ill as to be within the scope of the Mental Health Act 1983, and his property has been put under the control of the court (called the Court of Protection) under s. 93(2) of the Act, then he cannot make contracts involving that property.

Where contracts for necessaries (e.g. food, clothing, shelter) are made, then a reasonable price is payable for them. This is much the same as with minors (*see* Chapter 13).

These basic, common law, rules of contract law apply in a similar manner to those who are only temporarily lacking in capacity like drunkards and (presumably) those under the influence of drugs etc.

Marriage (which is discussed in more detail in Chapter 15) too must be an act of free will, so if a person is unaware of the circumstances then consent cannot be said to be genuine and the marriage is voidable (it can be undone). The Matrimonial Causes Act 1973 provides:

12 A marriage celebrated after 31st July 1971 shall be voidable on the following grounds only, that is to say—

(*c*) that either party to the marriage did not validly consent to it, whether in consequences of duress, mistake, unsoundness of mind or otherwise;

(*d*) that at the time of marriage, either party, though capable of giving a valid consent, was suffering (whether continuously or intermittently) from mental disorder within the meaning of the Mental Health Act 1983 of such a kind or to such an extent as to be unfitted for marriage.

Furthermore, to make a will a person needs to understand the nature of what he is doing, as Cockburn CJ said in *Banks* v. *Goodfellow* (1870):

> As to the testator's capacity, he must, in the language of the law, have a sound and disposing mind and memory. In other words, he ought to be capable of making his will with an understanding of the nature of the business in which he is engaged, a recollection of the property he means to dispose of, of the persons who are the objects of his bounty, and the manner in which it is to be distributed between them. It is not necessary that he should view his will with the eye of a lawyer, and comprehend its provisions in their legal form. It is sufficient if he has such a mind and memory as will enable him to understand the elements of which it is composed, and the disposition of his property in its simple forms.

It seems, then, that a will can only be made during a lucid interval. The person need not be cured. He could revert to illness the following day, but his will must be made when he had capacity to do it. (There is more about wills in Chapter 16.)

As for the criminal law, the mentally disordered person's position must be regarded in line with the statutory provisions, particularly the Mental Health Act 1983. If a minor offence has been committed the police might well choose not to charge the mentally disordered person at all, but allow him to return to his relatives or enter an appropriate hospital informally (voluntarily). Alternatively, he might be committed compulsorily to hospital on a medical certificate without going through the criminal courts. If the alleged crime is more serious, and the person has been charged, and remanded in custody, then, again under the 1983 Act, he can be transferred to hospital. If he is taken to court for trial, he may be declared unfit to plead or unfit to stand trial if he does not understand what is happening. He can then be sent to hospital (under the Criminal Procedure (Insanity) Act 1964). If he can plead, but his defence at the trial is insanity, and if it succeeds, he is sent to hospital. Even if he does not raise the defence, or if it is raised and not accepted by the jury he can still be sent to hospital by the judge. If he is sentenced to imprisonment he can be later transferred to hospital.

The defence of insanity is governed by rules called the M'Naghten Rules, after a case in 1843 where Daniel M'Naghten shot Sir Robert Peel's secretary. He was acquitted because of his insanity and committed to hospital. The Rules emerged from a House of Lords debate on the case. The leniency of the result had caused a public outcry. The House requested that the judges clarify the requirements of the insanity defence. These are, briefly, the Rules they laid down:

(*a*) everyone is presumed sane until proved otherwise;

(*b*) it is a defence to prove that when committing the alleged offence the accused was labouring under such a defect of reason, from disease of the mind, as not to know, the nature and quality of his act, or (if he did know it) that what he was doing was wrong;

(*c*) where an act is committed by someone under an insane delusion about what is going on around him, and this prevents him from understanding what he is doing, then his responsibility is measured in accordance with his appreciation of the circumstances i.e. that what he imagined as true, was accurate.

Where the defence is raised, because of the general presumption of sanity, the defence counsel must establish (on a balance of probabilities) that the accused was insane. If this works, the accused is not guilty by reason of insanity, and hospitalised, unless he appeals, for an unlimited time. The defence is not often raised, perhaps three or four times each year.

Against a charge of murder there is a statutory defence called diminished responsibility contained in the Homicide Act 1957. If successful it has the effect of reducing a conviction for murder to a conviction for manslaughter (and the result is not automatically life imprisonment nor indefinite detention in a mental hospital). In order to establish the defence it must be shown (on a balance of probabilities) that at the time of the crime the accused (1957 Act, s.2.):

was suffering from such abnormality of mind (whether arising from a condition of arrested or retarded development of mind or any inherent causes or induced by disease or injury) as substantially impaired his mental responsibility for his acts and omissions in doing or being a party to the killing.

Chapter 10

Corporations and Unincorporated Associations

LEGAL PERSONALITY

In the last chapter we considered the differences between natural and legal (or juristic) persons. Each has its own identity and capacity. In this chapter we look more closely at precisely what legal persons are, how they are created, and how they differ from other groups and associations, like partnerships and social clubs.

A legal person is created by the process of incorporation. It is a corporation—from the latin *corpus*, a body. It has a separate legal identity apart from the human beings who work for it. As Lord Halsbury LC said (in *Salomon* v. *Salomon and Co. Ltd.* (1897)):

> It seems to me impossible to dispute that once the company is legally incorporated it must be treated like any other independent person with its rights and liabilities appropriate to itself and that the motives of those who took part in the promotion of the company are absolutely irrelevant in discussing what those rights and liabilities are.

The people come and go, but the corporation lives on, unless it is brought to an end by the proper legal processes. Sometimes this survival capability is called perpetual succession.

Corporations come in two types: corporations sole and aggregate. A corporation sole is an official position which has a separate legal identity from the man or woman who occupies it from time to time, like the monarch or the Archbishop of Canterbury. There is a great deal of property vested in such positions. It may be used by the incumbents, but it is not their personal property. When the job changes hands there is no need to revest the property in the new occupant because the corporation lives on continuously through the change (perpetual succession). New corporations sole are not easily created; it can only be done by statute; they are not common.

On the other hand, corporations aggregate are everywhere. For example, there are about three quarters of a million companies registered in England and Wales. Such corporations are usually classified according to method of creation.

CREATING CORPORATIONS

By Royal Charter

This is issued by the monarch after a request (called a petition) to the Privy Council. Trading corporations are not formed by charter today although the East India Co. and the Hudson Bay Co. were set up in this way (in 1600 and 1670). Examples of modern-day chartered corporations are the BBC, the Institute of Chartered Accountants and the Chartered Institute of Secretaries and Administrators. Liability of members is not usually limited, but since trading is not usual either this is not important.

By Act of Parliament

Statutory corporations are generally large bodies of a public nature such as Gas and Electricity Boards. They are created by an Act of Parliament which sets out their powers (e.g. borrowing) and duties. As examples, the National Coal Board was created by the Coal Industry Nationalisation Act 1946, and the British Railways Board by the Transport Act 1962.

By registration

This is done under the Companies Acts and is the way most trading corporations are established.

INCORPORATION BY REGISTRATION

This method of creating a corporation, a registered company in this case, involves the deposit of certain documents with the Registrar of Companies at 55 City Road, London EC1, or Crown Way, Maindy, Cardiff. It is usual to take them along by hand, but it can be done by post. These documents are as follows.

(a) The Memorandum of Association. This document will regulate the external affairs of the company. It is a sort of charter. Those who are considering dealing with the company can refer to it. It includes the name of the company, the address of the registered office, the objects of the company (the purpose for which it is created), a statement of how liability is limited, the amount of share capital and its division into shares (a public company must have at least £50,000), and the association clause. This is the declaration of the members that they wish to be associated as a company. Each subscriber takes at least one share, the rest are distributed later, according to the contract between the members. Each must sign and the signature must be dated and witnessed by at least one person, who must also sign.

(*b*) The Articles of Association. This document must also be formally executed by the members. It is the internal document, containing the regulations for internal management. It can be written especially, or the model set out in Table A of the Companies Act 1948 could be adopted. The document will contain rules about the issue and transfer of shares and dividends, general meetings, voting rights, accounts, audits, the appointment and powers of directors, the managing director and the secretary.

(*c*) A statement of names. These are those of the proposed first directors and secretary, signed by or on behalf of the subscribers and containing the director's consent to act.

(*d*) A statement of the share capital.

(*e*) The statutory declaration. This is usually made by the solicitor who is acting for those setting up the company. The declaration is that the registration requirements have been satisfied. The Registrar may be satisfied with this as sufficient evidence of compliance. When he is satisfied he issues a certificate of incorporation, and publishes the fact in the London Gazette.

There are significant advantages to incorporating a business, particularly in the area of limited liability. In exchange, the company must regard itself as being open to public scrutiny. The documents deposited with the Registrar are public. They can be inspected by anyone, who has paid the appropriate fee. Furthermore, each year after incorporation a company issuing share capital must make an annual return to the Registrar. This must include such matters as the address of the registered office, a summary of the position regarding the issue, holding and transfer of shares, the extent of the company's indebtedness, details of the directors and secretary, and the accounts and reports as presented to the annual general meeting.

CAPACITY OF CORPORATIONS

It is important to keep in mind the artificial nature of the personality of corporations when considering matters of legal capacity.

In the criminal law, for example, it is difficult to imagine a company being held criminally liable for activities that require the accoutrements of the human body, for example, perjury, bigamy, rape. However, there is a principle within the criminal law called identification. It has been developed along the fictional lines that the minds of certain superior officers within a corporation compose its personality and their acts are its acts.

Lord Denning said (in *Bolton* v. *Graham* (1957)):

A company may in many ways be likened to a human body. It has a brain and nerve centre which controls what it does. It also has hands which hold the tools and act in accordance with directions from the centre. Some of the people in the company are mere servants and agents who are nothing more than hands to do the work and cannot be said to represent the mind or will. Others are directors and managers who represent the directing mind and will of the company, and control what it does. The state of mind of these managers is the state of mind of the company and is treated by the law as such.

Whilst it may be mildly diverting to imagine a company being jailed for incest, it is important to note that there have been heavy fines levied on corporations for such criminal offences as involve commercial fraud. Indeed the Law Commission has issued a Working Paper, No. 44, on the Criminal Liability of Corporations. Furthermore, a corporation can be vicariously liable for the crimes of its servants which do not require a mental element (called *mens rea*; *see* Chapter 14). The doctrine of identification is not the same as holding an employer liable for his/its employees' activities. It actually equates the acts of the superior officers of the company with the company itself. Their crimes are the company's own acts for which it can be punished, not those of someone else for which it must answer.

In the law of tort the position is quite similar. Of course, corporations can be held vicariously liable for torts committed by their employees whilst they are acting within the course of their employment (*see* Chapter 12), but corporations have been held personally liable too. In *Lennards Carrying Co.* v. *Asiatic Petroleum* (1915) the managing director was found to have been the "directing mind and will of the corporation". In general, corporations can own and dispose of land and all other property just as natural persons can, provided that the source of its status (charter, statute or memorandum of association) permits it.

For capacity in the law of contract, again reference must be made to the status source. A chartered corporation will have powers from its charter, but in theory it has the full contractual capacity of a natural, sane, adult, despite any limits within the charter. However, and naturally, if it persists in acting beyond its powers (*ultra vires*), then it risks having its charter revoked. Short of that, any member can seek an injunction to stop the activity. This was seen in *Jenkin* v. *Pharmaceutical Society* (1921) where the Society was prevented by such an injunction from setting up an industrial committee, a trade union activity which was outside its charter of 1843. It was similarly prevented from organising an insurance scheme.

A statutory corporation's activities outside its statutory powers are *ultra vires* and void.

On the face of it, that would appear to be the position with a registered company's activities outside the objects clause within its memorandum of association. After all, the registered documents are public, and so those who contract with companies are presumed to be aware of the contents of their objects clauses, that is, of what the company was set up to do.

However, these objects clauses are often very widely drawn. For example, in *Bell Houses Ltd.* v. *City Wall Properties Ltd.* (1966) a company in housing development had drafted part of its objects to read:

> To carry on any other trade or business whatsoever which can in the opinion of the board of directors be advantageously carried on by the company in connection with, or as ancillary to, any of the above business or the general business of the company.

This was held to cover the mortgage broking in which the company had dabbled. Further to wide objects clauses, the European Communities Act 1972, implementing a directive designed to harmonise company law amongst the European Communities, provides:

> 9(1) In favour of a person dealing with a company in good faith, any transaction decided on by the directors shall be deemed to be one which it is within the capacity of the company to enter into, and the power of the directors to bind the company shall be deemed to be free of any limitation under the memorandum or, articles of association; and a party to a transaction so decided on shall not be bound to enquire as to the capacity of the company to enter into it or as to any such limitation on the powers of the directors, and shall be presumed to have acted in good faith unless the contrary is proved.

It follows from this that, if someone makes an *ultra vires* contract with a company, not aware that it is *ultra vires*, then provided that it has been decided upon by the board of directors or (presumably) someone delegated by them specifically for the purposes of that contract, it is deemed to be within the powers of the company, but only from his point of view. He can enforce it. The company cannot. He must, of course, have acted in good faith; that is, without actual notice of the limitations of the objects clause. His good faith is presumed, unless the company can show otherwise.

This lack of good faith was established as one of several grounds for the benefit of 9(1) not being available in *International Sales and Agencies Ltd.* v. *Marcus* (1982).

COMPARISONS BETWEEN CORPORATIONS AND UNINCORPORATED ASSOCIATIONS

Formation

A registered company, as we have seen in this chapter, is formed by the deposit of certain documents with the Registrar of Companies, whereas a partnership is formed by agreement. It can be express or implied. It can be written, oral, put into a deed or inferred from the conduct of the parties. However, joint ownership of property is not enough, nor is just sharing the income (particularly if it is simply the recovery of an existing debt or taken as a salary or an annuity).

The Partnership Act 1890 is very important here. Unless the agreement provides to the contrary, its contents will form the legal framework of the partnership firm. The definition within the 1890 Act, s. 1(1), is:

> Partnership is the relation which subsists between persons carrying on a business in common with a view of profit.

Number of members

A company, whether public or private, must have at least two members; there is no upper limit. On the other hand, a partnership firm cannot consist of more than 20 partners unless they are solicitors, accountants, stockbrokers, stockjobbers, patent agents and certain other professional people.

Separate personality

A company has, as has been noted, a legal identity quite separate and apart from those who set it up. As Lord Macnaghten said (in *Salomon* v. *Salomon and Co. Ltd.* (1897)):

> The company is at law a different person altogether from the subscribers to the memorandum, and though it may be that after the incorporation the business is precisely the same as it was before, the same persons are managers and the same hands receive the profits the company is not in law the agent of the subscribers or trustee for them.

This famous case was about a boot business. Mr Salomon set up a limited company, with himself and his wife and children as shareholders. The company bought the business from him for about £40,000. £10,000 of this was paid with debentures. These are loan shares which are repaid before unsecured creditors if a company fails. This company did fail owing about £7,800 to unsecured trade creditors. The assets were only about £6,000. The unsecured creditors were left unpaid because the debenture holders had to be paid first. Mr Salomon was one. The company was a different legal person.

This veil of incorporation, as it is known, is lifted sometimes, when the court suspects particularly scurrilous activity. For example, in *Daimler* v. *Continental Tyre and Rubber Co.* (1916) the principle of separate identity was disregarded in order to expose a trading organisation controlled by the enemy in wartime.

By contrast a partnership firm has no separate identity apart from the members who comprise it. It may, however, sue and be sued in the firm's name. The partners own the firm's property and they are liable on the firm's contracts.

Spheres of activity

A company may only trade in accordance with the objects clause within its memorandum of association. Although this might in fact be very widely drawn, as we have seen. It can, also, be altered if the appropriate procedures are followed. Furthermore, the impact of the European Communities Act 1972, also seen earlier in this chapter, must be taken into consideration.

With a partnership the objects will have been agreed between the members of the firm. If there is a formal document they will most probably be included in it. By a (unanimous) resolution they can be changed. They cannot be discovered from public registered documents by outsiders and potential traders with the firm. Privacy is an advantage of partnerships.

Agency

A member of a company is not thereby qualified as its agent. Agents must be specially appointed before they can bind the company by their acts.

However, each general partner is an agent of the firm—as the 1890 Act, s. 5, says:

Every partner is an agent of the firm and his other partners for the purpose of the business of the partnership; and the acts of every partner who does any act for carrying on in the usual way of business of the kind carried on by the firm of which he is a member bind the firm and his partners, unless the partner so acting has in fact no authority to act for the firm in the particular matter, and the person with whom he is dealing either knows that he has no authority, or does not know or believe him to be a partner.

The transfer of shares

A public company is one (a) which is limited by shares (or by guarantee) and has a share capital (whichever is the case, the share capital must meet a minimum requirement, currently £50,000); and (b) whose memorandum states that the company is public, and which has been properly registered as a public company. The name of a public limited company must always end with "Public Limited Company" (PLC will do). Shares are usually freely transferable, subject only to restrictions in the articles of association.

Any company not meeting the definition of "public" will be a private company. Again, shares are transferable, but much less freely. There are likely to be far greater restrictions in the articles.

A partner cannot transfer his share in the firm without the consent of all the other partners. The firm is the product of an agreement between the specific individuals initially and each is individually involved. A share can be "assigned", however. This might be, for example, as security for a loan. The 1890 Act, s. 31(1), provides that the assignee does not take the full place of the partner:

An assignment by any partner of his share in the partnership, either absolute, or by way of mortgage or redeemable charge, does not, as against the other partners, entitle the assignee, during the continuance of the partnership, to interfere in the management or administration of the partnership business or affairs, or to require any accounts of the partnership transactions, or to inspect the partnership books, but entitles the assignee only to receive the share of profits to which the assigning partner would otherwise be entitled, and the assignee must accept the account of profits agreed to by the partners.

Management

The members of a company are not entitled to participate in management unless they are appointed onto the board of directors from whom this work is expected. Partners are entitled to share in management, unless their agreement stipulates otherwise.

Liability

A company can be expected to pay its debts, until its assets are exhausted. Limitation of liability applies to members, not the company itself. The extent to which this protection is effective depends upon the way the company was created. It could be a company limited by shares.

This is the usual kind of limited liability company. Each shareholder is liable only to the extent of his shareholding. If he has paid for the shares he holds no further call can be made upon him; if he has not, then he is responsible only for the amount that he still owes. Alternatively, the company might be limited by guarantee, where the members guarantee to pay a particular amount in the event of the company going into liquidation. The size of the guarantee will be stated in the memorandum of association. This is the extent of the members' liability provided that no shares are issued by the company. If shares are issued, then their liability extends to them. This is very rare. Limited liability is the most obvious advantage of incorporation (there are a very few companies with unlimited liability). A member of such a company is liable for its debts without limit.

General partners are liable to the extent of their personal wealth for the debts of the firm.

It is possible to set up a limited partnership under the Limited Partnerships Act 1907. They are rare. They must be registered. A statement signed by all the members must be sent to the Registrar. It must contain the firm's name, the nature and general place of business, the full name of each partner, when the firm was created and (if it is set) its duration, the particulars of contribution whether in cash or otherwise of each limited partner and a statement that the firm is a limited partnership. The limited partner is liable only to the extent of his contribution. He cannot participate in management, only advise. He cannot bind the firm. Any limited partnership must contain at least one general partner, whose liability, of course, is unlimited.

Taxation

The dividends paid to the members of a company are always taxed as investment income—although directors' salaries will be earned income, whereas partners' income from the firm is taxed (usually) as earned income.

Accounts and auditors

Companies, as we saw earlier in this chapter, must make an annual return. Their accounts must be audited by professionally qualified auditors, whereas partnership accounts are private, and need not be audited professionally, although they usually are.

Termination

A company, having been created by process of law, must be legally
"killed" (wound up). It possesses perpetual succession, that is, it
survives all involved natural persons, until it is wound up. This could
be a voluntary winding-up by the members (if the company can meet
its debts) or by creditors (if it seems unable to meet them).
Alternatively, the winding up could be compulsory—ordered by the
court. This will be on the petition of the company, a creditor or a
contributory (someone who is liable to pay in on winding-up).
Petitions by contributories are very rare. There are seven grounds
upon which a company might be compulsorily wound up:

(*a*) it is unable to pay its debts;

(*b*) the number of members has fallen below two;

(*c*) the company was registered as a public company, but it failed
to satisfy the minimum capital requirement;

(*d*) the company does not commence business within a year of
being incorporated;

(*e*) the company suspends business for a whole year;

(*f*) the members have passed a special resolution to have the
company wound up (this is unusual because it would be cheaper and
easier to wind up voluntarily); and

(*g*) the court is satisfied that it would be just and equitable to wind
the company up.

By contrast a partnership firm is dissolved. This might be achieved
with or without the aid of a court, and, subject to the partnership
agreement. The 1890 Act, s.32, provides for dissolution, without the
aid of the court:

Subject to any agreement between the partners a partnership is
dissolved—

(*a*) if entered into for a fixed term, by the expiration of that
term;

(*b*) if entered into for a single adventure or undertaking, by the
termination of that adventure or undertaking;

(*c*) if entered for an undefined time, by any partner giving notice
to the other or others of his intention to dissolve the partnership.

Note also that by virtue of s.33(1):

Subject to any agreement between the parties, every partnership is
dissolved as regards all the partners by the death or bankruptcy of
any partner.

Further, by virtue of s.34 of the Act, a partnership is in every case dissolved by the happening of any event which makes it unlawful for the business of the firm to be carried on or for the members of the firm to carry it on in partnership.

On the other hand, s.35 provides that on application by a partner the court may decree a dissolution of the partnership in any of the following cases:

(*a*) (This paragraph concerned the insanity of a partner and has been replaced by the Mental Health Act 1983, s.96(1)(*g*), under which a judge can dissolve a firm if one member is a patient within the Act i.e. broadly speaking, mentally too disordered to manage his affairs);

(*b*) when a partner, other than the partner suing becomes in any other way permanently incapable of performing his part of the partnership contract;

(*c*) when a partner, other than the partner suing, has been guilty of such conduct as, in the opinion of the court, regard being had to the nature of the business, is calculated to prejudicially affect the carrying on of the business;

(*d*) when a partner, other than the partner suing, wilfully or persistently commits a breach of the partnership agreement, or otherwise so conducts himself in matters relating to the partnership business that it is not reasonably practicable for the other partner or partners to carry on the business in partnership with him;

(*e*) when the business of the partnership can only be carried on at a loss;

(*f*) whenever in any case circumstances have arisen which in the opinion of the court render it just and equitable that the partnership be dissolved.

TRADE UNIONS

There are about 500 trade unions in England and Wales. Many are small staff associations, recruiting within individual workplaces. The vast majority of the unionised workforce are to be found in the 112 unions affiliated to the Trades Union Congress (TUC). There are 12 million workers in those unions, less than 250,000 elsewhere. Trade unions were originally seen as unlawful conspiracies. Now they enjoy a special status in the law. They are not corporations, they have no separate legal personality, but they can make contracts and their property is held by trustees for them. They are capable of suing and being sued in their own names. Their liability in tort is covered by the Trade Union and Labour Relations Act 1974, and the Employment Act 1982. It is constantly under review. Presently, where an action is not taken in contemplation or furtherance of a trade dispute, tortious liability can exist for negligence, nuisance, breach of statutory duty, etc. which has resulted in personal injury, or which arises from a breach of duty involving the occupation, ownership, possession, control or use of property. Under the Employment Act 1982, individuals are enabled to bring actions in tort against trade unions for damages and/or injunctions.

Under the Employment Act 1980 immunity was removed in respect of secondary action, unless the action was aimed at supplies to or from the employer involved in the dispute. Lawful picketing was restricted to the employees' own place of work.

Under the Trade Union and Labour Relations Act 1974, collective agreements between a trade union and an employer about wages, hours, conditions of work etc. are presumed not to be legally enforceable, unless they are written and they state that they are to be legally binding.

Trade unions are required to keep properly audited accounts, and to make an annual return to the Registrar of Friendly Societies.

Chapter 11

Freedom under the Law

RIGHTS OR LIBERTIES?

In English law there is no written constitution nor any Bill of Rights to enshrine individual freedoms. Indeed, the idea of rights may not be entirely appropriate here. It is a matter of liberties rather than rights. Professor Williams wrote:

> A liberty... means any occasion on which an act or omission is not a breach of a duty... A right exists where there is a positive law on the subject; a liberty where there is no law against it.

Furthermore it is tempting to examine the topic of civil liberties from a comfortable point of view. Dr O'Higgins wrote:

> A basic question is whether the effectiveness with which civil liberties are protected should be assessed from the point of view of a conventional middle-class citizen comfortably employed with conventional politics or whether it should be assessed from the point of view of the black; the poor; the subversive; the atheist; the "lunatic fringe" etc.

So while it is true to say that all societies require limitations upon total individual freedom to do, say, write, meet, etc., and it is also true that any civilised society will attempt to maximise the liberty and minimise the restriction upon an individual's freedom, it must be borne in mind that such pure theory may not be reflected every day, on the streets. Moreover, whereas our discussion centres upon civil liberties in the United Kingdom there is an international context into which our liberties must be placed. Since the Second World War a number of international agreements, treaties, conventions and so on have been drawn up to protect, stabilise and increase civil liberties.

As examples consider the following:

(*a*) the Universal Declaration of Human Rights—United Nations

Organisation. This was adopted by the General Assembly on 10th December 1948;

(b) the European Convention on Human Rights and Fundamental Freedoms 1950—Council of Europe. This is not an institution of the European Communities, but an international organisation of 21 west European states which was formed in 1949; it was the first post-war attempt at unifying Europe. Twenty of the 21 are parties to the convention—Liechenstein being the exception. The convention came into force on 3rd September 1953.

PERSONAL LIBERTY

An individual is allowed to move freely. His personal liberty can only be curtailed on specific and narrowly defined grounds:

(a) he is unfit to plead to a criminal charge in court, or is detained otherwise through mental illness;

(b) he has been sentenced to imprisonment;

(c) he has been committed to jail for contempt of court;

(d) he is detained in pursuance of another court order;

(e) he is detained in order to bring him before a court (i.e. arrested and not granted bail, see Chapter 14);

(f) he is a minor under a care order;

(g) he is detained to prevent the spread of serious illness;

(h) he is an illegal immigrant or awaiting deportation or extradition.

A person wrongfully detained can sue for false imprisonment and/or malicious prosecution as appropriate. These are essentially actions which follow the event. During wrongful imprisonment the prerogative writ called habeas corpus may be applied for. This was considered in Chapter 4 when we were dealing with the supervisory jurisdiction of the Divisional Court of the Queen's Bench Division. It is to this court that applications for habeas corpus are made.

FREEDOM OF ASSOCIATION

People join together in association for various reasons, of which the following are examples:

(a) to facilitate the expression of a collective viewpoint (get their points across more powerfully); and/or

(b) to increase job security or the quality and conditions of work; and/or

(c) for social reasons.

There are few restrictions on the freedom of individuals to associate, provided that neither the purpose of their association nor the means it employs are against the general law, (e.g. to overthrow the government by force).

Some professions restrict the activities of individuals; for example, in the Police Act 1964, s.47(1), it is provided as follows:

> Subject to the provision of this section, a member of a police force shall not be a member of any trade union, or of any association having for its objects, or one of its objects, to control or influence the pay, pensions or conditions of service of any police force.

Otherwise, the general law has basic controls within it. The crime of conspiracy (under the Criminal Law Act 1977) applies to those who agree together to commit a crime, to defraud or to act so as to outrage public decency or corrupt public morals. There is also a tort of conspiracy. This is committed where a group of people decide to do something unlawful, or to do something lawful using unlawful means with the object of injuring someone else. If he is injured he can sue them. In *Huntley* v. *Thornton* (1957) the plaintiff obtained compensation. He had refused to go out on a strike called by his union. The district committee expelled him. The national executive did not ratify this decision, but the district committee made it impossible for the plaintiff to carry on his trade in the area. This amounted to a tortious conspiracy. They had set out to injure him, not to protect their own interests.

There are also restrictions on association which are placed in the interests of preserving public order. Under the Public Order Act 1936 for example:

> any person who in any public place or at any public meeting wears uniform signifying his association with any political organisation or with the promotion of any political object shall be guilty of an offence.

The police can allow the wearing of uniforms, but only where the peace is not likely to be disturbed. This section was designed to combat the rise of the fascists. In *R.* v. *Charnley* (1937) successful prosecutions were brought against "blackshirts". These actions show that full regalia is not required for a uniform here. Armbands, emblems, etc., are enough. Members of the Ku Klux Klan were prosecuted in 1965, IRA supporters in 1975.

Under the Prevention of Terrorism (Temporary Provisions) Act 1976 (replacing the 1974 Act) special powers of interrogation, detention and exclusion from mainland Britain were introduced, along with new offences connected with membership and support of proscribed organisations. The original Act was passed in 48 hours in November 1974, within a week of the dreadful Birmingham pub bombings, when 21 people died and over 180 were injured. The Act was last reviewed and its continuance approved in March 1983. However, there are critics of the Act who point to the statistical evidence of the failure of the measures to combat terrorism and advocate fresh considerations of the need for and the form of special counter-terrorist legislation. For example, between November 1974 and December 1982, 5,555 people had been detained under the Act for interrogation. Only 261 were subjected to exclusion orders (shifting them back to Ireland), and 98 were charged with offences under the Acts, 23 were fined, 22 were sentenced to one year or less in jail, 21 to 5 years or more. It is argued by some that these results could be at least equalled without emergency powers, and that retention of the provisions begins to appear as an unjustified restriction of liberty—but there are strong and passionately held views on both sides.

FREEDOM OF ASSEMBLY

There are many restrictions on the freedom to hold public assemblies—meetings and processions. They fall into two categories: control of the place of assembly and control over the conduct there once the assembly has gathered.

Location

The highway
The use of the highway is controlled by the criminal law and the law of tort.

The key criminal provision is the Highway Act 1980, s.137(1), which states:

> If a person, without lawful authority or excuse, in any way wilfully obstructs the free passage along a highway he shall be guilty of an offence.
> A constable may arrest without warrant any person whom he sees committing an offence against this section.

The power of arrest is important. It is in daily use at demonstrations. The local authority cannot give permission for an obstruction of the highway. The fact that only part of the highway is blocked, and not for long, is not a defence. The use being made of the highway is relevant. In *Nagy* v. *Weston* (1965) a lay-by was used for five minutes by a hot-dog salesman. This was not a reasonable use. Lord Parker CJ said:

> It depends upon all the circumstances, including the length of time the obstruction continues, the place where it occurs, the purpose

for which it is done, and of course whether it does in fact cause an actual obstruction as opposed to a potential obstruction.

It was a busy road. The lay-by also contained a bus stop. Lajos Nagy was convicted.

The controls contained in the civil law of tort, on the other hand, are less commonly seen. They include the torts of trespass, public nuisance and private nuisance. The landowners of the highways are (usually) the highway authorities. An assembly on a highway would not be the purpose for which access to the land is permitted, thus (technically) a trespass. A public nuisance is caused by unreasonable use of the land affecting the public at large. Unless an individual has been especially injured (beyond the general effect on others) an action in public nuisance can be brought only by the Attorney-General. In private nuisance, the individual whose reasonable use of his property is adversely affected can sue; this may occur as a result, for example, of blocking an access. In *Hubbard* v. *Pitt* (1976) a firm of estate agents obtained an injunction against a group of pickets (from the Islington Tenants Campaign) who were standing around outside their offices.

Open Spaces

These usually belong to the Crown or to a local authority. Under the Local Government Act 1972, s.235, district and London Borough Councils are enabled to make byelaws for the good rule and government of their areas. (We saw this in Chapter 3, when considering delegated legislation.) There are likely to be regulations about assemblies in open spaces. It is likely that the written permission of the local authority will be necessary.

A popular open space in this context is Hyde Park in London. The Department of the Environment, Royal Parks Division, published in 1969 a document of "Policy and Procedure for the Use of Hyde Park for Special Events":

Applications may be considered from any organisation (religious, political or otherwise) for permission to hold assemblies and events in Hyde Park. Normally, the Speaker's Corner/Reformer's Tree areas will be used for assemblies/rallies, but for special events other areas are permissible (e.g. Cockpit, Serpentine Road).

The formal regulations are to be found in the Royal and other Parks and Gardens Regulations 1977.

The fact that there was no right to assemble in Hyde Park, at Speaker's Corner or anywhere else, was pointed out by Cockburn CJ (in *Bailey* v. *Williamson* (1873)):

Whatever enjoyment the public have been allowed to have of these parks and royal possessions for any purpose has been an enjoyment which the public have had by the gracious concession of the Crown.

Trafalgar Square, similarly, may be used only in accordance with regulations, the Trafalgar Square Regulations 1952. They contain a list of prohibited acts (which include bathing and paddling!) and acts for which written permission is required (which include "organising, conducting or taking part in any assembly, parade or procession").

Near Parliament

Under the Seditious Meetings Act 1817, s.23, no meeting of 50 people or more can take place within a mile of Westminster Hall "for the purpose or on the pretext of considering of or preparing any petition, complaint, remonstrance, declaration or other address to the king..." or to the Houses of Parliament for "alteration of matters in Church or State" when either or both Houses is sitting. Any such gathering is an unlawful assembly.

There is an even older provision, the Tumultuous Petitioning Act 1661, under which it is an offence for more than ten persons at any one time to repair to the Queen or to Parliament to present any address.

Apart from these statutes, every session Parliament directs the Metropolitan Police Commissioner to see to it that free access to the Houses is maintained. Under the Metropolitan Police Act 1839, s.52, sessional orders are made under which police constables "take care that the passages leading to this House be kept free" and they "disperse all assemblies or processions of persons causing or likely to cause obstruction or disorder".

Meetings in Public Buildings

At election time the Representation of the People Act 1983, s.95(1), provides:

A candidate at a parliamentary election shall be entitled for the purpose of holding public meetings in furtherance of his candidature to the use at reasonable times between the receipt of the writ and the date of the poll of—
  (a) a suitable room in the premises of any school to which this section applies;
  (b) any meeting room to which this section applies.

The section applies to local authority, publicly funded properties. Notice must be given and a fee can be charged. A deposit against damage can be required. In 1934 a meeting of the British Union of Fascists was cancelled because of the size of the deposit required for using the White City Stadium in London. At other times a reasonable policy must be followed. A set rule against particular groups or parties might be challenged in the courts as an improper use of public property, or an arbitrary use of discretion.

Processions
There are no general powers to ban meetings in advance but with processions the position is different. The Public Order Act 1936, s.3(1), provides:

> If the chief officer of police, having regard to the time or place at which and the circumstances in which any public procession is taking place or is intended to take place and to the route taken or proposed to be taken by the procession, has reasonable ground for apprehending that the procession may occasion serious public disorder, he may give directions imposing upon the persons organising or taking part in the procession such conditions as appear to him necessary for the preservation of public order, including conditions prescribing the route to be taken by the procession and conditions prohibiting the procession from entering any public place specified in the directions.

The chief officer can also restrict the use of flags, banners and so on so as to preserve the peace. If he believes that such restrictions may not be enough he can apply to the appropriate local council for an order prohibiting all public processions, or any class of procession, such as political processions, for a period of up to three months. The council can make such an order with the consent of the Home Secretary. In the Metropolitan Police Area the Commissioner can make such an order himself, with the consent of the Home Secretary.

There seems to be no general formal requirement for notice of a procession. One was recommended by the Metropolitan Police Commissioner in his evidence to the Scarman Inquiry into the disorder in Red Lion Square on 15th June 1974. There are various local Acts of Parliament which do make such requirements within the areas to which they relate; e.g. the Bournemouth Corporation Act 1971, the Oxfordshire County Council Act 1971, the Torbay Corporation Act 1971, the County of South Glamorgan Act 1976. However, Lord Scarman did not recommend such a change in the law. He reported:

> In the few instances where no notification is given, the police have

so far experienced no difficulty in finding out that a demonstration is planned. An effective demonstration needs a degree of advance publicity: the police, therefore, are seldom ignorant of what is planned.

The conduct of those who attend the assembly or procession

Those who take part in public meetings or processions, and those who seek to disrupt them, could commit any from a range of criminal offences:

(*a*) assaulting a constable in the execution of his duty, or anyone assisting the constable (Police Act 1964 s.52(1));

(*b*) resisting or wilfully obstructing such an officer or assistant (1964 Act s.51(3));

(*c*) obstruction of the free passage along a highway (Highways Act 1980, s.137(1));

(*d*) destruction of or damage to another's property, without lawful excuse (Criminal Damage Act 1971, s.1);

(*e*) possession of offensive weapons in public places (Public Order Act 1936, s.4, and the Prevention of Crime Act 1953, s.1);

(*f*) trespass upon consular or diplomatic premises (Criminal Law Act 1977, s.9);

(*g*) offensive conduct with intent to provoke a breach of the peace. This includes threatening, abusive or insulting words, behaviour, signs and visible representations (Public Order Act 1936, s.5);

(*h*) affray (a common law crime, i.e. not created by statute). This consists of fighting or an unlawful show of force (such as brandishing weapons) which is regarded as likely to terrify any reasonable person nearby;

(*i*) Unlawful assembly, another common law crime, which is committed by participation in a gathering of three or more people with a common purpose of committing an offence involving violence or of achieving an object (lawful or unlawful) in such a way that a reasonable person nearby fears an imminent breach of the peace. The meeting could start peacefully; but as soon as a few of them decide to act so as to cause bystanders to fear a breach of the peace, then the assembly becomes unlawful;

(*j*) rout, which is a common law crime committed when an unlawful assembly takes steps towards carrying out their common purpose;

(*k*) riot, which is the most serious of these common law crimes committed where three or more (usually many more) people with a common purpose in mind have begun to carry out their aim with the intent to assist each other by force if necessary, and they have displayed such violence as to alarm at least one person nearby, who is of reasonable firmness and courage.

A famous example is *Field* v. *Receiver of Metropolitan Police* (1921) where a crowd of people broke into an empty house to gather fuel for the bonfire around which they were celebrating Peace Night 1919. The next door neighbour of the house having its woodwork liberated was alarmed. The gathering was a riot.

Under the Riot (Damages) Act 1886, where the assembly has been tumultuously as well as riotously gathered together, there can be paid compensation for property damage out of the police rate (i.e. from public funds);

(1) acting in a disorderly manner so as to break up a public meeting is an offence (Public Meeting Act 1908, s.1), as is inciting others to do so. This Act does not apply to election meetings, but a similar offence is to be found within the Representation of the People Act 1983, s.97.

FREEDOM OF SPEECH AND EXPRESSION

Professor Dicey, one of our greatest constitutional lawyers, wrote in 1885:

> Freedom of discussion is . . . in England little else than the right to write or say anything which a jury, consisting of twelve shopkeepers, think it expedient should be said or written. Such "liberty" may vary at different times and seasons from unrestricted license to very severe restraint, and the experience of English history during the last two centuries shows that under the law of libel the amount of latitude conceded to its expression of opinion has, in fact, differed greatly according to the conditions of popular sentiment.

So it is today. The extent of the freedom of the individual to say what he likes or write what he feels is far from an absolute right. There are both civil and criminal law restrictions on these freedoms. The restraint upon the spoken word depends not just on what is said, but on where it is said and the job the person voicing his opinion has. In Parliament, for example, there is a great deal of freedom from actions in the tort of defamation. On the other hand, people like to discuss their work, but if the worker's work is covered by the Official Secrets Acts 1911–1939, then his freedom of discussion is very restricted.

Even if a person is free to express his opinions he may not be able to find anyone to listen to them; reasons for this include:

(*a*) no-one will hire him a hall; or

(*b*) public open spaces are not available; or

(*c*) the police threaten to prosecute for obstruction of the highway; or

(*d*) the police disperse the assembly to avoid a breach of the peace; or

(*e*) newspaper editors burn his letters; or

(*f*) publishers return his manuscript for books; or

(*g*) private printers refuse to take on his work; or

(*h*) printers have had his work printed but he cannot post it to his audience because it is offensive, obscene or prejudicial to public safety or to security; or

(*i*) booksellers and libraries refuse to stock the work; or

(*j*) the advertising media refuse his copy; or

(*k*) a licence to broadcast is refused.

Perhaps the media do wish to publish a person's views. There are many restrictions (short of outright censorship) which might prevent it—the law on obscenity, contempt of court, official secrets, "D" notices, treason, sedition, incitement to disaffection, racial and sexual discrimination, privacy, criminal and blasphemous libel and the tort of defamation. Even if put into dramatic form, there are limits on freedom of expression in theatres and cinemas.

(*a*) *Obscenity.* There are criminal offences contained in the Obscene Publications Acts 1959 and 1964, including the offence of publication of obscene material. The Acts were designed to protect works of art and outlaw pornography. The tastes of juries and magistrates and the massive profits to be had from publishing pornography despite criminal sanctions have reduced their effectiveness.

A related statute is the Children and Young Persons (Harmful Publications) Act 1955, which is designed to outlaw horror comics—illustrating crimes, violence, cruelty, "incidents of a repulsive or horrible nature"—which would tend to corrupt the young.

(*b*) *Contempt of court.* There are, of course, various restrictions upon the reporting of trials (e.g. the general ban on publishing the name of the accused in a juvenile court), but this topic of contempt is wider and more vague. It seems to be an offence to publish material which may be prejudicial to a fair criminal trial, or civil proceedings, scandalising the court (like abusing the judge), contempt in the face of the court, and material which interferes with the course of justice. The most recent changes in the law on this matter were made by the Contempt of Court Act 1981 and the County Court (Penalties for Contempt) Act 1983.

(*c*) *Official secrets.* The Official Secrets Act 1911–1939 cover offences involving the disclosure of matters undermining national security at one extreme and the unauthorised release of even the broadest detail of official information at the other. They cover everybody who holds a public office: ministers, civil servants, the armed forces, even the royal gardeners.

(*d*) *"D" notices.* These are confidential letters, sent at the request of government departments to newspapers, periodicals, and radio and television news editors requesting that certain material not be published in the interests of national defence or security. To ignore a "D" notice is not an offence, but it might be evidence of a breach of the Official Secrets Acts. Anyway, they are rare and virtually always obeyed.

(*e*) *Treason.* This ancient common law crime (in theory still carrying the death penalty) is committed by a person who conspires or incites the murder or overthrow of the monarch, levies war against her or adheres to her enemies (e.g. by broadcasting enemy propaganda). There is a marginally less serious offence called treason felony which involves inviting foreigners to invade British territory or inciting rebellions against the monarch.

(*f*) *Sedition.* This is a very broad common law crime, committed by expressing opinions with the intent as Sir James Stephen wrote:

> to bring into hatred and contempt, or excite disaffection against . . . the government and constitution . . . either House of Parliament, or the administration of justice . . . or to raise discontent or disaffection among Her Majesty's subjects, or to promote feelings of ill-will and hostility between different classes of such subjects.

So it seems to cover any criticism of the existing structure of authority within the state, provided that it is expressed with sufficient force. Examples of this offence are very rare nowadays.

(*g*) *Incitement to disaffection.* There exist a number of statutory offences generally related towards those who attempt to persuade members of the armed forces or the police away from their duties: the Incitement to Mutiny Act 1797, the Army Act 1955, the Air Force Act 1955, the Naval Discipline Act 1957, the Aliens Restriction (Amendment) Act 1919, the Incitement to Disaffection Act 1934 and the Police Act 1964. Recent instances include the cases in the mid 1970s involving Pat Arrowsmith and her friends who distributed leaflets to soldiers suggesting leaving the army or deserting rather than serving in Northern Ireland.

(*h*) *Racial and sexual discrimination.* The Race Relations Act 1976 and the Sex Discrimination Act 1975 seek to outlaw unjustifiable discrimination on the grounds of sex or race. They each provide a mechanism of complaint for the victim of such action.

(*i*) *Privacy*. As long ago as 1880 Dr Cooley described privacy as "the right to be let alone". There is no general right to privacy in English law. Protection against interference is piecemeal and include the torts of defamation, trespass to land, and nuisance, breach of copyright and breach of confidence. There have been many suggestions for a more general law, for example the famous Younger Report in 1972, but little has been achieved.

(*j*) *Criminal and blasphemous libel*. The tort of defamation will be dealt with in Chapter 12. Libel is generally a tort, but if it is likely to lead to a breach of the peace, then it can be the subject of a criminal prosecution. Blasphemous libel, on the other hand, is committed where a person publishes in a permanent form any matter attacking the Christian doctrine or the Bible, or the doctrine of the church of England, or God, Christ or other sacred persons. Recently "Gay News" and its editor, Mr Lemon, were convicted of this offence. (*R.* v. *Lemon* (1979)).

(*k*) *The censorship of films and plays*. Theatre censorship was abolished by the Theatres Act 1968, but the presentation of obscenity is still criminal. Films are censored (to an extent) by local authorities. Certificates are attached to films indicating their views and recommendations: "U" (universal)—suitable for all ages; "P.G." (parental guidance)—parents may consider some scenes unsuitable for young children; "15" (AA)—persons under the age of 15 will not be admitted; "18" (X)—persons under the age of 18 will not be admitted.

Chapter 12

The Law of Tort

TORT: GENERAL ISSUES

A tort is a civil wrong. We met the law of tort first in Chapter 1 while classifying the law as between civil and criminal law. Sometimes students new to legal study have difficulty with the word tort. Professor Williams (in *Learning the Law*) wrote:

> This word conveys little meaning to the average layman, and its exact definition is a matter of great difficulty even for the lawyer; but the general idea of it will become clear enough if one says that torts include such wrongs as assault, battery, false imprisonment, trespass, conversion, defamation of character, negligence and nuisance. It is a civil wrong independent of contract: that is to say, it gives rise to an action for damages irrespective of any agreement not to do the act complained of.

The point of taking action in tort is to obtain compensation. There are other ways: private insurance, social insurance, compensation for criminal injuries, welfare benefits, etc., but if your legal rights have been infringed, then you can sue for compensation in a tort action. Your rights are the key—not your injury.

There is no automatic right to compensation in tort law simply because the plaintiff has suffered injury. A corner shop going out of business because of the pressure of a supermarket brings about financial injury and loss, but no legal right has (usually) been infringed, so no action lies. On the other hand, there are certain rights which the law takes so seriously that if they are infringed an action can be brought. There is no need to establish injury. *Damnum* means physical or financial damage or loss, *injuria* means the infringement of a legal right. It follows from the above that *damnum sine injuria* (physical etc. loss without the infringement of a legal right) is not actionable, whereas *injuria sine damno*, the opposite, is.

For example, in the famous case of *Bradford Corporation* v. *Pickles* (1895) Mr Pickles had excavated a hole on his land so as to reduce the water supply to the corporation waterworks down the hill from the spring up the hill. (He claimed to be working minerals.) The gesture was made, it was alleged, so as to induce the corporation to buy his land. Lord Halsbury said:

> The acts done, or sought to be done, by the defendant were all done upon his own land, and the interference whatever it is, with the flow of water is an interference with water, which is underground and not shown to be water flowing in any defined stream, but is percolating water, which, but for such interference, would undoubtedly reach the plaintiff's works, and in that sense does deprive them of the water which they would otherwise get. But although it does deprive them of water which they would otherwise get, it is necessary for the plaintiffs to establish that they have a right to the flow of water, and that the defendant has no right to do what he is going... The landowner had a right to do what he had done whatever his object or purpose might be, and although the purpose might be wholly unconnected with the enjoyment of his own estate.

He had, obviously, caused injury, but no legal right had been infringed.

Incidentally, this case also highlights another general principle of the law of tort: that (with only a few exceptions, which we will consider later) it is not much concerned with motive. Broadly, tort law is about what the defendant did, not why he did it, and what the plaintiff suffered as a reasonably foreseeable consequence. Lord Halsbury again:

> This is not a case in which the state of mind of the person doing the act can affect the right to do it. If it was a lawful act, however ill the motive might be, he had a right to do it. If it was an unlawful act, however good his motive might be, he would have no right to do it.

On the other hand, there are a number of cases in libel (a form of defamation) where the plaintiff has not really suffered much at all. Similarly in trespass to land. The law regards these wrongs as especially bad and tends to compensate beyond loss. Indeed actual loss need not be proved. Such torts are said to be actionable *per se*.

There are also instances where the courts have awarded exemplary damages, where the activity of the defendant has been regarded as especially outrageous, but such events are very rare. The broad line of policy in tortious liability is founded on fault—that the defendant should answer for loss which is his fault. This fault must be proved. It is argued that much of the money available to compensate for, say, road accident injuries, is soaked up in proving that the plaintiff's injuries are attributable to the defendant's fault.

There are instances where the defendant is liable even where the injury was clearly not his fault. These include the liability of an employer for the torts of his employees (called vicarious liability), and those instances where liability is said to be strict. These include actions under the tort named after the case *Rylands* v. *Fletcher* (1866) which concerned the flooding of mine shafts by a reservoir of water built on the instructions of the defendants. Blackburn J said:

> The person who for his own purposes brings on his lands and collects and keeps there anything likely to do mischief if it escapes, must keep it in at his peril, and, if he does not do so, is prima facie answerable for all the damages which is the natural consequence of its escape.

VICARIOUS LIABILITY

This is the liability of one person for acts committed by someone else. In tort law the usual instance is the liability of an employer for the torts of his employee. It is important to note that the employer is not liable instead of the employee, but liable as well. In practice the point may not matter to a plaintiff faced with an employer carrying an insurance policy and an impecunious employee. The justifications for this liability have been various:

(*a*) the plaintiff has a financially sound defendant (usually with insurers who will pay, raise the premiums generally, so everybody who insures pays; at least it spreads the load);

(*b*) the potential of vicarious liability will increase standards of training, supervision and safety within the enterprise;

(*c*) the employee is merely an extension of the employer, taken on as the business grew and diversified, so the torts are really those of the employer, committed indirectly.

The employer will not be answerable for all the torts of everyone he employs. In strange terminology, a distinction is drawn between servants and independent contractors, so that the employer is not usually liable for the torts of his independent contractor.

Servants and independent contractors

We know that the distinction is important, but how is it made? There is no single test. There are various guidelines which emerge from the cases. (Each case is decided on its own facts.) These guidelines include the so-called control test; that is, the servant can be told what to do and how to do it, but the independent contractor only what to do. This test is not much use in an age of accelerating technology. The employee may have been chosen for his special expertise, he probably was. The employer does not really control his methods of work. Any control in an overall sense would not separate out the independent contractor. There are other tests:

(*a*) the method of payment (servants by wage or salary, independent contractors by lump sum);

(*b*) the supply of tools, premises, etc.;

(*c*) taxation (servants on PAYE, independent contractors taking care of their own tax);

(*d*) pension schemes;

(*e*) the power of appointment and dismissal (called the right to hire and fire; an employer would have individual powers of this kind over servants); and

(*f*) the integration test, suggested by Denning LJ (in *Stevenson, Jordan and Harrison Ltd.* v. *MacDonald and Evans* (1952)):

It is often easy to recognise a contract of service when you see it, but difficult to say wherein the difference lies. A ship's master, a chauffeur, and a reporter on the staff of a newspaper are all employed under a contract of service; but a ship's pilot, a taxi-man, and a newspaper contributor are employed under a contract for services. One feature which seems to run through the instances is that, under a contract of service, a man is employed as part of the business, and his work is done as an integral part of the business; whereas, under a contract for services, his work, although done for the business, is not integrated into it but is only accessory to it.

The lack of any single test leads to apparent inconsistencies. For example, in *Morren* v. *Swinton and Pendlebury UDC* (1965) an engineer was held to be the servant of a local authority despite the lack of control over his work, because his contract of employment made him part of the organisation. Whereas, in *Market Investigations* v. *Minister of Social Security* (1969) a lady interviewer was held to be a servant because the manner of her interviewing was controlled, yet she was hardly integrated: she could work when she wanted, and for other similar organisations as well if she chose to.

The distinction is always made when required, but not always in a predictable way. Its importance, as we noted, lies in the fact that only very rarely does an employer find himself answering vicariously for the torts of his independent contractor. However, it is not the case either that he will always have to answer for the torts of his servant.

Servants

An employer is vicariously liable for the torts of his servants committed during the course of their employment. It is another problem: was the act which injured the plaintiff done while the employee was within his course of employment or not? The answer, from the cases, seems to be based more on degree than logic. This may reflect the policy (quite widely advocated) that wherever an injury can be compensated by insurance it ought to be—and if this means stretching the course of employment, well ... One judge actually said "this court looks around to see who is best able to pay."

The measure of the course of employment is readily visible in *Hilton* v. *Thomas Burton* (1961) where some demolition contractors decided to take the employer's van (they had permission) to a cafe eight miles away, for tea. They left the site at about 3.30 pm. When they reached the cafe it was time to finish work. They drove back again. The driver's negligence resulted in one of his colleagues being killed. His widow sued. The employer's insurers claimed that the men were outside the course of their employment. Diplock J said:

> I think that the true test can best be expressed in these words: was the second defendant doing something that he was employed to do? If so, however improper the manner in which he was doing it, whether negligent or fraudulently, or contrary to express orders, I have got to look at the realities of the situation. What were the circumstances, and what was the purpose for which this journey to the cafe and back was taken. Looking at the realities of the situation, it seems to me to be clear beyond a peradventure that what happened was this: the four men having taken the view that they had done enough work to pass muster, were filling in the rest of their time until their hours of work had come to an end. They decided to go to the cafe after sitting and chatting on the job for some time, to fill in the time until they could go home and draw their pay. This seems to me to be a plain case of what, in the old cases, was sometimes called going out on a frolic of their own. It had most tragic consequences; but it does not seem to me that it is possible to hold (though I would like to do so if I could), looking at the realities of the situation, that on the course of that journey the second defendant was doing anything that he was employed to do.

It is interesting to compare this case with the decision in *Rose* v. *Plenty* (1976) where a Co-op milkman in Bristol, in the face of an express prohibition from his employers, used a boy, Leslie Rose, 13 years of age to help him on his round. The boy's leg was broken when the float was driven negligently. Despite the prohibition, the employers were held vicariously liable. Lord Denning said:

> In considering whether a prohibited act was within the course of the employment, it depends very much on the purpose for which it is done. If it is done for his employer's business, it is usually done in the course of his employment, even though it is a prohibited act.

This would seem to echo the true test mentioned at the beginning of what we noted from the judgment of Diplock J in *Hilton* v. *Thomas Burton* (1961).

Independent contractors

As we have noted, vicarious liability here is rare and limited. It could arise where the tortious activity was authorised or done under the employer's instructions; or where the instructions were carelessly given, or where the tort was one of strict liability (like *Rylands* v. *Fletcher*, noted earlier in this chapter), or where the work ordered is of exceptional danger to the public (like work on the highway) or where the duty the work has been commissioned to fulfil is not delegable to anyone else (like the employer's duty to provide proper equipment, premises and staff—it is a personal duty).

GENERAL DEFENCES

There are special defences available to the defendant when faced with allegations of particular torts, we will note some of them later, but there are also a number of general defences which are available to combat allegations of many torts. It is important to realise that when dealing with particular torts the tendency is to look from the plaintiff's point of view (i.e. what must the plaintiff prove in order to succeed, etc.), whereas here we are looking from the reverse angle. We are about to consider the defences that might be raised in reply.

Volenti

This is one of the most important of the general defences. It is properly called *volenti non fit injuria*. Recalling that *injuria* means the infringement of a legal right and not injury in the usual sense, this phrase means "to him who consents, no harm is done".

Sometimes the defence is considered as falling into two parts: certain harm and accidental harm. If you climb into the boxing ring to fight you are likely to be punched. If this took place elsewhere it would be actionable as a tort, but if you were to sue the boxer you would lose because you would be taken to have consented to the normal consequences of boxing. This has been seen in the case of *Simms* v. *Leigh Rugby Football Club* (1969), where a player whose leg was broken in a tackle lost his action. The accident was within the rules of the game. On the other hand, of course, if the tackle had been outside those rules then he might not have been taken to have consented. In *Gilbert* v. *Grundy* (1978), for example, almost £4,000 in damages and costs were awarded to the owner of a broken leg following "deliberate and/or reckless foul play outside the laws of the game".

The issue of accidental harm is more subtle. Where the plaintiff places himself in a position where, if an accident were to happen he might well be injured, then in general he will be taken to have consented to run the risk of it happening. In *Hall* v. *Brooklands Auto Racing Club* (1933) a spectator was badly injured when a car crashed off the track. The court was satisfied that reasonable precautions had been taken by the organisers. They took the plaintiff to have consented to run the risk of accidental harm in attending a race-track and standing near the railings. (No car had left the track before in the 23 year history of the club.)

There are two groups of people who are not generally taken to consent to run the risk of accidental harm in what they do: employees and rescuers.

In *Smith* v. *Baker* (1891) we can see the employee, a man drilling holes in rock for railway contractors, carrying on working despite the fact that he knew that a nearby crane was carrying rocks over his head. Almost irresistibly he was struck by a falling rock. His action was defended with *volenti*. Lord Halsbury said:

> I think that a person who relies on the maxim must show a consent to the particular thing done. Of course, I do not mean to deny that a consent to the particular thing may be inferred from the course of conduct, as well as proved by express consent; but if I were to apply my proposition to the particular facts of this case, I do not believe that the plaintiff ever did or would have consented to the particular act done under the particular circumstances. He would have said, "I cannot look out for myself at present. You are employing me in a form of employment in which I have not the ordinary means of looking out for myself; I must attend to my drill. If you will not give me warning when the stone is going to be slung, at all events let me look out for myself, and do not place me under a crane which is lifting heavy stones over my head when you keep my attention fixed upon an operation which prevents me looking out for myself!"

Thus it is said that knowledge of the risk is not enough, the plaintiff must have actually consented to run it. It seems that the only employees who do that will be those who are handsomely paid to take risks, like test pilots etc.

The rescuer can be seen in *Haynes* v. *Harwood* (1935) where a horse and van had been left unattended by the defendants. The horses bolted when a boy threw stones at them, and a policeman was badly injured when he caught one of them to save bystanders, including many children, from injury. One of the defences raised was *volenti*. It was held that where a situation of danger is brought about by negligence and someone is put at risk and a rescue is made or attempted, then the rescuer acts out of a spirit of moral duty rather than of consent to run the risk, and volenti cannot be used against him. Maugham LJ said:

> In deciding whether such a rescuer is justified in putting himself into a position of such great peril, the law has to measure the interests which he sought to protect and the other interests involved. We have all heard of the reasonable man whom the law postulates in certain circumstances; the reasonable man here must be endowed with qualities of energy and courage, and he is not to be deprived of a remedy because he has in a marked degree a desire to save human life when in peril.

Statutory authority

It may be that the defendant admits that he did the act complained of as causing the plaintiff's injury, but that he has authority within a statute to carry on with that activity. The extent of the defence depends entirely upon the interpretation put upon the statute in question by the court. They might see the authority as absolute—something in the nature of a duty. This happened in *Vaughan* v. *Taff Vale Railway* (1860) where sparks escaped from a steam engine causing extensive damage. The statute under which the railway was operated afforded a defence. Had the company not taken all reasonable precautions, been negligent, it might have been otherwise. Alternatively, the statute might be seen as just permissive, so that an activity can be carried on provided the rights of others are observed. This happened in *Metropolitan Asylum District* v. *Hill* (1881) where the contruction and operation of a hospital in Hampstead as a reception centre for smallpox and other infectious and contagious diseases was held to constitute a nuisance to those nearby, and an injunction was awarded.

Act of God

In *Tennent* v. *Earl of Glasgow* (1864) Lord Westbury defined this defence as involving "circumstances which no human foresight can provide against and of which human prudence is not bound to recognise the possibility". The defence is almost unknown today, Professor Rogers wrote:

> not because strict liability is thought to be desirable but because increased knowledge limits the unpredictable.

The case of *Nichols* v. *Marsland* (1876) is an illustration. A rainstorm "greater and more violent than any within the memory of witnesses" caused damage when some ornamental lakes overflowed. The defence of act of God was successfully pleaded.

Necessity

This is another rare defence. The defendant admits the activity, but claims that it was done in order to prevent greater harm. In *Cope* v. *Sharpe* (1912), for example, a gamekeeper deliberately destroyed some of the plaintiff's heather in order to create a fire-break and stop a fire spreading to the land where his pheasants were kept. The fire was extinguished before it reached the fire-break, but the defence of necessity was accepted by the court. His fear had been reasonable; so had his action.

Inevitable accident

This is virtually unknown, of dubious value, but is quoted in some books as a general defence. It depends upon an injury having been sustained as a result of an accident which no reasonable man could have been expected to provide against. The difference between this and the act of God defence is that here the elements are not the exclusive players. *Stanley* v. *Powell* (1891) is cited. It concerned a hunting accident where a shot fired at a pheasant ricocheted off an oak tree and injured one of the party. The court held that in the absence of negligence the defendant, who fired the gun, was not liable.

Contributory negligence

This is not strictly a general defence since it only serves to reduce liability, it does not enable the defendant to escape it. We will include it in our examination of the tort of negligence.

REMOTENESS OF DAMAGE

The court must be able to see a clear link between what the defendant did and what the plaintiff suffered. Without it the damage is said to be too remote a consequence, and the action fails. It is not quite the same thing as pleading a defence.

If several things happen between the activity of the defendant and the injury complained of the chain of events is called a chain of causation. Provided it remains unbroken the necessary connection between the action and injury exists. Anything which breaks the chain of causation is called a *novus actus interveniens*.

These principles can be applied to a very old case, *Scott* v. *Shepherd* (1773). It was the fair day at Milborne Port, 28th October 1770, in the evening. The defendant threw a lighted gunpowder firework into a crowded covered market. It fell onto Yate's gingerbread stall. A bystander called Willis, in order to protect himself and Yate's goods, picked it up and threw it across the market. It landed on Ryal's stall. He picked it up and threw it to another part of the market, where it exploded in the plaintiff's face, and he lost an eye. There was a lengthy chain of causation, but no break, no *novus actus interveniens*. Nothing had happened which was not a natural consequence of the defendant's act.

However, in *McKew* v. *Holland & Hannen & Cubitts (Scotland) Ltd.* (1969) the chain was broken. The plaintiff was injured at work. The defendants were responsible. As a result, sometimes, and without much warning, he temporarily lost the use of his left leg. He had been out to look over a flat with his wife, child and brother-in-law. The access to it was a steep flight of stairs, without a handrail. On the way down he felt his leg give way, and he pushed his child out of the way, and in order not to fall head first he jumped, and broke his right ankle. He claimed for this injury too. Lord Reid said:

> If a man is injured in such a way that his leg may give way at any moment he must act reasonably and carefully. It is quite possible that in spite of all reasonable care his leg may give way in circumstances such that as a result he sustains further injury. Then that second injury was caused by his disability which in turn was caused by the defender's fault. But if the injured man acts unreasonably he cannot hold the defender liable for injury caused by his own unreasonable conduct. His unreasonable conduct is *novus actus interveniens*. The chain of causation has been broken and what follows must be regarded as caused by his own conduct and not by the defender's fault or the disability caused by it.

The test of remoteness

Apart from a strictly factual approach to causation (it either followed or it did not), the courts also set a limit to the defendant's liability for what he has actually caused. He will be called to account only for the damage which is of a kind that the reasonable man should have foreseen—not the precise nature, nor the precise manner in which it was inflicted—but the kind of damage which should reasonably have been foreseen. So his liability is not limited by the extent of the loss, provided the kind of loss was foreseeable.

The rule comes from an Australian case called *The Wagon Mound* (1961) in which the defendants spilt oil onto seawater. Sparks from welding nearby set the oil alight and the plaintiff's wharf was destroyed. The damage was a direct result of the spillage, but the kind of damage, fire damage, was not reasonably foreseeable. It seems that to ignite this oil on that water is not easy. Obviously, clogging up the wharf with oil would have been foreseeable.

The case of *Hughes* v. *Lord Advocate* (1963) is also instructive. Some Post Office workmen were away at tea. They were working on cables reached by a ladder, down through a manhole. They had a tent over the manhole. They put a tarpaulin over the entrance to the tent, having lifted out the ladder and left it nearby. Two boys (eight and ten) went exploring. They went down the manhole, using the ladder and one of the paraffin lamps the men had set to mark the site. On the way out of the tent one of the lads knocked the paraffin lamp into the manhole. There was a violent explosion. Flames reached thirty feet. The boy fell into the hole and was badly burnt. He was able to recover damages because it was foreseeable that a child might get onto the site, break a lamp, and be burnt. The lamp exploding was not foreseeable, but the type of injury was.

The point about the extent of injury enabling the defendant to escape liability, provided the type of injury is foreseeable is nowhere clearer seen than in the so called thin-skull cases. In *Smith* v. *Leech Brain & Co.* (1962) for example, the plaintiff's husband was burnt on the lip by molten metal. It was the defendant's fault. The burn set off a latent cancer in him, and he died. The kind of injury, the burn, was foreseeable, the extent was not, but the defendants were liable for all, his injury.

NEGLIGENCE

Negligence is the most important of the torts. It is committed when a person fails to live up to a standard of care expected of him, as a matter of law, and someone else is injured as a result. It is often claimed that in order to succeed in an action for negligence the plaintiff must prove:

    (*a*) that the defendant owed him a duty of care; and

    (*b*) that he acted in breach of that duty; and

    (*c*) that as a result the plaintiff suffered damage. (This resultant damage, of course, is subject to the issues about remoteness which we considered earlier in this chapter.)

So the action could be regarded as something of a hurdle race: duty, breach, resulting damage. It is a neat and convenient way to examine the tort, but, as Lord Pearson said (in *Home Office* v. *Dorset Yacht Co.* (1970)):

> The analysis is logically correct and often convenient for purposes of exposition, but it is only an analysis and should not eliminate consideration of the tort of negligence as a whole.

We will return often to the idea of negligence (for example in Chapter 14 it will be seen as an element in some crimes), but here we consider it as a matter which is actionable in itself, as a tort.

The duty of care

The foundation stone of much of the modern development of the tort is a case called *Donoghue* v. *Stevenson* (1932) which arose from the events of 28th August 1928, in Vincenti Minchella's ice cream parlour in Paisley, near Glasgow. Mrs Day Donoghue drank some ginger beer, bought for her by her friend, only to discover, in the opaque bottle, the remnants of a decomposing snail. She had not bought the product, so a breach of contract action was not possible for her, so she sued the manufacturer for negligence. The case that finally wound its way into the House of Lords, and thereafter in English law, (remember that the law in Scotland is different), was upon the question whether the manufacturer owed her, a consumer not a buyer, a duty of care.

The judgment of Lord Atkin is very important. It goes wider than the set point, it explores generally when a duty of care is owed, by whom and to whom. Unless the plaintiff can show himself to have been owed such a duty of care by the defendant, his action in negligence will fail (fall at the first hurdle, as it were). Lord Atkin explained the law in terms of neighbours—not necessarily the person next door, but the person whose welfare in the circumstances in question, ought to have been of concern to the defendant. It is, of course, an application of the Biblical entreaty, "love thy neighbour". Lord Atkin said:

> The rule that you are to love your neighbour becomes in law, you must not injure your neighbour; and the lawyer's question, Who is my neighbour? receives a restricted reply. You must take reasonable care to avoid acts or omissions which you can reasonably foresee would be likely to injure your neighbour. Who, then, in law, is my neighbour? The answer seems to be—persons who are so closely and directly affected by my act that I ought

reasonably to have them in contemplation as being so affected when I am directing my mind to the acts or omissions which are called in question.

Clearly, then, the manufacturer, David Stevenson, owed the consumer a duty of care. This is not to say that there are no limits set to the size of neighbourhood. There is a case popularly called the pregnant fishwife case, *Bourhill* v. *Young* (1943) which shows a plaintiff who was not owed a duty of care. Euphemia Bourhill was a pregnant (eight months) fish wife getting off a tram in Edinburgh. Her basket of fish was being lifted onto her back by the driver of the tram. She was standing at the rear, offside of the tram. John Young was a motor cyclist. He overtook the tram on the inside and crashed into a car which was turning right, in front of the tram. He was killed. Mrs Bourhill heard the crash. She did not see it. She saw the blood on the road. Her child was still-born. She blamed the motor cyclist, and sued his estate. To win, she would first need to establish that John Young had owed her a duty of care at the time of the crash. Lord Russell said:

> In considering whether a person owes to another a duty a breach of which will render him liable to that other in damages for negligence, it is material to consider what the defendant ought to have contemplated as a reasonable man.
>
> Can it be said that (the motor cyclist) could reasonably have anticipated that a person, situated as was the (plaintiff), would be affected by his proceeding towards Colinton at the speed at which he was travelling? I think not. His road was clear of pedestrians. The (plaintiff) was not within his vision, but was standing behind the solid barrier of the tramcar. His speed in no way endangered her. In these circumstances I am unable to see how he could reasonably anticipate that, if he came into collision with a vehicle coming across the tramcar into Glenlockhart Road, the resultant noise would cause physical injury by shock to a person standing behind the tramcar. In my opinion, he owed no duty to the (plaintiff) and was, therefore, not guilty of any negligence in relation to her.

She was beyond the area of foreseeable danger; as was the plaintiff mother in *King* v. *Phillips* (1953). She was 70–80 yards away, upstairs in her house, from the taxi which was reversing over her son's tricycle. Naturally the boy screamed in protest, but he was hardly hurt at all. The boy was owed a duty of care, but not the mother. These cases have to be read now in the light of the House of Lords decision in

McLoughlin v. *O'Brien* (1982) where a mother was held to have been owed a duty of care even though she was not at the scene of the road accident which injured her husband and two of her children, and killed the third child. Lord Wilberforce placed a new line of limitation on claims. He said that it is necessary to take into account:

(*a*) the class of persons claiming (relative, friend, bystander);
(*b*) their proximity to the accident (in time and space); and
(*c*) the means by which the nervous shock, which forms the basis of cases like these, was caused.

The mother here satisfied these three considerations. It remains to be seen whether future claimants will be measured in the same way, or whether the lines will be redrawn or whether (as some writers recommend) it is time for legislation in this area.

Having considered some of the limits which have been placed upon the expansion of the neighbour principle, we must note the remarkable manner in which it has been instrumental in the spread of negligence liability. At the (considerable) risk of over-simplification, we could examine several different threads of development.

Acts causing physical damage

In *Dutton* v. *Bognor Regis UDC* (1972) the plaintiff recovered for damage to her house due to inadequate foundations which ought to have been spotted by the local council building inspector.

In *Yianni* v. *Evans* (1981) defective foundations again caused damage and went unnoticed by a surveyor instructed by a Building Society for a prospective mortgagor; the plaintiff's claim succeeded. Of course, it is very difficult to isolate physical from financial loss in cases like these.

Acts causing financial loss

In *Ross* v. *Caunters* (1979) a solicitor drew up a will, but used the husband of a beneficiary as a witness. Under the Wills Act 1837, s.15, the gift in the will could not go to the beneficiary, so she sued the solicitor in negligence, and won.

In *Junior Books* v. *Veitchi* (1982) specialists laid a floor in a factory inadequately. It was not dangerous but it needed replacing. It had cracked badly. The plaintiffs wanted the cost of replacing it, and compensation for the cost of shifting the machinery to do it, and loss of profit while the machinery was out of use. The House of Lords allowed all this, because, as specialists, they ought to have known what was required and the consequences of not supplying it.

Statements causing physical damage

In *Clay* v. *Crump* (1964) land was being redeveloped. An architect

said a particular wall could be left standing. He did not examine it. It
fell on the plaintiff, who was an employee of the building contractors
on the site. Lord Justice Ormerod applied the words of Lord Atkin
(which we noted earlier in this chapter); he said:

> The question is . . . whether, according to established principles of
> law, the architect owed a duty to the plaintiff. Is this a case in which
> it can be said that the plaintiff was so closely and directly affected
> by the acts of the architect as to have been reasonably in his
> contemplation when he was directing his mind to the acts or
> omissions which are called in question? In my judgment, there
> must be an affirmative answer to that question. The architect, by
> reason of his contractual arrangement with the building owner,
> was charged with the duty of preparing the necessary plans and
> making arrangements for the manner in which the work should be
> done. This involved taking precautions or giving instructions for
> them to be taken so that the work could be done with safety. It
> must have been in the contemplation of the architect that builders
> would go on the site as the whole object of the work was to erect
> buildings there. It would seem impossible to contend that the
> plaintiff would not be affected by the decisions and plans drawn up
> by the architect.

Statements causing financial loss

In the very important case of *Hedley Byrne* v. *Heller and Partners*
(1964) a new stream of authority arose, but it was based on Lord
Atkin's neighbour principle. The plaintiffs were advertising agents.
They needed to enquire into the financial stability of a company
called Easipower Ltd. They were advancing credit to them. The
plaintiffs asked their bankers to enquire. They asked Easipower's
bankers, who provided a favourable reference, but carrying an
exclusion clause: "for your private use and without responsibility on
the part of this bank or its officials." The plaintiffs relied on the
reference. Easipower went into liquidation. The plaintiffs lost
£17,661.92½. They sued Easipower's bankers. They lost because of
the effectiveness of the exclusion cause, but the central importance of
the case lies in the discussion in the judgments of the House of Lords
about what the position would have been without the exclusion
clause.

Lord Reid commented upon the impact of Lord Atkin's neighbour
principle in *Donoghue* v. *Stevenson* (1932), he said:

> The appellants' first argument was based on *Donoghue* v.
> *Stevenson*. That is a very important decision, but I do not think

that it has any direct bearing on this case. That decision may encourage us to develop existing lines of authority, but it cannot entitle us to disregard them. Apart altogether from authority, I would think that the law must treat negligent words differently from negligent acts. The law ought so far as possible to reflect the standards of the reasonable man, and that is what Donoghue v Stevenson sets out to do. The most obvious difference between negligent words and negligent acts is this. Quite careful people often express definite opinions on social or informal occasions even when they see that others are likely to be influenced by them; and they often do that without taking that care which they would take if asked for their opinion professionally or in a business connection. The appellant agrees that there can be no duty of care on such occasions... I therefore turn to the authorities to see what more is required. The most natural requirement would be that expressly or by implication from the circumstances the speaker or writer has undertaken some responsibility... A reasonable man, knowing that he was being trusted or that his skill and judgment were being relied on, would, I think, have three courses open to him. He could keep silent or decline to give the information or advice sought: or he could give an answer with a clear qualification that he accepted no responsibility for it or that it was given without that reflection or inquiry which a careful answer would require: or he could simply answer without any such qualification. If he chooses to adopt the last course he must, I think, be held to have accepted some responsibility for his answer being given carefully, or to have accepted a relationship with the inquirer which requires him to exercise such care as the circumstances require.

Lord Morris added:

if in a sphere in which a person is so placed that others could reasonably rely upon his judgment or his skill or upon his ability to make careful inquiry, a person takes it upon himself to give information or advice to, or allows his information or advice to be passed on to, another person who, as he knows or should know, will place reliance upon it, then a duty of care will arise.

Breach of duty

Whilst the existence of a duty of care owed by defendants to plaintiffs is a complex and developing matter of law, if such a duty was owed, then the issue of its breach (the second hurdle) is a matter of fact in each case. Broadly, the court will look at what the defendant did and what the plaintiff suffered and judge the risk that the defendant was running of causing the plaintiff's injury, and the measures which would have been necessary to prevent that risk being run. In short, the court will ask itself whether the defendant acted reasonably in the circumstances. One definition of negligence describes it as "doing what a reasonable man would not do, or failing to do what a reasonable man would do". You do not have to be perfect, just reasonably careful.

In *Bolton* v. *Stone* (1951) the plaintiff was injured by a cricket ball which had travelled so far and so high that it sailed over the defendant cricket club's perimeter fence (17 foot high, and 78 yards from the wicket). It was a straight drive. A ball had left the cricket ground only five or six times before, and never hit anyone outside. There was a risk. There were measures which could obviate it—close the ground perhaps. Lord Oaksey said:

> The standard of care in the law of negligence is the standard of an ordinarily careful man, but in my opinion an ordinarily careful man does not take precautions against every foreseeable risk. He can, of course, foresee the possibility of many risks, but life would be almost impossible if he were to attempt to take precautions against every risk which he can foresee. He takes precautions against risks which are reasonably likely to happen.

So the duty of care which the club owed to those in the neighbourhood of their activities had not been breached. They had acted reasonably.

In *Paris* v. *Stepney Borough Council* (1951) a council fitter had sight only in one eye. He was using a hammer to move a bolt on a vehicle when a chip of metal flew into his good eye, and he was blinded. The defendants had not provided goggles. It seems that it was not usual for that kind of job. On the facts (and only by a majority) the House of Lords held that the duty of care had been breached. The seriousness of the risk (total loss of sight) and the foreseeable chance of it happening on the one hand, and the simple precaution (goggles being provided) necessary to obviate it on the other, were regarded, on balance, as sufficient evidence to show lack of reasonable care in this case.

Resulting damage

The third element or hurdle is that the damage the plaintiff complains of must have resulted from the breach of the duty that was owed him by the defendant. Again, it is a matter of fact, the damage resulted or it did not. In *Barnett* v. *Chelsea and Kensington Hospital Management Committee* (1968) a nightwatchman came to the casualty department of the hospital, complaining of vomiting after having drunk tea. The nurse contacted the doctor, a Dr Banerjee, by telephone, who recommended that he go home to bed and call his own doctor. A few hours later he died of arsenical poisoning. His widow sued. Clearly a duty of care was owed. Plainly, in not even examining the man, the duty had been breached, but, on the evidence it seems that when he called at casualty he was already bound to die. There was nothing which could have been done for him which would have saved his life. This sad case shows that if the damage does not, in fact, result from the breach of the duty owed, then the plaintiff's case in negligence must fail.

Contributory negligence

Where the plaintiff is in part the cause of his own injury then the blame is shared, on a percentage basis, and he receives less from the defendant than he would have had he not been contributorily negligent. This is the position today, under the Law Reform (Contributory Negligence) Act 1945. Before the 1945 Act contributory negligence was a complete defence.

The matter is topical with the compulsory wearing of seat belts. Even before the criminal law was changed in January 1983, an action for injury sustained in a road accident could result in reduced damages if the plaintiff had failed to wear a seat belt where, had it been worn, his injuries would have been less serious. These were the circumstances in *Froom* v. *Butcher* (1975). The plaintiff here had his damages reduced by 20 per cent. Lord Denning explained:

> Negligence depends on a breach of duty, whereas contributory negligence does not. Negligence is a man's carelessness in breach of duty to others. Contributory negligence is a man's carelessness in looking after his own safety. He is guilty of contributory negligence if he ought reasonably to have foreseen that, if he did not act as a reasonable prudent man, he might be hurt himself. Before 1945 a plaintiff who was guilty of contributory negligence was disentitled from recovering anything if his own negligence was one of the substantial causes of the injury. Since 1945 he is no longer defeated altogether. He gets reduced damages. The present law is contained in s.1(1) of the Law Reform (Contributory Negligence) Act 1945, which says:
>> "Where any person suffers damage as the result partly of his own fault and partly of the fault of any other person or persons, a claim in respect of that damage shall not be defeated by reason of the fault of the person suffering the damage, but the damages recoverable in respect thereof shall be reduced to such extent as

the court thinks just and equitable having regard to the claimant's share in the responsibility for the damage."

A popular case in this area is *Sayers* v. *Harlow UDC* (1958). Eileen Sayers had popped into a public convenience before catching the bus to London. She could not get out. She shouted and waved for fifteen minutes. She tried to climb out. She put her left foot on the seat, her right on the toilet-roll holder. She grasped the cistern pipe with her left hand and the top of the door with her right. She gave up. As she was returning to ground level the toilet roll rotated and she fell, and was injured. Her climbing attempt was unsuccessfully argued as a *novus actus interveniens*, breaking the chain of causation (we considered such things earlier in this chapter). The defendants were held liable in negligence, but Eileen Sayers was found 25 per cent to blame, and her damages were reduced accordingly.

Res ipsa loquitur

Sometimes the plaintiff suffers in such a way that it appears fairly obvious that the defendant must have been negligent—*res ipsa loquitur* (the thing speaks for itself). This is a rule of evidence law. Where the plaintiff can show:

(*a*) that the defendant was in control of the activity which caused his injury; and

(*b*) that the injury was of such a kind as would not have occurred unless someone had been negligent;

then the burden shifts, very unusually in English law, to the defendant to show that he had not been negligent. If he can give another reasonable explanation for the plaintiff's injuries then the burden shifts back to the plaintiff to establish negligence in the normal way. An early example is *Scott* v. *London and St Katherine's Docks* (1865) where a customs officer going about his business was hit on the head by six bags of sugar as he passed by the defendant's warehouse. They had no explanation to offer. Erle CJ said:

There must be reasonable evidence of negligence. But where the thing is shewn to be under the management of the defendant or his servants, and the accident is such as in the ordinary course of things does not happen if those who have the management use proper care, it affords reasonable evidence, in the absence of explanation by the defendants, that the accident arose from want of care.

OCCUPIER'S LIABILITY

The liability of an occupier for injuries sustained by someone on his premises depends upon whether that person was a lawful visitor or a trespasser.

All lawful visitors are protected by the Occupiers' Liability Act 1957, but the protection does not extend to trespassers. There are three categories of lawful visitor:

(a) persons with an express permission to visit the occupier's premises (e.g. friends invited for a party);

(b) persons with an implied permission to visit the occupier's premises (i.e. persons not specifically excluded such as customers in a shop, door-to-door salesmen);

(c) persons who enter by operation of law (e.g. police in execution of a search warrant, gas and electricity meter reading).

Under the Occupiers' Liability Act 1957, s.2(2), the occupier owes a common duty of care to all his visitors. It is defined as:

a duty to take such care as in all the circumstances of the case is reasonable to see that the visitor will be reasonably safe in using the premises for the purposes for which he is invited or permitted to be there.

This is not an absolute duty and can therefore be discharged by the occupier taking reasonable care; what this means will depend on all the circumstances of the case.

The occupier is the person who has sufficient degree of control over the premises to be expected to take responsibility for them. For example, in a block of flats the tenants are occupiers of their living accommodation but the landlord is occupier of the hall/landings, stairway and lifts.

An occupier may attempt to exclude or limit his liability by putting up a notice. The notice may state "Trespassers will be prosecuted" and is an attempt to keep people off the premises. What is the effect of such a notice? As far as concerns children who go on such premises and are injured it would probably have little or no effect. As far as adults are concerned the Occupiers' Liability Act, s.2(4), states that if damage is caused to a visitor by a danger of which he has been warned, the fact of a warning notice is not enough. The warning notice must be brought to the visitor's attention and the contents of the notice must be so clear as "to enable the visitor to be reasonably safe". In law, in fact, it will only very rarely be possible for the occupier to prosecute trespassers; the normal remedy is to sue for damages for the tort of trespass to land.

If the visitor enters as a result of a contract e.g. to watch motor racing or to watch a film then a further restriction on notices is imposed by the Unfair Contract Terms Act 1977, s.2. This prevents an occupier from excluding or restricting his liability for death or personal injury resulting from his being in breach of the common duty of care under the Occupiers' Liability Act, e.g. at a motor race in failing to erect an adequate safety barrier.

Towards the trespasser no statutory duty is owed. Particularly, towards the trespassing adult. It has been said that there is no duty owed towards trespassing adults at all—but this goes too far. There is a duty. It is referred to as a duty of common humanity. It is, of course, far less onerous than that imposed by the Occupiers' Liability Act 1957, but it nervertheless exists. In the famous old case of *Bird* v. *Holbrook* (1828), for example, the defendant set a spring gun in his garden to protect his tulips. The plaintiff entered to retrieve a pea-hen, and was severely injured when the gun went off. The plaintiff received damages. He was a trespasser, but was owed the duty of common humanity, which, in this instance might have been satisfied by warning signs.

Liability towards children

The Occupiers' Liability Act states that the occupier must be prepared for children to be less careful than adults. Therefore, if the occupier expects children to enter his premises as visitors e.g. a public park or a children's playground, then those premises must be safe for their use since he owes them the common duty of care. This requires that the characteristics of children be taken into account so that if there is an allurement on the land that can injure children the occupier will be liable. An allurement is something which is "fatal and fascinating".

In *Glasgow Corporation* v. *Taylor* (1922) a child of seven died after eating poisonous berries in a public park. The berries looked like cherries and were very tempting to children. Because the shrub had no warning notice or anything which prevented the children reaching the berries the occupiers were held liable.

If, however, the child is not a lawful visitor, but a trespasser, then the 1957 Act does not apply, and the plaintiff is left to establish that the basic duty of common humanity has been breached. There was a milestone of a case decided on this point: *British Railways Board* v. *Herrington* (1972). Here a six year old boy called Peter Herrington ran from land belonging to the National Trust onto the property of British Railways through a hole in the fence. He was severely injured on the electric line. The employees of the defendants had been aware of the hole in the fence for weeks, perhaps months. They had done nothing effective to mend it. Lord Reid said:

An occupier does not voluntarily assume a relationship with

trespassers. By trespassing they force a "neighbour" relationship on him. When they do so he must act in a humane manner—that is not asking too much of him—but I do not see why he should be required to do more. So it appears to me that an occupier's duty to trespassers must vary according to his knowledge, ability and resources. It has often been said that trespassers must take the land as they find it. I would rather say that they must take the occupier as they find him.

So the question whether an occupier is liable in respect of an accident to a trespasser on his land would depend on whether a conscientious humane man with his knowledge, skill and resources could reasonably have been expected to have done or refrained from doing before the accident something which would have avoided it. If he knew before the accident that there was a substantial probability that trespassers would come I think that most people would regard as culpable failure to give any thought to their safety.

So, to satisfy the duty of common humanity the fence ought to have been repaired—especially in the light of the occupier's knowledge that children played nearby. The defendants were liable to Peter Herrington.

Generally, whether this duty has been discharged will depend on the particular facts. In *Pannet* v. *McGuiness and Co. Ltd.* (1972) the defendants were demolishing a warehouse. This involved lighting large bonfires which employees of the defendants were supposed to supervise but failed to do. A child of five, trespassing on the property, fell into one of the fires and was badly burned. The Court of Appeal held the defendants liable. This was because the fires were attractive to children, and the defendants knew that children trespassed on the site. To discharge their duty of common humanity the defendants should have ensured that the fires were properly supervised at all times.

NUISANCE

The tort of nuisance concerns the unjustifiable interference with your right to enjoy your land (i.e. to live there reasonably comfortably). The tort has a public and private category.

Public nuisance

Public nuisance, logically since its effect is so broad, is usually a crime, but it is actionable in tort by an individual too where he has suffered more than the public have generally. As to the general aspect of public nuisance, Denning LJ (as he then was) sat in a case called *Attorney-General* v. *P.Y.A. Quarries* (1957), which concerned the public nuisance of blasting, flying stones, dust and vibrations from a quarry, and he said:

> A public nuisance is a nuisance which is so widespread in its range or so indiscriminate in its effect that it would not be reasonable to expect one person to take proceedings on his own responsibility to put a stop to it, but that it should be taken on the responsibility of the community at large.

Concerning the individual bringing an action, note that in *Castle* v. *St. Augustines Links Ltd.* (1922) a taxi driver on the way from Deal to Ramsgate was severely injured when a golf ball, driven from the thirteenth tee of a golf course smashed the windscreen. The evidence showed that balls often went into the road. "The thirteenth" was declared a public nuisance, and the taxi driver, because he had especially suffered, was able to obtain individual compensation.

Private nuisance

There are a number of characteristics which make up an actionable private nuisance, but it has none of the general character of public nuisance. It concerns the complaint of one person about another person or persons' activity.

The activity complained of must interfere with the plaintiff's enjoyment of his land. It is usually a general state of affairs rather than one isolated act (a large bonfire, an all night party, an explosion). The interference must be unreasonable; we live in towns, on estates, and there are certain activities we have to put up with. The alleged nuisance must have either been created by the defendant or be the result of his neglect of some specific duty imposed by the law, or it must be carried on (continued) by him, having been created by someone else. Usually actual damage must be proved. The plaintiff must be someone with an interest in the land over which the alleged nuisance is having an effect.

So that in *Malone* v. *Laskey* (1907) the injured woman was the wife of the manager of the company which was the subtenant of the house. It was unfortunate that the cistern in the lavatory had fallen on her head, but not actionable in nuisance. She had no interest in the land. This event illustrates another aspect of the tort. Although the injury followed a single event, the reason for it lay in the continuing state of the property caused by vibrations from the defendants' machinery in the adjoining premises.

S.C.M. v. *Whittall* (1971) was about a power cut and consequent loss of production when a cable was cut by a workman. Referring to the need for a continuing characteristic in nuisance, Thesinger J said:

> While there is no doubt that a single isolated escape may cause the damage that entitles the plaintiff to sue for nuisance, yet it must be proved that the nuisance arose from the condition of the defendants' land or premises or property or activities thereon that constituted a nuisance. I am satisfied that one negligent act that causes physical damage to an electric cable does not thereby constitute a nuisance.

The defendant must have been acting in an unreasonable manner. This is not easy to assess, but it concerns the measure of what one must put up with in a social environment, and what exceeds that. Furthermore, there are standards of comfort and convenience which are more than one can expect.

In *Andreae* v. *Selfridge* (1938), for example, the plaintiffs ran an hotel. Nearby, the defendants, who were demolition contractors, were busily at work. This was an actionable nuisance not in itself but to the extent that it developed an excessive amount of dust and noise, over and above what is normally to be expected in such circumstances. However, in *Bridlington Relay* v. *Yorkshire Electricity Board* (1965) the plaintiffs demanded a high standard of interference-free television reception. They traded in relaying the signal to the public. The defendants' power lines nearby disturbed reception. Buckley J said:

> In my judgment, the plaintiff could not succeed in a claim for damages for nuisance if what I may call an ordinary receiver of television by means of an aerial mounted on his own house could not do so. It is, I think, established by authority that an act which does not, or would not, interfere with the ordinary enjoyment of their property by neighbours in the ordinary modes of using such property cannot constitute a legal nuisance.

So the plaintiffs were expecting too much.

Another factor taken into account is the character of the neighbourhood. One arrogant judge once said "... what would be a nuisance in Belgrave Square would not necessarily be so in Bermondsey." Furthermore the motive for the activity complained of is relevant. In *Christie* v. *Davey* (1893) a woodcarver, who did not much enjoy music, retaliated when piano and singing lessons were given next door. He blew whistles, knocked on trays and boards, hammered, shrieked and shouted. His neighbours' use of their property was held to be reasonable, his was not. (This is a rare example of the motive for action being counted as relevant in tort.)

There are various defences that can be raised by the defendant in the face of a private nuisance action. We considered most of them earlier in this chapter: *volenti*, statutory authority and act of God. In addition he might claim that the nuisance was created by a third party (someone else), or he might allege the right to be a nuisance by "20 years' user". This interesting defence arises where an activity has been carried on for so long (20 years at least) that it has hardened into a right—despite the fact that it might have been actionable as a nuisance over the years. It is now too late.

The point was raised in *Sturges* v. *Bridgman* (1879), where the plaintiff, a doctor in Wimpole Street, London, had built a consulting room in his back garden which was close to the workshop of the defendant's confectionery business. The plaintiff complained of the interference. The defendant raised "20 years user" because the machinery had been in use for many years. The defence failed. The extra room had only just been built. The interference there was in question. The time had only just begun to run.

The obvious remedies for nuisance are damages and/or an injunction. Indeed it may well be that damages are not enough in this tort. An injunction will be wanted to stop the activity. (We considered the common law nature of damages and the equitable remedy of injunction in Chapter 2.) Further to these, the plaintiff could abate (put an end to) the nuisance himself. No unnecessary damage can be done. If it involves going onto the defendant's property then notice of the intention must be given, unless, of course, it is an emergency.

TRESPASS

Trespass is one of the oldest actions in English law. It is concerned with the direct infringement of the plaintiff's rights. (An indirect infringement might be actionable in nuisance.) It is likely that the infringement will have been made intentionally. Careless infringement is probably now part of the empire of negligence, but since there is no need for the plaintiff to specify the tort in his action this does not matter much. Actual damage must be proved if the infringement was careless. (It must usually be proved if the infringement was indirect.) Intentional, direct infringement of the plaintiff's rights is actionable *per se* i.e. without proof of damage. These are some of the rights taken very seriously by the law, we considered such matters earlier in this chapter. Broadly, trespass falls into three categories, which will be examined in turn.

To land

This has been defined as the unjustifiable, direct, intentional interference with the plaintiff's possession of land. So the plaintiff must be in possession of the land affected. He need not be the owner. The one in control, who intends to exclude others is in possession (a tenant perhaps, but probably not a bed and breakfast customer).

The interference must be direct. It could be entry, or refusal to leave having been invited in (say to a party) and asked to go. It could be placing things on the land (perhaps tossing garden pests like slugs into next-door's vegetable patch). It could be tunnelling under the ground, or flying above it. Here, however, the Civil Aviation Act 1949, s.40(1), gives immunity to aircraft, flying at a reasonable height, although it also makes them strictly liable for any damage they cause.

The main defences are that the defendant entered because there is a public or private right of way across the land, or because the person in possession gave permission, or under the Civil Aviation Act 1949, or because (as may be pleaded by an official such as a policeman or electricity board meter reader) another statute gives him the right to enter (this is the defence of statutory authority again). Further defences are necessity, or entering to put a stop to (abate) a nuisance, or that the defendant entered to recover his own goods of which he had been deprived by the plaintiff.

Of the remedies available to the plaintiff, damages are the most obvious. An injunction might be appropriate. There are various self-help remedies, like ejectment (using only reasonable force) of the trespasser. This was used in *Hemmings* v. *Stoke Poges Golf Club* (1920), where the plaintiff and his wife were ejected from a cottage which had been let to them in connection with their employment. Proper notice to quit had been given. The plaintiffs refused to leave. They were removed, as was their furniture, but no unreasonable force was held to have been used. There used to be problems with "squatters" in that trespass actions had to be mounted to remove them. The matter has now been absorbed into the criminal law. The Criminal Law Act 1977 created a variety of crimes connected with entering and remaining in property to which someone else was entitled as possessor.

To the person

This category of trespass can be considered in three parts: assault, battery and false imprisonment. Assault and battery will be considered in Chapter 14 because they overlap to an extent with the criminal law.

Briefly, an assault is committed where the defendant puts the plaintiff in fear of an imminent battery, and a battery is the intentional, direct application of force to the plaintiff's body. So, in *Tuberville* v. *Savage* (1669), when the defendant said "If it were not assize-time, I would not take such language from you", with his hand placed upon his sword, this did not amount to an assault. This was because it was assize-time and the judges were in town and so the plaintiff knew he was not about to be filleted. The opposite was held to be the case in *R*. v. *Cotesworth* (1704) when someone who spat in a doctor's face was found to have committed a battery (which involves some physical contact).

False imprisonment consists of an unlawful restraint directly and intentionally being placed upon the plaintiff's liberty. The restraint need not be by lock and key, but it must be such that liberty is confined. As Patterson J. explained in *Bird* v. *Jones* (1945):

> Now the facts of this case appear to be as follows. A part of Hammersmith Bridge which is ordinarily used as a public footway was appropriated for seats to view a regatta on the river, and separated for that purpose from the carriage way by a temporary fence. The plaintiff insisted on passing along the part so appropriated, and attempted to climb over the fence. The defendant, being clerk of the Bridge Company, seized his coat, and tried to pull him back: the plaintiff, however, succeeded in climbing over the fence. The defendant then stationed two policemen to prevent, and they did prevent, the plaintiff from proceeding forwards along the footway; but he was told that he might go back into the carriage way, and proceed to the other side of the bridge, if he pleased. The plaintiff would not do so, but remained where he was above half an hour; and then, on the defendant still refusing to suffer him to go forwards along the footway, he endeavoured to force his way, and, in so doing, assaulted the defendant: whereupon he was taken into custody . . . I have no doubt that, in general, if one man compels another to stay in any given place against his will, he imprisons that other just as much as if he locked him up in a room: and I agree that it is not necessary, in order to constitute an imprisonment, that a man's person should be touched. I agree, also, that the compelling a man to go in a given direction against his will may amount to imprisonment. But I cannot bring my mind to the conclusion that, if one man merely obstructs the passage of another in a particular direction, whether by threat of personal violence or otherwise, leaving him at liberty to stay where he is or to go in any other direction if he pleases, he can be said thereby to imprison him.

The person imprisoned, it seems, need not know about it at the time. In *Meering* v. *Graham White Aviation* (1919) the plaintiff was unaware of the two men outside the room in which he was being quizzed about thefts from the factory. They would have hindered his departure. This amounted to false imprisonment.

Obviously, if there is a justification for the restraint, then it is not false; for example, lawful arrest, sentence to imprisonment by a court, confinement under the mental health legislation, reasonable chastisement by parents, are all lawful restraints.

The remedy would be damages, perhaps an injunction. Habeas corpus might be available (*see* Chapters 4 and 11). Self-help could be appropriate (breaking out, using only reasonable force).

Trespass and other interference with goods

Under the Torts (Interference with Goods) Act 1977, interference includes trespass to goods, conversion of goods, negligence or any other tort so far as it results in damage to goods or to an interest in goods.

Trespass to goods is an intentional, unjustifiable, direct interference with the plaintiff's possession of goods. It could be damage to goods, moving them somewhere else, or just messing around with them. The defendant can sometimes plead that a third party has a better right than the plaintiff to the goods. An interesting case on trespass to goods is *Kirk* v. *Gregory* (1876) where the "master of the house" died in a state of delirium tremens. There was a party going on, and the deceased's sister in law decided to move some of his valuables (jewellery etc.) from where he was lying to a place of safety, from where some of it was stolen. She was held to have trespassed with regard to those goods, despite her good faith.

Conversion consists in the defendant acting in such a way in connection with goods that it amounts to a complete denial of, or is totally inconsistent with, the plaintiff's ownership of them. (Interference with possession will not do.) This might be taking, destroying, or selling the goods.

As a remedy the plaintiff might claim damages, perhaps an injunction; the court can order the return of the goods, indeed the plaintiff could take them back himself (a course called recaption) provided that only reasonable force is used.

DEFAMATION

This is not an easy tort to define. Professor Winfield offered:

> It is the publication of a statement which tends to lower a person in the estimation of right-thinking members of society generally; or which tends to make them shun or avoid that person.

The tort falls into two categories: libel and slander. Libel is defamatory material published in a permanent form—like writing,

photographs, films, waxworks, statues, records etc. and broadcasting
for general reception (because the Defamation Act 1952 says so).
Libel is actionable *per se* (without proof of damage). If it tends
towards a breach of the peace it could also be a crime (slander cannot
be). Slander is defamatory material published in a temporary (or
transient) form—like speech, gestures etc. It is regarded rather less
seriously. Damage must be proved, except in the following four
instances where slander is also actionable *per se*:

(*a*) where there is an imputation of (imprisonable) crime;

(*b*) where there is an imputation of contagious or infectious
disease;

(*c*) an imputation of unchastity or adultery in a woman (under the
Slander of Women Act 1891, s.1);

(*d*) where there is an imputation designed to disparage the plaintiff
in any office, profession, trade or business held or carried on by him
when the material was published (under the Defamation Act 1952,
s.2).

So, with these exceptions, the plaintiff in a slander action needs to
show loss. It must be monetary or calculated in money terms—like
loss of a job. Otherwise, defamation is actionable without proof of
damage.

The plaintiff has to prove three other things to establish the action,
and we shall examine each in turn.

Defamatory nature of the publication

The plaintiff must show the statement was defamatory. It might be
overtly defamatory, a bald statement which fulfils the requirements
of Winfield's definition above. Or it might be an apparently innocent
statement which carries a defamatory meaning called an innuendo.
Lord Reid explained (in *Lewis* v. *Daily Telegraph* (1964)):

> Sometimes it is not necessary to go beyond the words themselves,
> as where the plaintiff has been called a thief or a murderer. But
> more often the sting is not so much in the words themselves as in
> what the ordinary man will infer from them, and that is also
> regarded as part of their natural and ordinary meaning... In this
> case it is, I think, sufficient to put the test in this way. Ordinary men
> and women have different temperaments and outlooks. Some are
> unusually suspicious, and some are unusually naive. One must try
> to envisage people between these two extremes and see what is the
> most damaging meaning they would put on the words in question.

A famous case on innuendo is *Tolley* v. *Fry* (1931). The plaintiff
was a famous amateur golfer. The defendants made chocolate. They

published advertisements in the Daily Sketch and Daily Mail which included a caricature drawing of the plaintiff with a bar of chocolate sticking out of his pocket. There was also a limerick:

> The caddy to Tolley said, "Oh Sir,
> Good Shot, Sir! That ball, see it go, Sir.
> My Word, how it flies,
> Like a cartet of Fry's,
> They're handy, they're good, and priced low, Sir."

The golfer sued for libel. He said that people would think that he had taken money, and lost his amateur status. The action succeeded.

Reference to the plaintiff

The statement must be understood to refer to the plaintiff. People must be able to spot who is being referred to. In *Hulton* v. *Jones* (1910) a newspaper published a story about Artemus Jones who was having a pretty good time in Dieppe with a French lady, despite being a churchwarden from Peckham. The publishers thought the name fictitious. They were mistaken. A barrister of the same name sued successfully. He showed that people had taken the tale to refer to him.

Under the Defamation Act 1952, s.4, it is possible to make an offer of amends in cases like this, if the publication was done innocently and without carelessness and a suitable apology is published. It is not uncommon to see disclaimers in books and at the cinema—"all characters fictitious" and so on. Of course, they do not protect a careless publisher.

Publication

The statement must have been published. This means that someone other than the plaintiff must be made aware of the statement. Otherwise the effect in Winfield's definition (above) could not be achieved.

Publication to the plaintiff's spouse is publication. Everyone who repeats the publication is a potential defendant, from the newspaper proprietor to the paper boy. Every new publication constitutes a fresh cause of action. (However an agent such as a newspaper seller can claim to have been an innocent disseminator, and thus avoid liability for having published the statement if he can establish that he did not know about the libel, and would not have known if he had been carrying on his business properly.)

In *Huth* v. *Huth* (1915), however, an improper opening of a letter by a butler was held not to constitute publication. "Publishing ill of the dead" is not defamation; nor is it possible to defame a "class" of people (e.g. by saying that all lawyers are crooks) unless the class is so small that each member can claim to be identifiable, when each can sue.

Defences

Apart from the defendant simply denying that the statement was defamatory, or that it referred to the plaintiff, or that it had been published, there are certain special defences available in this tort.

Justification

The defendant produces evidence that the statements are true both in substance and in fact. Slight inaccuracies, especially where lists of allegations are published will not render the defence useless, provided that the bulk of the statement was true. This is provided for in the Defamation Act 1952, s.5, and in cases like *Alexander* v. *North-Eastern Railway Co.* (1865), where a sign was exhibited which read:

> North-Eastern Railway. Caution. J. Alexander... was charged before the magistrates of Darlington, on 28th September for riding in a train from Leeds for which his ticket was not available and refusing to pay the proper fare. He was convicted in the penalty of £9 1s10d, including costs, or three weeks' imprisonment.

The said Mr Alexander had actually only been ordered to spend two weeks in jail. He sued for libel, and lost.

This can be a risky defence to raise, because in effect it is an emphatic repetition of the allegedly defamatory statement. If the defence fails, damages escalate.

Fair comment on a matter of public interest

Opinion is free, and its expression (on matters of public interest) is not actionable—unless it is activated by malice. Lord Denning explained the need for and the nature of the defence in *Slim* v. *Daily Telegraph* (1968):

> The right of fair comment is one of the essential elements which go to make up our freedom of speech. We must ever maintain this right intact. It must not be whittled down by legal refinements. When a citizen is troubled by things going wrong, he should be free to "write to the newspaper": and the newspaper should be free to publish his letter. It is often the only way to get things put right. The matter must, of course, be one of public interest. The writer must get his facts right: and he must honestly state his real opinion. But that being done, both he and the newspaper should be clear of

any liability. They should not be deterred by fear of libel actions.

The requirement of honesty here involves an absence of malice (spite, ill-will). In *Thomas* v. *Bradbury* (1906) the plaintiff published a book called "Fifty years of Fleet Street". There appeared an extremely critical review in the magazine "Punch", which was owned by the defendants. The plaintiff successfully sued. The defence of fair comment failed because, on the evidence, the reviewer was seen to have been motivated by malice.

An important distinction between justification and fair comment as defences here is that when raising justification the truth or accuracy of the statement must be established, whereas when raising fair comment the essential feature is that the opinion was honestly held. It need not be true.

Privilege

This is a defence in that certain statements made at certain times cannot amount to actionable defamation. It is not that the individual involved does not suffer; it is simply that the public interest in the statement being made is seen to outweigh the injury to the individual. Privilege might be absolute or qualified.

Absolute privilege is as wide as it sounds. Anything can be said or written. Nothing can be done about it. This complete freedom of speech is closely confined to several occasions:

(*a*) statements made by members of either House within Parliament (under the Bill of Rights 1688), reports, papers, votes and proceedings ordered to be published by either House (under the Parliamentary Papers Act 1840);

(*b*) all statements made in the course of judicial proceedings, whether by the judge, barrister or solicitor, jury member, witness or a party to the case, provided that the statement relates to the proceedings;

(*c*) communications between senior "officers of state" (probably not below the rank of minister);

(*d*) fair, accurate and contemporaneous reporting in newspapers and on radio and television of judicial proceedings in the United Kingdom (under the Law of Libel Amendment Act 1888).

It was interesting to see that in *Church of Scientology* v. *Johnson-Smith* (1972), Hansard, the verbatim report of proceedings in Parliament, could not even be referred to as providing evidence of ill-will sufficient to defeat the defences of fair comment and qualified privilege. The case arose from statements made outside Parliament, in a television interview.

The other aspect of the defence is qualified privilege. It affords less protection than absolute privilege, but it is better than nothing. There are a number of occasions upon which it can be relied upon. They have in common a quality of reciprocity, as Lord Atkinson explained (in *Adam* v. *Ward* (1917)):

> Where the person who makes a communication has an interest or a duty, legal, social or moral, to make it to the person to whom it is made, and the person to whom it is made has a corresponding interest or duty to receive it. This reciprocity is essential.

So there must be a relationship of this kind between the maker of the statement (a duty to make it) and the person to whom it is made (an interest in receiving it). Where a statement is made in circumstances such as these, then it is protected. It is not actionable as defamation. An example of such a relationship would be that between your present or previous employer or school master or course tutor and a prospective employer, when writing a reference about you.

Fair and accurate reports of Parliamentary proceedings, judicial proceedings and the meetings of other public bodies (like local authorities and the United Nations) are also protected by qualified privilege.

A crucially important point about this kind of qualified privilege is that it can be defeated with evidence of malice in the maker of the statement. In *Egger* v. *Viscount Chelmsford* (1964) the plaintiff was a judge of Alsatian dogs whom, in a letter to a dog club in Northern Ireland, the committee of the Kennel Club refused to approve, despite the fact that she was on their list of judges. The action for libel succeeded against the five members of the committee whose protection in qualified privilege had been destroyed by evidence of their malice. It failed against the three who were not shown to have been motivated in that way (their defence was successful). The other two members of the committee died before the verdict.

Apology

Under the Defamation Act 1952, s.4, the defendant can make an apology for what he published. The statement must be shown to have been put into a newspaper or periodical without malice or gross negligence. Further, the defendant must show he published an apology before the action began, or straight afterwards. The apology must be accompanied by a payment of money into court by way of amends.

Apart from this statutory apology it is wise to apologise quickly and publicly. It can reduce the size of (mitigate) the damages awarded against the defendant.

Chapter 13

The Law of Contract

THE FORMATION OF CONTRACTS

A contract is an agreement which the law will enforce. It is at least an agreement. There are other requirements too. It is sometimes said "all contracts are agreements but not all agreements are contracts". A contract consists of five basic elements. The two most basic ones, offer and acceptance, form the agreement. In addition, both parties must contribute something to the bargain. This contribution (e.g. money, work, goods) has the special name of consideration. Unless a promise is put into a deed it will not be binding upon the person who made it (called the promisor) unless the other party (the promisee) has also contributed to the bargain (provided consideration). Thus "I promise to deliver" is not binding on me, but "I promise to deliver in return for your promise to pay" probably would be.

So offer, acceptance, and consideration are three of the essential ingredients. Further to these the parties must intend to make the sort of bargain which has legal overtones; they must intend to be legally bound. If a young man asks a girl out for the evening, and she agrees but neglects to attend at the appointed place and time, then he would be disappointed certainly, but hardly in the position to sue for breach of contract! It was a social agreement. Such agreements are presumed not to carry the intention to be legally bound which is another essential ingredient for a contract.

The fifth requirement is that both parties must be able to make contracts. The law protects the weak and the infirm, those of less than full contractual capacity—mainly the mentally disordered (permanently or just drunk) and the young.

So the five elements in any "simple" contract are offer, acceptance, consideration, the intention to be legally bound and capacity. We now need to took a little closer.

OFFERS

The party making the offer is called the offeror; the party to whom it is made is called the offeree. An offer is a statement of the terms by which the offeror is prepared to be bound. If an offer is accepted then the agreement exists. If the other three elements are present, a contract exists. Then the person who offered to buy and the person who agreed to sell are bound. If either fails to do as he promised it might amount to a breach of contract.

Some statements, however, are not offers, though they may look like them. They cannot be accepted so as to form contracts.

Most of the law of contract is common law. That is, it has been developed over the years by the judges, case by case, by analogy with earlier cases. (We examined this in Chapter 3.) It follows, then, that whenever a statement of a point of contract law is made it is usually based upon the decision of a judge in a case brought before him. Therefore, when examining contract law it is very important to examine (and remember) cases. They are the basis of the contract law.

For example, on this point of statements which are not offers, but look like them. Clearly, there must be at least one case in which one party was alleging the existence of a contract and the other denying it on the basis that there was no offer made, thus no acceptance, thus no contract. Such a case is *Pharmaceutical Society* v. *Boots* (1953). Here it was alleged that in a supermarket shop layout the sales were made at the shelves. It was defended on the basis that a contract is made at the cashdesk. It was important because the sale of certain medicines must be made under the supervision of a pharmacist. The Pharmacy and Poisons Act 1933 said so. The pharmacist was near the cashdesk not the shelves. This is what the judge, Somervell LJ said:

> Is a contract to be regarded as being completed when the article is put into the receptacle, or is this to be regarded as a more organised way of doing what is done already in many types of shops—and a bookseller is perhaps the best example—namely, enabling customers to have free access to what is in the shop, to look at the different articles, and then ultimately, having got the ones which they wish to buy, to come up to the assistant saying: "I want this"? The assistant in 999 times out of 1,000 says: "That is all right," and the money passes and the transaction is completed. I agree with what the Lord Chief Justice has said, and with the reasons which he has given for his conclusion, that in the case of an ordinary shop, although goods are displayed and it is intended that customers should go and choose what they want, the contract is not completed until, the customer having indicated the articles which he needs, the shopkeeper, or someone on his behalf, accepts that offer. Then the contract is completed. I can see no reason at all, that being clearly the normal position, for drawing any different implication as a result of this layout.

The Lord Chief Justice, I think, expressed one of the most formidable difficulties in the way of the plaintiffs' contention when he pointed out that, if the plaintiffs are right, once an article has been placed in the receptacle the customer himself is bound and would have no right, without paying for the first article, to substitute an article which he saw later of a similar kind and which he perhaps preferred. I can see no reason for implying from this self-service arrangement any implication other than that which the Lord Chief Justice found in it, namely, that it is a convenient method of enabling customers to see what there is and choose, and possibly put back and substitute, articles which they wish to have, and then to go up to the cashier and offer to buy what they have so far chosen. On that conclusion the case fails, because it is admitted that there was supervision in the sense required by the Act and at the appropriate moment of time.

Judgments are often as lucid as this. Wherever possible the cases should be read in law reports or casebooks. They are the raw material of the law.

It follows from this case that price tags in shops are not offers. They are called invitations to treat. It is the same if the goods are not on the shelves inside but in the window on display. This was established in *Fisher* v. *Bell* (1960). Here the outcome of the case depended upon whether goods (flick-knives) on display in a shop window were being offered for sale. If it had been so then the shopkeeper would have been guilty of an offence under the Restriction of Offensive Weapons Act 1959; but it was not so. Lord Parker said:

It is clear that, according to the ordinary law of contract the display of an article with a price on it in a shop window is merely an invitation to treat. It is in no sense an offer for sale, the acceptance of which constitutes a contract.

Similarly, a classified advertisement is an invitation to the readers to make offers. So that if a car is advertised in the classified advertisements columns of the local evening paper at, say, £500 and if there are 50 replies from people who are willing to buy the car, then is there to be one sale followed by 49 breach of contract actions? No, the advertisement was an invitation to treat, so the replies must be offers. Now the advertiser can choose between the offers as to which he will accept. Of course, he is still free not to sell at all, should he so choose. An interesting case on the point is *Partridge* v. *Crittenden* (1968) where a man was acquitted of offering for sale a bramblefinch, contrary to the Protection of Birds Act 1954, on the basis that the display of an advertisement in *Cage and Aviary Birds* constituted an invitation to treat and not an offer.

This advertisement in the paper must be distinguished from a reward poster on a wall. In the paper the reader makes an offer, if he is interested. With a reward case the reader is asked to do something—give information leading to a murderer, find a lost cat—and if he does then the advertiser is bound to pay the reward. Problems with rewards are rare, but it is important to understand that the nature of the transaction is very different. An advertisement is an invitation to treat. A reward poster is an offer—"if you do this, I will pay".

The position was dramatically illustrated by the famous case of *Carlill* v. *Carbolic Smokeball Co.* (1893). Medicine was advertised— the carbolic smokeball. Full page advertisements were placed in such papers as the *Illustrated London News*:

Coughs cured in 1 week
Snoring cured in 1 week
Whooping cough relieved the first application
Hay fever cured in every case

There were 18 such claims. The advertisers went further, they said: "£100 reward", and they named their deposit account. It was a very substantial sum in 1892. The reward was to be paid to anyone who bought and used the smokeball, and caught influenza. There was an epidemic. Mrs. Carlill bought and used a smokeball and caught 'flu, claimed the £100, and was refused. She sued. Bowen LJ said:

We were asked to say that this document was a contract too vague to be enforced. The first observation which arises is that the document itself is not a contract at all, it is only an offer made to the public. The defendants contend next, that it is an offer the terms of which are too vague to be treated as a definite offer, inasmuch as there is no limit of time fixed for the catching of the influenza, and it cannot be supposed that the advertisers seriously meant to promise to pay money to every person who catches the influenza at any time after the inhaling of the smoke ball. It was urged also, that if you look at this document you will find much vagueness as to the persons with whom the contract was intended to be made—that, in the first place, its terms are wide enough to include persons who may have used the smoke ball before the advertisement was issued; at all events, that it is an offer to the world in general, and, also, that it is unreasonable to suppose it to be a definite offer, because nobody in their senses would contract themselves out of the opportunity of checking the experiment which was going to be made at their own expense. It is also contended that the advertisement is rather in the nature of a puff or a proclamation than a promise or offer intended to mature into a contract when accepted.

But the main point seems to be that the vagueness of the document shows that no contract whatever was intended. It seems to me that in order to arrive at a right conclusion we must read this advertisement in its plain meaning, as the public would understand it. It was intended to be issued to the public and to be read by the public. How would an ordinary person reading this document construe it? It was intended unquestionably to have some effect, and I think the effect which it was intended to have, was to make people use the smoke ball, because the suggestions and allegations which it contains are directed immediately to the use of the smoke ball as distinct from the purchase of it. It did not follow that the smoke ball was to be purchased from the defendants directly, or even from agents of theirs directly. The intention was that the circulation of the smoke ball should be promoted, and that the use of it should be increased ...

Was it intended that the £100 should, if the conditions were fulfilled, be paid? The advertisement says that £1,000 is lodged at the bank for the purpose ... it was intended to be understood by the public as an offer which was to be acted upon. But it was said there was no check on the part of the persons who issued the advertisement. The answer to that argument seems to me to be that if a person chooses to make extravagant promises of this kind he probably does so because it pays him to make them, and, if he has made them, the extravagance of the promises is no reason in law why he should not be bound by them.

It was also said that the contract is made with all the world—that is, with everybody; and that you cannot contract with everybody. It is not a contract made with all the world. There is the fallacy of the argument. It is an offer made to all the world; and why should not an offer be made to all the world which is to ripen into a contract with anybody who comes forward and performs the condition?

When an offer is accepted an agreement (and perhaps a contract) is made. If it remains unaccepted it will not last for ever. There are various ways in which an offer might be brought to an end.

Rejection

This is self-explanatory.

Revocation

This is the withdrawal of the offer by the offeror. Provided that revocation is effectively communicated to the offeree—by the offeror or a reliable third party—and provided this is done before acceptance—then the offer is revoked. It no longer exists to be accepted.

Counter-offers

If an offer is answered with another offer then the first offer is destroyed. In *Hyde* v. *Wrench* (1840) a farm was offered at £1,000; the offeree suggested £950 (a counter-offer); the offeror refused (whereupon the counter-offer died); the offeree then suggested £1,000—as an acceptance of the first offer. The court held that this had been destroyed by the counter-offer. Careful businessmen always check that both sides are agreed at the end of negotiations.

Lapse of time

Obviously, if an offer is open for a fixed time it lapses afterwards. If it is not, then it lapses after a reasonable time, and this depends on the circumstances. In *Ramsgate Victoria Hotel Co.* v. *Montefiore* (1866) an offer to buy shares on 8th June 1864 was held to have lapsed by 23rd November when the offeree tried to accept.

Delays

There have been cases which involve delays between offer and acceptance during which the goods involved have been damaged. Such a case was *Financings* v. *Stimson* (1962) where, while the offeror was awaiting a finance company's response to his offer to buy a car on hire purchase terms, the vehicle was wrecked by thieves. The offer lapsed then. It was held that the offer was made to buy the car in its condition when inspected.

Death

The general rule is that the death of either offeror or offeree terminates negotiations. If the subject matter does not involve the dead party's personal activity—if his executors could carry out the deal—and if the offeree had not heard of the death when he accepted, then a contract might be made.

ACCEPTANCE

An acceptance is the unconditional assent of the offeree to all the terms of the offer. Obviously a conditional acceptance is not good enough. Counter offers can be regarded as conditional acceptances, as in *Hyde* v. *Wrench* above.

Sometimes the phrase "acceptance subject to contract" is used, typically when houses are being bought and sold. The parties agree "subject to contract". Both then go away and contact surveyors, building societies, etc. Meanwhile, the contract is being prepared. The court will not hold the parties bound by such an agreement, as Jessel MR said (in *Winn* v. *Bull* (1877)):

> It comes, therefore, to this, that where you have a proposal or agreement made in writing expressed to be subject to a formal contract being prepared, it means what it says; it is subject to and is dependent upon a formal contract being prepared.

Meanwhile the estate agent's board outside the house might say "under offer" or "sold—subject to contract". A contract is envisaged, but not yet made. The buyer needs time to get a survey done, raise a mortgage, etc. The seller may get a better offer. If he accepts it he is not in breach of contract. There is no contract with the first "buyer", only an agreement. "All agreements are not contracts." Making this second agreement is called gazumping. Anyway, the seller is likely to be the buyer in another deal somewhere else. House sales are usually done in "chains".

When an offeree decides to accept the offer he must communicate his decision. The offeror must know he is now a party to an agreement. This can be seen in the case of *Felthouse* v. *Bindley* (1862) where a horse was to be sold by auction. The seller's uncle had offered to buy it. He said, "if I hear no more about him, I consider the horse mine at £30 15s." As Willes J explained:

> The nephew might, no doubt, have bound his uncle to the bargain by writing to him: the uncle might also have retracted his offer at any time before acceptance. It stood an open offer; and so things remained until 25th February, when the nephew was about to sell his farming stock by auction. The horse in question being catalogued with the rest of the stock, the auctioneer (the defendant) was told that it was already sold. It is clear, therefore, that the nephew in his own mind intended his uncle to have the horse at the price which he (the uncle) had named, £30 15s.: but he had not communicated such his intention to his uncle, or done anything to bind himself. Nothing, therefore, had been done to vest the property in the horse in the plaintiff down to 25th February, when the horse was sold by the defendant. It appears to me that, independently of the subsequent letters, there had been no bargain to pass the property in the horse to the plaintiff, and therefore that he had no right to complain of the sale.

The action was brought by the disappointed uncle against the auctioneer—alleging that he had bought the horse from his nephew and so the auctioneer had no right to sell it. He lost. There had been no contract formed between uncle and nephew. No acceptance had been communicated. The rule is sometimes phrased: "silence does not constitute acceptance". A similar argument applies to situations where books, records, etc., are sent unrequested to householders with notes saying "if you do not tell us you do not want this we will send you the bill". Now we have the Unsolicited Goods and Services Act 1971 which provides that where goods do arrive unsolicited they become the property of the recipient after six months. He need not pay anything. If he takes the step of informing the sender, then unless they are collected within 30 days, the goods become his. Meanwhile they should be kept reasonably safe (e.g. not left out in the rain).

There are two exceptions to the rule that acceptance must be communicated. The first one we have already met. It concerns rewards. The offeror of a reward does not expect to be told—indeed he does not need to be in order to be bound to pay up. In *Carlill* v. *Carbolic Smokeball Co.*, which we considered earlier in this chapter, another unsuccessful excuse put forward was that the company had not been told that the plaintiff had bought and was using the smokeball. That is, that acceptance had not been communicated. But this was a reward case, and, as Bowen LJ said:

> If I advertise to the world that my dog is lost, and that anybody who brings the dog to a particular place will be paid some money, are all the police or other persons whose business it is to find lost dogs to be expected to sit down and write me a note saying that they have accepted my proposal? Why, of course, they at once look for the dog, and as soon as they find the dog they have performed the condition. The essence of the transaction is that the dog should be found, and it is not necessary under such circumstances, as it seems to me, that in order to make the contract binding there should be any notification of acceptance.

The other exception is about the post. Where the post is the appropriate means of communication between the parties then, unless the parties have agreed otherwise, the following rules apply.

(*a*) The letter containing the offer is effective when the offeree receives it. Obviously, you cannot accept an offer you have not heard about. (Consider returning a lost cat out of the goodness of your heart and then finding a postcard on a tree offering a reward for its recovery. Can you claim it?)

(*b*) A letter of revocation is effective when it is received—because the revocation (withdrawal) of an offer must be communicated to the offeror before acceptance.

(*c*) A letter of acceptance is valid as soon as it is posted, or put into the hands of a post office employee who can take letters for posting.

This third rule might seem a bit strange. It applies even if the letter of acceptance goes astray in the post, so the offeror is not told he is bound in a contract. However, the rule comes from judgments in difficult cases like *Byrne* v. *Van Tienhoven* (1880). Here the defendants, in Cardiff, posted an offer to the plaintiffs in New York on 1st October. On 8th October, however, they had changed their minds, and they posted a letter of revocation. Meanwhile, the plaintiffs had received the offer and had accepted by telegram on 11th October, and sent a letter confirming acceptance on 20th October. The letter of revocation did not arrive until 25th October. The court was faced with two innocent parties. One regarded the offer as revoked, the other was convinced that he had accepted it. The court held that the letter of acceptance was valid when posted, and so the revocation arrived too late. The contract had been formed, probably on 11th, but if not by the telegram certainly by the letter of 20th. Both were sent before the revocation arrived. As has been noted, the parties can avoid this rule if they wish. In *Holwell Securities* v. *Hughes* (1974) the offeror said that he required "notice in writing" of the acceptance. Thus the letter of acceptance had to reach him before the contract could be formed.

CONSIDERATION

As was explained earlier in this chapter, consideration is the technical name given to the contribution each party makes to the bargain—"I promise to pay if you promise to deliver"—"You can be the proud owner of this car for £1,500", and so on. Lord Dunedin defined consideration (in *Dunlop Pneumatic Tyre Co.* v. *Selfridge* (1915)) like this:

An act or forbearance of one party or the promise thereof is the price for which the promise of the other is bought and the promise thus given for value is enforceable.

In practical terms, consideration is the point of making the bargain. It is what you wanted to get out of it. If you do not receive it (if the consideration fails) then it usually amounts to a breach of contract. Professor Atiyah wrote:

Consideration means a reason for the enforcement of a promise. Nobody can seriously propose that all promises should become enforceable; to abolish the doctrine of consideration, therefore, is simply to require the courts to begin all over again the task of deciding what promises are to be enforceable.

There have been many cases over the years which have developed the idea of consideration to such an extent that there seem to be several rules which must be obeyed before consideration can properly be said to exist. This is crucial, of course, because it is one of the five essentials of a contract. Without any one of them no contract exists. Again, in practical terms, this means that whilst I may promise to do something for you unless that promise is part of a contract, unless I receive something in return, then I can break my promise. There is nothing you can do. With very few exceptions (e.g. promises in deeds), a promise for nothing (a gratuitous promise) is not binding. Let us return to these developed rules:

The first is that "consideration must be valuable but it need not be adequate". This means that provided something of value is given, in the absence of fraud or improper pressure, then it will be enough. In *Thomas* v. *Thomas* (1842) £1 each year towards the ground rent of a house was held to be enough to bind a promise to allow a woman to live in her late husband's house. It was not a market price, but it had value. His natural love and affection for her was not enough. It has no commercial value. But £1 would do.

Similarly, in *Chappell & Co.* v. *Nestlé's* (1960), the issue arose whether three chocolate bar wrappers, which were later thrown away by a record company, could be of value as consideration, and thus part of a deal where the wrappers and 1s. 6d. formed the price paid for a copy of a record called "Rockin' Shoes". Lord Somervell said:

> The question, then, is whether these wrappers were part of the consideration ... I think they are part of the consideration. They are so described in the offer. "They", the wrappers, "will help you to get smash hit recordings". They are so described in the record itself—"all you have to do to get such new record is to send three wrappers from Nestlé's 6d milk chocolate bars, together with postal order for 1s 6d". This is not conclusive but, however described, they are, in my view, in law part of the consideration. It is said that when received the wrappers are of no value to Nestlé's. This I would have thought irrelevant. A contracting party can stipulate for what consideration he chooses. A peppercorn does not cease to be good consideration if it is established that the promisee does not like pepper and will throw away the corn. As the whole object of selling the record, if it was a sale, was to increase the sales of chocolate, it seems to me wrong not to treat the stipulated evidence of such sales as part of the consideration.

Consideration, however, cannot exist in doing what you are already bound to do in a contract with the same other party (called existing contractual duty), although if you do more you could expect extra payment. In *Stilk* v. *Myrick* (1809) a sailor could not recover extra pay he was promised (the promise was not binding) for working on a voyage to cover for two deserters out of a crew of eleven. On the other hand, in *Hartley* v. *Ponsonby* (1857), on similar facts, the sailor did get his extra pay because the desertion was 19 of 36, leaving only four or five able seamen. He had done more than his existing contractual duty. He had "bought" the promise of extra pay.

Another aspect of this first rule concerns the part payment of debts. It is of no extra value to be paid less than you are owed. So it was that in *D & C Builders* v. *Rees* (1965) the builders' promise to accept £300 in full settlement of a debt of £482 was not binding on them, and they could successfully sue for the balance. It would not be the same, of course, if part payment were to be made early or in a different form (e.g. £300's worth of bricks) or with a chattel (£300 and a bucket) or by a third party (A owes B but B accepts less from C)—all with the agreement of the creditor—because none of these is "straight" part payment. They all contain a little extra and, as we know, three second-hand chocolate bar wrappers will do. If a little extra is paid the promise is binding but straight part payment will not discharge a debt. It has no value. Consideration must be valuable.

The second of these so-called rules is that "consideration must not be past". The rule sounds strange, but it is not difficult. Suppose I sell you a horse. After we have agreed the price and I have the cash and you have the horse you ask me about its temperament. I say that the horse is sound and free from vice. This turns out to be less than accurate. You want to enforce my promise against me. You cannot. At the time I made my promise about the horse the deal was over. You can only sue me for a broken binding promise (part of a contract). This promise was not binding. At the time I made it the only possible consideration from you (the money for the horse) was already in the past—used up. The rule is sometimes stated as "past consideration is no consideration", and the facts of this story happened in *Roscorla* v. *Thomas* (1842).

Similarly, in *Re McArdle* (1951) a man left his house to his widow in his will, for her life, and then to his children. There were improvements made to the house, for which the children subsequently promised to pay a contribution. This they neglected to do. Nothing could be done. When the promise was made the improvements had already been done. It was a gratuitous promise.

On the other hand, suppose I ask you to work for my company. You do so for a while. Later I promise to pay you. Since (*a*) I asked you to do it, and (*b*) it is the kind of thing that would normally be paid for, then despite the fact that I promised after you worked I have to pay. In a sense my request carried an implied promise of payment. These were the circumstances of *Stewart* v. *Casey* (1892) (which is sometimes called *Re Casey's Patents* (1892)). It followed a very old case called *Lampleigh* v. *Braithwait* (1615) in which a man asked another to travel to the king and beg a reprieve from hanging for him. It was successful. The man promised to pay £100. He failed to do so, but he was held bound by his promise to pay for the act since it had been performed at his request.

The final rule has an even stranger name: "consideration must move from the promisee". It is part of a doctrine of contract law called privity. Only the parties to a contract have rights under it, and only they have obligations. There are very few exceptions to this. In *Tweddle* v. *Atkinson* (1861), for example, a couple were engaged. Their parents promised each other that they would each pay some money to the couple when they married. One set of parents paid, the other did not; the father died before he had had a chance to. The couple sued his estate. The action failed, because the only appropriate plaintiffs were the other set of parents. The couple had provided no consideration. They were not parties to the contract. They could not, therefore, sue on it.

In Chapter 2 we discussed the nature of equity. We observed that it is composed of a number of principles developed over the years in the interests of justice and fairness between the parties when a strict observance of the common law rules would lead to unfairness and injustice. In *Central London Property Trust Ltd.* v. *High Trees House Ltd.* (1947), commonly called *High Trees*, such a principle emerged when the argument concerned consideration. A landlord had gratuitously promised to halve the rent he could legally have demanded from a company renting the whole of a block of flats from him. It was wartime and it was proving difficult for the company to let the flats and pay the full rent. After the emergency the landlord wanted to restore the position and claim the full rent. He also questioned his ability to claim the back rent. Strictly, he had a right to the money, but the court said that they would not have allowed it if formally asked. This on the basis of the unfairness to the company who had relied on the promise, which had been made knowing it would be relied upon (they cut the rents to fill the block). This rare and very limited principle of equity is called estoppel. Where it is recognised, it can make a gratuitous promise binding provided it was acted upon by the promisee.

THE INTENTION TO BE LEGALLY BOUND

This is the fourth essential ingredient in any simple contract. In order to assist the courts to decide whether or not it exists two presumptions are made.

(*a*) That in social and domestic agreements there is no intention to be legally bound. This was seen in *Balfour* v. *Balfour* (1919). The defendant was a civil servant stationed in Sri Lanka. He and his wife came to England on leave. When it was time to return, he left his wife in England for the good of her health. They agreed that he would pay her £30 per month while they were apart. Later the wife divorced him and he stopped paying. She sued him, unsuccessfully. As Atkin LJ said:

> It is necessary to remember that there are agreements which do not amount to contracts ... it is quite common and it is the natural and inevitable result of the relationship of husband and wife that the two spouses should make arrangements between themselves ... They are not contracts because the parties did not intend that they should be attended by legal consequences.

But it is only a presumption. It is not a rule. When the court sees fit it will hold social agreements to have been contracts. For example, in *Simpkins* v. *Pays* (1955), where an old lady, her grand-daughter and the lodger jointly entered a competition. The entry went in under the old lady's name. The grand-daughter won £750. The lodger had to sue for his share. This social agreement was held, despite the usual presumption, to have been a contract. He was paid.

(*b*) The other presumption is that in commercial agreements there is an intention to be legally bound. So, in *Edwards* v. *Skyways* (1964), where a promise to make a sort of redundancy payment to some surplus pilots was referred to as *ex gratia* (out of goodwill), it was nevertheless held to have been binding. It was a commercial agreement.

Again, the presumption has been rebutted. In *Rose & Frank* v. *Crompton* (1923) an agreement for the sale of paper tissues contained an "honourable pledge" clause stating: "This arrangement is not entered into, nor is this memorandum written, as a formal or legal agreement, and shall not be subject to legal jurisdiction in the law courts." The parties were not bound. This was because they had expressly agreed not to be. This kind of clause is found in football pools agreements. In *Jones* v. *Vernons Pools Ltd.* (1938), the action for an unpaid win was lost, because the agreement was not a contract. If you "do the pools" check the rules for such an honour clause as this.

CAPACITY

As was discussed earlier in the chapter, the law protects those of less than full contractual capacity. The mentally disordered (whether temporarily through drink or drugs or mentally ill) can avoid contracts made whilst unaware of events, if it can be shown that the other party knew of the incapacity. Minors are also closely protected. They are people under the age of 18. Contracts involving minors are usually considered under the following three headings.

Valid, binding contracts

These are made either for necessaries (like food, clothing and shelter) or they are beneficial contracts of service. If it is alleged that a minor is bound in a contract for necessaries, two things must be proved. First that the goods or services could (as a matter of law) have been necessaries; secondly, that they were (as a matter of fact) actually necessary. So in the famous case of *Nash* v. *Inman* (1908) a minor was not bound in a contract for clothing, not because the goods could not have been necessaries (clothing) nor because they were unsuitable for him (he was an undergraduate at Cambridge), but because he already possessed a large number of such clothes. The lesson to the tailor was not to sell children goods they do not need. Even if they had been necessaries the price payable would have been a reasonable price only, whatever the agreed price might have been.

The other type of (potentially) binding contract is a "beneficial contract of service". That is, a good apprenticeship or something similar, as in *Doyle* v. *White City Stadium* (1935) where a licence to box was held to be binding according to the rules of the British Boxing Board of Control. This was so even though it meant the minor (a boxer) would lose his fight fee. He had been disqualified in the second round. The apprenticeship agreement, or whatever other arrangement is in question, is scrutinised by the court; if, taken as a whole, it is regarded as being reasonable, and for the minor's benefit, then it is binding. Otherwise, it is not. Here, the boy wanted to fight for a living. This fight was for the Heavyweight Championship of Great Britain. Taken as a whole the contract was for his benefit. He had to learn to fight fairly.

Valid but voidable contracts

Where the contract is of one of four kinds, the minor can avoid it. Up until the time it is avoided the contract is valid, so that any liability under it arising before then must be met. The four types are said to concern property of a permanent kind which involves continuing obligations. They include contracts concerning land (particularly buying or renting it, e.g. renting a flat), contracts subscribing for or buying company shares, partnership contracts and marriage settlements.

Absolutely Void

Such cases will normally be contracts within the Infant's Relief Act 1874;

All contracts, whether by specialty or by simple contract, henceforth entered into by infants for the repayment of money lent or to be lent, or for goods supplied or to be supplied (other than necessaries), and all accounts stated with infants, shall be absolutely void.

"By specialty" means formal contracts, made (usually) by deed; "by simple contract" means all other contracts, no matter how complicated. The term "accounts stated" generally means all admissions of indebtedness.

We met the Law Commission in Chapter 3. We noted its importance in law reform. There has been a Working Paper published recently—No. 18—on Minors' Contracts. One suggestion made in it is that the age of protection, as it were, ought to be lowered from 18 to 16 years.

THE CONTENTS OF CONTRACTS

While negotiating the contract the parties will make many statements. Not all of them will be part of the contract. Those which induce the deal but do not form part of it are called representations. If they prove to have been lies (or just inaccurate) then the innocent party might consider action for misrepresentation. This will be considered later in this chapter. It is easy to tell which statements have become terms of the contract when it takes a written form; but there are millions of oral contracts made every day. It is more difficult to establish whether or not a particular statement formed part of an oral contract. Every statement which did form part of the contract, written or oral, is a contractual term.

These terms are not all of equal importance. The major ones are called conditions, the minor ones warranties. The innocent party to a breach is entitled to damages for a breach of either sort of them. For a breach of condition he is also entitled to cancel the contract and regard himself as free of it. We will consider this distinction again later in this chapter, when dealing with consumer law.

Express and implied terms

The terms within a contract will comprise many, but not necessarily all, of the statements made by the parties during negotiations: "I want some boots fit for fell walking", "this one has done 50,000 miles" and so on. Collectively all these terms can be referred to as express terms.

There may well be more in the contract than the express terms. Terms are implied into contracts by statutes, and also by the courts. A common example of a statute which does this is the Sale of Goods Act 1979. Sections 12–15 of that Act imply terms about the title of the seller of goods, the quality of those goods, correspondence with description and so on. These will be examined more closely later in this chapter when we look at consumer law. There are other statutes which imply terms into contracts. They include the Trading Stamps Act 1964, the Defective Premises Act 1972, the Carriage of Goods by Sea Act 1971 and the Marine Insurance Act 1906.

The courts are not keen to imply terms into contracts. They will only do so where:

(a) the parties are in the same trade and the term required is commonly accepted in the trade as usual, or

(b) the contract would not make business sense without it.

In these cases their policy is based on the idea that the term is already part of the deal, although it has not been included expressly. This is how three judges have explained it:

In *Reigate* v. *Union Manufacturing Co.* (1918), Scrutton LJ said:

> A term can only be implied if it is necessary in the business sense to give efficacy to the contract, i.e. if it is such a term that it can confidently be said that if at the time the contract was being negotiated someone had said to the parties "What will happen in such a case?" they would both have replied: "Oh, of course, so and so will happen; we did not trouble to say that; it is too clear".

In *Shirlaw* v. *Southern Foundries (1926) Ltd.* (1939), MacKinnon LJ said:

> Prima facie that which in any contract is left to be implied and need not be expressed is something so obvious that it goes without saying; so that, if while the parties were making their bargain an officious bystander were to suggest some express provision for it in their agreement, they would testily suppress him with a common, "Oh, of course".

In *Trollope & Colls Ltd.* v. *North West Metropolitan Regional Hospital Board* (1973), Lord Pearson said:

> An unexpressed term can be implied if and only if the court finds that the parties must have intended that term to form part of their contract. It is not enough for the court to find that such a term would have been adopted by the parties as reasonable men if it had

been suggested to them: it must have been a term that went without saying, a term which although tacit, formed part of the contract which the parties made for themselves.

The case called *The Moorcock* (1889) is a good illustration. In this case the problem concerned a river bed. A mooring had been hired for a steamship called *The Moorcock* in the tidal part of the Thames. When the tide ebbed she grounded and was damaged. The owners of the jetty claimed no responsibility for the river bed or its condition. It was under the control of the Thames Conservators. The contract had made no mention of the river bed, but both parties realised that the tide would go out. So the question which arose was whether the court ought to imply a term into the contract about the condition of the river bed. Bowen LJ said:

> I think if they let out their jetty for use they imply that they have taken reasonable care to see whether the berth, which is the essential part of the use of the jetty, is safe, and if it is not safe, and if they have not taken such reasonable care, it is their duty to warn persons with whom they have dealings that they have not done so.

The court implied the term. The owners could then be liable for breach of it.

Exclusion clauses

An exclusion (or exemption) clause is a term which, if found to be part of a contract and effectual, will enable one party to avoid liability he would otherwise carry. A limitation clause is similar, but, obviously, seeks to limit rather than exclude responsibility—"the company is responsible for the first £100 only of any loss" and "all cars parked at owners' risk" are commonly found examples.

The courts frown on such clauses. They militate against the very nature of contracts—the assumption of rights and obligations. However, where the parties agree to their inclusion, the court must recognise their freedom of contract. Recent statutes have undermined this freedom to some extent. Some exclusion clauses, while they may be part of a contract, have been deprived of their effectiveness.

In order for an exclusion clause to be relied upon three points must be established:

(*a*) that the clause was incorporated into the contract, and
(*b*) that it covered the damage complained of, and
(*c*) that it is not affected by statutory interventions or by common law rules of invalidity.

Incorporation can be achieved by signature or notice.
Scrutton LJ said (in *L'Estrange* v. *Graucob* (1934)):

When a document containing contractual terms is signed, then, in
the absence of fraud or, I will add, misrepresentation, the party
signing it is bound, and it is wholly immaterial whether he has read
the document or not.

The courts are very strict about signatures. You are bound by what
you sign, whether or not you have read the document, and if you have
read it, whether or not you understand it. So an exclusion clause can
enter a contract by means of a signature on a contractual document.
(*See also* the cases on duress and undue influence discussed later.)

Otherwise, a notice must be used—a sign or a poster. This notice
must be effectively brought to the attention of the other party to the
contract, and this must be done before the contract is made, while the
other party can still refuse to make a deal on the basis that the other
party restricts his obligations under it.

As to effectiveness of communication, Lord Denning said (in
Thornton v. *Shoe Lane Parking* (1971)):

I do not pause to inquire whether the exempting condition is void
for unreasonableness. All I say is that it is so wide and so
destructive of rights that the court should not hold any man bound
by it unless it is drawn to his attention in the most explicit way. In
order to give sufficient notice, it would need to be printed in red ink
with a red hand pointing to it—or something equally startling.

Even the most startling communication is useless if it comes too
late. It must be before formation (pre-contractual, not post-
contractual). In *Olley* v. *Marlborough Court Hotel* (1949), for
example, a couple booked into an hotel for a week. They paid in
advance, at the desk. When they went to their room they saw a sign
which said "the proprietors will not hold themselves responsible for
articles lost or stolen unless handed to the manageress for safe
custody". The lady's furs were stolen. This clause was not part of the
contract. The hotel could not rely on it. It had been communicated
effectively enough, but post-contractually. The contract had been
made at the desk.

Once the clause has been established as a term of the contract it
must be shown to cover the damage complained of. In *Andrews* v.
Singer (1934) a clause which read "all conditions, warranties and
liabilities, implied by statute, common law or otherwise" was useless
to protect a breach of an express term. The contract was for "new

Singer cars". One of the cars supplied was not new.

Finally, the clause must not be invalidated by statute or the various common law rules of invalidity. There are several statutes which disallow exclusion of liability. As examples: under the Road Traffic Act 1972, s.148, a driver cannot exclude his liability towards his passengers and s.143 of this Act makes passenger insurance compulsory. The Road Traffic Act 1960, the Carriage of Passengers by Road Act 1974, the Transport Act 1962 and the Carriage by Railway Act 1972 all taken together provide that neither the buses nor the railway can exclude or limit liability for the death or personal injury of their passengers. They can limit liability for luggage, but only so far as would be held reasonable under the most recent and important statute of this kind. The Unfair Contract Terms Act 1977 includes the following provisions;

2(1) A person cannot by reference to any contract term or to a notice given to persons generally or to particular persons exclude or restrict his liability for death or personal injury resulting from negligence.

(2) In the case of other loss or damage, a person cannot so exclude or restrict his liability for negligence except in so far as the term or notice satisfies the requirement of reasonableness.

3(1) This section applies as between contracting parties where one of them deals as consumer or on the other's written standard terms of business.

(2) As against that party, the other cannot by reference to any contract term—

(a) when himself in breach of contract, exclude or restrict any liability of his in respect of the breach; or

(b) claim to be entitled—

(i) to render a contractual performance substantially different from that which was reasonably expected of him or

(ii) in respect of the whole or any part of his contractual obligation, to render no performance at all, except in so far as (in any of the cases mentioned above in this subsection) the contract term satisfies the requirement of reasonableness.

Furthermore, the 1977 Act provides, in s.6, that the terms implied into contracts for the sale of goods by the Sale of Goods Act 1979 cannot be excluded at all in a consumer sale, and only so far as would be reasonable in any other sale, for example, between a wholesaler and retailer. This reflects the protective attitude often taken towards the weaker party in situations of inequality of bargaining power. The Act says:

6(1) Liability for breach of the obligations arising from—
(*a*) section 12 of the Sale of Goods Act 1979 (seller's implied undertakings as to title etc.);
(*b*) section 8 of the Supply of Goods (Implied Terms) Act 1973 (the corresponding thing in relation to hire-purchase), cannot be excluded or restricted by reference to any contract term.
(2) Against a person dealing as consumer liability for breach of the obligations arising from—
(*a*) section 13, 14 or 15 of the 1979 Act (seller's implied undertakings as to conformity of goods with description or sample or as to their quality or fitness for a particular purpose);
(*b*) section 9, 10 or 11 of the 1973 Act (the corresponding things in relation to hire-purchase), cannot be excluded or restricted by reference to any contract term.
(3) As against a person dealing otherwise than as consumer, the liability specified in subsection (2) above can be excluded or restricted by reference to a contract term, but only in so far as the term satisfies the requirement of reasonableness.

As to limitations on effectiveness aside from statutes, exclusion clauses are not generally allowed to protect third parties. That is, if the contract is made between A and B, and it contains a clause purporting to protect C then that protection is ineffectual. Furthermore if the nature or extent of the clause is misrepresented by the party who later seeks to rely on it then its effect will be limited to his statement, despite the actual wording. So if he says it excludes X but in fact it seeks to exclude liability for X, Y and Z, the clause is likely to be held to protect only against X.

VITIATING ELEMENTS: THINGS THAT CAN GO WRONG AND SPOIL CONTRACTS

Having considered the formation of contracts, and their contents once formed, we now need to look at a collection of ways in which the contract could be spoilt (vitiated). These will include the lack of formality, where a contract needs to be made in a particular form, mistakes of various kinds, misrepresentation, duress, undue influence, illegality and vagueness.

Lack of form

Most contracts are just as valid and enforceable (given the evidence) whether they are made orally or in writing. However, formality is sometimes required:
(*a*) conveyances of land, leases for longer than three years, the

transfer of British ships, or shares in them all need deeds (formal, sealed documents);

(b) bills of exchange, promissory notes, marine insurance contracts, bills of sale, most consumer credit agreements are all examples of transactions which need to be made in writing;

(c) guarantees (where someone says he will answer for another's liability if he fails to do so) and contracts for the "sale or other disposition of land" need written evidence of their existence before they can be enforced by court proceedings.

This requirement of writing for contracts dealing in land comes from the Law of Property Act 1925:

> 40(1) No action may be brought upon any contract for the sale or other disposition of land or any interest in land, unless the agreement upon which such action is brought, or some memorandum or note thereof, is in writing, and signed by the party to be charged or by some other person thereunto by him lawfully authorised.

This means that either the contract must be made in writing or at least some written evidence of it must exist before anyone can be sued on it. This is what the person to be charged means. The written evidence must acknowledge the existence of a contract (an agreement to make one will not do), it must contain all the material terms (the names of the parties, the subject matter, etc.), and it must be signed or, at least, the defendant ("the person to be charged") must have written or had his signature printed on it. More than one document can be used, for instance, where a signed document refers to an unsigned one or, as in *Pearce* v. *Gardner* (1897) where a letter and its envelope were taken together.

Of course, many contracts that do not specifically require formality are made in a formal way. The importance of written evidence when starting an action for breach of contract, for example, cannot be over-emphasised; but some contracts have special requirements without which they are not valid at all or (in the case of those needing written evidence) unenforceable.

Mistake

Signed documents

We have already noted in this chapter the seriousness of the courts' attitude towards signatures on documents. It is settled that a mistake about the contents of a signed document will be no excuse. The signer is bound. In *Saunders* v. *Anglia Building Society* (1970), for example, a 78-year old lady who had lost her reading glasses was held bound by her signature on a document which had been prepared by a crook and had the effect of transferring her house to him. Since this case, to escape the binding nature of your signature you would need to prove that the document signed was radically different from the one thought to have been signed; secondly, that the signing had not been done negligently (carelessly); thirdly, that had the true contents of the document been known, it would not have been signed. The old lady in the case could have established this last one, but not the others. The document was not radically different and she had been careless in that she had signed without asking independent advice about the contents which she could not read.

It seems that to escape liability you have to be blind, illiterate and without a friend—as Byles J explained (in *Foster* v. *MacKinnon* (1869)):

> It seems plain on principle and on authority that if a blind man, or a man who cannot read or who for some reason (not implying negligence) forbears to read, has a written contract falsely read over to him, the reader misreading to such a degree that the written contract is of a nature altogether different from the contract pretended to be read from the paper which the blind or illiterate man afterwards signs; then, at least if there be no negligence, the signature so obtained is of no force. And it is invalid not merely on the grounds of fraud, where fraud exists, but on the ground that the mind of the signer did not accompany the signature; in other words, that he never intended to sign, and therefore in contemplation of law never did sign, the contract to which his name is appended.

Mistakes about the identity of the other party

If someone makes a contract with you and he is lying about who he is, should it matter? Particularly, if he sells the goods he has obtained from you to an innocent third party, should you be able to recover the goods from that third party who bought them in good faith? The answer seems to be no. Unless you can prove that the identity of the other party to the contract was so important to you that you would not have sold to anyone else, then your mistake does not matter, even though it might have been induced by fraud. Naturally, if you can trace the other person before he has time to sell the goods on, then you can recover them because of the fraud (misrepresentation which we will examine soon), but not because of the mistake alone. You would probably have sold to anyone who appeared to be able to pay you. It was really a mistake about creditworthiness not identity that has left you with a useless cheque, no goods and little hope of catching the crook.

The courts have had to deal with such cases. A recent example is *Lewis* v. *Averay* (1972) where the crook pretended to be Richard Greene, the actor (who used to play Robin Hood on television). A car was sold for a cheque with a film studio pass as evidence of identity. It was sold on to a student before the cheque bounced. The original owner sued the student to get the car back. He lost. He had to establish that the contract between himself and the crook was spoilt (made void) by his mistake, thereby preventing the ownership passing to the student on the second sale. He had not parted with ownership. The crook could not sell it to the student. He failed. Lord Denning said:

> When a dealing is had between a seller like Mr Lewis and a person who is actually there present before him, then the presumption in law is that there is a contract, even though there is a fraudulent impersonation by the buyer representing himself as a different man than he is. There is a contract made with the very person there, who is present in person. It is liable no doubt to be avoided for fraud, but it is still a good contract under which title will pass unless and until it is avoided.

There have been cases where the identity of the other party to the contract has been recognised as having been essential to the contract. They are rare, and often criticised, because innocent third parties lose out. Such a case was *Cundy* v. *Lindsay* (1878) where linen was sold to a rogue, through the post. He called himself "Blenkiron & Co." The sellers were able to satisfy the court that they would only have dealt with that company, and not with the rogue, whose name was Alfred Blenkarn. Lord Cairns said:

> How is it possible to imagine that in that state of things any contract could have arisen between the respondents and Blenkarn, the dishonest man? Of him they knew nothing, and of him they never thought. With him they never intended to deal. Their minds never, even for an instant of time rested upon him, and as between him and them there was no consensus of mind which could lead to any agreement or any contract whatever.

It is worth observing that this was not a contract made after "face to face" negotiations, as was the case in *Lewis* v. *Averay* (1972).

Mistakes about the subject matter
If you are misled you may be able to complain, but if you are just

mistaken about the quality of what you buy, then the basic rule is *caveat emptor* (let the buyer beware). However, mistakes about the identity of the subject matter are sometimes recognised. In *Raffles* v. *Wichelhaus* (1864), for example, there was an agreement made concerning a cargo aboard a ship called the Peerless. The fact that there were two ships of that name in the harbour at the time, and the parties were at cross purposes about which ship was meant, led the court to the conclusion that no contract had actually been made at all. The parties were never truly agreed.

If the parties were mistaken about the existence of the subject matter, then this would be an operative mistake, enabling the court to conclude that no contract had been made. So in *Strickland* v. *Turner* (1852), where an annuity was taken out upon the life of a man who was already dead at the time, the court held that no contract had been made at all.

Misrepresentation

We noted earlier in this chapter that it is not every statement made during pre-contractual negotiations that becomes a term of the contract. Those that do not are called representations. If a representation proves false, it might be actionable as a misrepresentation. It must, however, have been a statement of fact, not opinion or future intentions, etc. and it must have been relied upon to the extent that it induced the contract. It must have been taken seriously.

In *Bisset* v. *Wilkinson* (1927) the statement in question was held just to have been an opinion. The seller of land had stated that it would support 2,000 sheep, but he had never used it for that purpose; so, as Sim J said:

> In ordinary circumstances, any statement made by an owner who has been occupying his own farm as to its carrying capacity would be regarded as a statement of fact ... This, however, is not such a case ... In these circumstances ... the defendants were not justified in regarding anything said by the plaintiff as to the carrying capacity as being anything more than an expression of his opinion on the subject.

In *Redgrave* v. *Hurd* (1881) statements made about income misled a solicitor into believing that a place in a partnership was worth more than documents produced to him showed. They were statements of fact. They had induced the contract. On the other hand, in *Attwood* v. *Small* (1838) the prospective purchaser sent surveyors in to check the accuracy of statements the seller had made about a mine. They were statements of fact too, but, obviously, they had not been relied upon.

Sometimes you can be liable for misrepresentation if you say nothing. Silence can amount to statements of fact. When completing a proposal for life assurance, for example, if you are silent about your fits and three dozen heart attacks, it amounts to misrepresentation. Such contracts are called *uberrimae fidei* (of the utmost good faith). There is a duty to disclose all relevant facts in such contracts.

When a court allows you to plead your mistake, the contract is void—it was not made—you were not truly agreed. When misrepresentation is the issue, the contract is valid but voidable at the option of the party misled. It is called a right to rescind the contract. It is a choice; if he wished he could continue with the deal. If the statement was made innocently, without fraud, and without negligence, then the court could grant the innocent party damage (money compensation), but this would be instead of rescission. If it had been an innocent but negligently made statement, damages are available as well as rescission. If it was fraudulent misrepresentation then heavier damages are available. The innocent party sues for deceit, which is a tort.

Rescission is a remedy from the area of law called Equity which we have noticed on several occasions already—particularly in Chapter 2. As an equitable remedy it is discretionary. It cannot be demanded. It will generally not be allowed after a long delay in applying for it (it looks as if the claimant has decided to carry on despite having been misled), nor if it would be unfair to an innocent third party (so in *Lewis* v. *Averay* (1972), above, the mistake was not allowed and nor was rescission because the car was in the hands of an innocent third party).

Some contracts contain exclusion clauses purporting to cover misrepresentation. The Misrepresentation Act 1967 (now amended by the Unfair Contract Terms Act 1977, which we met earlier in this chapter) says:

3 If a contract contains a term which would exclude or restrict—
(a) any liability to which a party to a contract may be subject by reason of any misrepresentation made by him before the contract was made; or
(b) any remedy available to another party to the contract by reason of such a misrepresentation,
that term shall be of no effect except in so far as it satisfies the requirement of reasonableness as stated in section 11(1) of the Unfair Contract Terms Act 1977; and it is for those claiming that the term satisfies the requirement to show that it does.

So exclusion must be reasonable, and if the parties are not of equal bargaining power it is unlikely to be so.

Duress and undue influence

When negotiating a contract the parties must have been acting free of the threat of force (e.g. with gun in one ear) and free of the unjustifiable influence of those who have power or authority over them. The use of threat of force is called duress and it prevents the formation of a contract, although some people argue that a contract is made but it is voidable. Undue influence does make contracts voidable. If the parties have a "special relationship" (e.g. doctor and patient, solicitor and client) then any contract between them will be assumed to have been the result of undue influence, and therefore voidable—unless the stronger party can rebut the presumption. He might show, for example, that independent advice was taken by the weaker party. Where no such relationship exists undue influence must be proved. It will not be presumed.

This was discussed in the recent case of *Lloyds Bank* v. *Bundy* (1975) where an old man was freed of mortgages held by his bank on his house, his only asset. He had executed them in reliance on advice from his bank manager. Eventually the mortgages outweighed the value of the house. Lord Denning took the opportunity to review many of the earlier decisions in this area:

> Gathering all together, I would suggest that through all these instances there runs a single thread. They rest on "inequality of bargaining power". By virtue of it, the English law gives relief to one who, without independent advice, enters into a contract on terms which are very unfair or transfers property for a consideration which is grossly inadequate, when his bargaining power is grievously impaired by reason of his own needs or desires, or by his own ignorance or infirmity, coupled with undue influences or pressures brought to bear on him by or for the benefit of the other. When I use the word "undue" I do not mean to suggest that the principle depends on proof of any wrong-doing. The one who stipulates for an unfair advantage may be moved solely by his own self-interest, unconscious of the distress he is bringing to the other. I have also avoided any reference to the will of the one being "dominated" or "overcome" by the other. One who is in extreme need may knowingly consent to a most improvident bargain, solely to relieve the straits in which he finds himself. Again, I do not mean to suggest that every transaction is saved by independent advice. But the absence of it may be fatal. With these explanations, I hope this principle will be found to reconcile the cases.

Illegality

Some contracts are declared illegal by statute, some at common law have been declared illegal on the grounds of public policy by the judges over the years. As examples, agreements for the collective enforcement of conditions regulating the price at which goods may be sold (e.g. black lists) are illegal under the Resale Prices Act 1976. Whereas agreements to commit a crime or a tort or fraud, to trade with the enemy in wartime, to prejudice international diplomacy, the administration of justice, or honesty in public life, to defraud the Inland Revenue or to promote immorality have all been declared illegal by the judges.

When an illegal contract is made the general effects (with rare exceptions) are that neither party can take action upon it to force performance by the other and property transferred under such a contract cannot be recovered.

In *Parkinson* v. *College of Ambulance Ltd.* (1925) one Colonel Parkinson placed £3,000 into the coffers of a charity in return for the promise of a knighthood in the Honours List. No knighthood appeared. No money was refunded. The contract was "prejudicial to honesty in public life" and illegal at common law. This case led to the passing of the Honours (Prevention of Abuses) Act 1925, which now governs the position.

Other contracts are not illegal but void of legal effect. The courts do not enforce rights and obligations in such deals. Again, they are identified by statutes and at common law. The Gaming Act 1845, s.18, says:

All contracts or agreements, whether by parole or in writing, by way of gaming or wagering, shall be null and void; and no suit shall be brought or maintained in any court of law and equity for recovering any sum of money or valuable thing alleged to be won upon any wager or which shall have been deposited in the hands of any person to abide the event on which any wager shall have been made.

So losers cannot be made to pay, nor can stakeholders.

Void contracts at common law (declared so by the judges on grounds of public policy) include:

(a) Agreements to oust the jurisdiction of the courts. These are deals where the parties agree not to take disputes to court. The judges do not mind agreements to go to some form of arbitration before going to court—but agreements which seek to oust them altogether are simply ignored, and the complaining party is welcomed into court.

(*b*) Agreements prejudicial to the sanctity of marriage. These would include a promise to procure a marriage for a fee and other such deals. Incidentally the agreement to marry is no longer a contract (Law Reform (Miscellaneous Provisions) Act 1970, s.1(1)).

(*c*) Contracts in restraint of trade. These contracts are found in business where there seem to be good reasons for restricting an individual to trade freely. Where the restraint is regarded as reasonable by the courts (as between the parties and in the public interest) then they are allowed; but where they are held unreasonable (because they are too wide or last too long) then they are not allowed. They are void to start with; they remain so unless declared reasonable. Sometimes only part of a restraining clause will be declared reasonable and allowed. The other part is said to be severed from the contract. It has no effect. In *Goldsall* v. *Goldman* (1915), for example, the buyer of a business which made imitation jewellery sought to restrain the seller from selling such goods or real jewellery for two years within the United Kingdom and various other areas of the world. The restraint on imitation jewellery in the United Kingdom was held to be reasonable in the circumstances, but the restraint on other goods and overseas was not. It was therefore void.

These contracts in restraint of trade tend to fall into three categories:

(*a*) between the buyer of a business and the seller;

(*b*) between an employer and an employee, to stop him working for the competition; and

(*c*) agreements (called solus ties) under which a garage or a public house might agree to take supplies from one petrol company or brewer in return for various financial advantages.

As examples of the employer-employee restraint consider the cases of *Fitch* v. *Dewes* (1921) where a solicitor was successfully restrained from working for another firm of solicitors within a seven mile radius of the town hall of Tamworth, and *Pearks* v. *Culten* (1912) where a counter-hand in a grocers in Southend was not restrained by the clause seeking to forbid employment for two years in any similar business within two miles of any of the chain of stores the company owned in which he had worked in the past 12 months. It was too much restraint. Validity seems to depend upon the importance of the employee and the trade the employer is trying to protect.

An interesting case on solus ties is *Esso* v. *Harper's Garage* (1968). Here there were two garages tied, one for four years and five months, the other for 21 years. The first was upheld as reasonable; the second was not reasonable: it was void.

Vagueness

The terms of a contract must be clear. The courts cannot enforce vague or ambiguous promises. Thus, in *Scammel* v. *Ouston* (1941), a statement that "the balance of the purchase price can be had on hire purchase terms" was too vague to be enforceable.

However, the courts are anxious to uphold a bargain whenever possible. So, if there is a way of clarifying uncertainty they will use it. So, in *Hillas* v. *Arcos* (1932) a vague term about an option to buy timber, which lacked such details as type and price, was clarified by reference to the previous course of dealings between the parties.

THE DISCHARGE OF CONTRACTS

Contractual liability does not go on forever. Contracts are brought to an end (discharged) in one of four main ways.

Performance

The contract ends when both parties have done as they agreed. I have paid, you have delivered. Our contract has been discharged by performance.

Obviously, the trouble starts where one party has not performed or he has tendered performance late when time was of the essence (i.e. an essential part of the agreement) of the deal, or has only partially performed. The general rule is that "part performance is no performance". That is, that in order to discharge the contract both sides must completely perform their side of the deal. It can be a harsh rule—as in *Cutter* v. *Powell* (1795) where a dead sailor's wife recovered nothing of her late husband's wages because he had died just before completing his voyage.

This rule has been mollified from time to time by the courts, in the interests of fairness, and several so-called exceptions now exist.

(*a*) Substantial performance. Where performance is nearly complete some payment is made to match the extent of the performance (on a basis called *quantum meruit* ("as much as he has earned")). One famous example is *Hoenig* v. *Isaacs* (1952) where a carpenter and decorator nearly completed a job, and did part of it badly. He was to be paid £750. He was awarded £750 less the cost of having the job put right—£56.

(*b*) Severable contracts. If a large contract can be seen as a series of smaller ones, for example instalment deliveries, then payment could be claimed (*quantum meruit* again) for the instalments actually delivered. Such a contract is sometimes called severable.

(*c*) Prevention. Obviously if the other party prevents full performance, then payment must be made for the performance achieved up to that time. The case of *Planche* v. *Colburn* (1831) involved an author commissioned to write a book about costume and ancient armour for a series called *The Juvenile Library*. He was to be paid £100. When the work was half-done the series was cancelled by the publishers. He recovered £50.

(*d*) Part performance accepted. If the other party accepts part performance (e.g. short delivery), then he must pay for what he has received.

Agreement

A contract is a creature of agreement. It can be discharged by agreement. The parties can just agree to end it. Technically this is binding because each side promises not to sue the other for breach. This comprises the necessary consideration.

There might be a slight problem, when one party has partly performed his side of the bargain. Here, the other party must compensate him in some way for what he has done before the contract can be discharged. This is called accord and satisfaction (i.e. agreement and compensation).

Breach

Any breach of contract qualifies the innocent party to recover damages. A serious breach will enable him to regard the contract as discharged and to regard himself as free of further obligations under it as well as claiming damages. Such a breach is a breach of condition. A condition, as has already been observed, is a major term in a contract. A warranty is not and its breach gives rise only to a claim for damages as compensation. A breach of warranty does not discharge the contract.

Frustration

If there is a period of time between formation and the date for performance then the contract could be discharged by frustration. It means supervening impossibility. For example:

(*a*) the whole foundation of the deal may be destroyed: in *Taylor* v. *Caldwell* (1863) the music hall hired under the contract burnt down before the concert date. The contract was discharged;

(*b*) the law might change: in *Re Shipton, Anderson and Co.* (1915) the Army, Supply of Food, Forage and Stores Act 1914 had rendered the performance of the contract illegal. The contract was for wheat which had now been requisitioned because of the war;

(*c*) personal services may not be available: in *Condor* v. *Barron Knights* (1966) a drummer signed to play every night, but he fell ill. He could only play four nights each week. The contract was discharged.

However, increased difficulty or the prospect of loss on the deal cannot be enough. Performance must be made impossible by the unforeseen event. In *Davis Contractors* v. *Fareham UDC* (1956) the fact that shortage of materials and labour meant that the estate would cost the builders far more to build was not enough. In *Amalgamated Investment* v. *John Walker* (1976) a preservation order placed on a warehouse rendering a £1,750,000 development site worth only £200,000 did not discharge the liability to pay the contract price. (The order was issued the day after formation of the contract.)

REMEDIES FOR BREACH OF CONTRACT

Damages

The object of an award of damages is to put the parties where they could have been had the contract not been breached. In *Victoria Laundry* v. *Newman* (1949) the breach was the late delivery of an extra boiler for the laundry. The loss claimed was two-fold. First the loss of extra business profit. Second the special loss of certain Ministry of Supply contracts. However, they had not told the boiler-makers about these special contracts. They would have been expected to foresee the loss of extra profits, but without information, they could not have been expected to foresee the further loss. Asquith LJ explained:

> It is well settled that the governing purpose of damages is to put the party whose rights have been violated in the same position, so far as money can do so, as if his rights had been observed... This purpose, if relentlessly pursued would provide him with a complete indemnity for all loss de facto resulting from a particular breach, however improbable, however unpredictable. This, in contract at least, is recognised as too harsh a rule. Hence, in cases of breach of contract the aggrieved party is only entitled to recover such part of the loss actually resulting as was at the time of the contract reasonably foreseeable as liable to result from the breach. What was at the time reasonably so foreseeable depends on the knowledge then possessed by the parties or, at all events, by the party who later commits the breach.

The rules about remoteness of damage emerged from a case called *Hadley* v. *Baxendale* (1854), where a replacement crankshaft for a mill was very late in being delivered. No damages were recovered because the carriers were unaware that no spare shaft was kept, and that the mill was at a standstill.

The plaintiff is always expected to keep his loss to a minimum (mitigate his loss). If I cancel my booking at your hotel you should at least try to re-let, even at a lower rate. You can recover the difference from me later. It would amount to the ordinary loss and reasonably foreseeable. Any extra loss could only be claimed if I had been made aware of the extra risk when we formed the deal.

In *The Heron II* (1967) a ship was chartered by the respondents to carry sugar. The ship arrived late and when the sugar was sold, because of a charge in the market price, a poorer price was obtained. The House of Lords held that the fall in the market price was not too remote a consequence of the breach of contract in arriving late. Their Lordships suggested that the test for remoteness of damage should be "real danger" or "serious possibility" of the events occurring. Or the facts the respondents should have recognised a "real danger" or "serious possibility" of the price of sugar falling and so were liable for it.

Other remedies

We have already met other remedies than just money compensation in Chapter Two. None can be demanded. Damages are available as a right. Only the amount (quantum) is open for discussion. Other remedies are from equity and therefore at the discretion of the court. They include:

(*a*) Specific performance—to make me do what I promised (although it cannot be used to enforce personal services);

(*b*) Injunctions—to stop me acting in breach of contract, like playing for another club when I have signed for you or, as in *Warner Bros.* v. *Nelson* (1937) where the actress Bette Davis was ordered not to breach her exclusive contract with the plaintiffs;

(*c*) Rescission—which we considered with misrepresentation. It means undoing the contract and putting the parties (as far as possible) back in their precontractual position. Note the difference from the purpose of an award of damages;

(*d*) Quantum meruit—where performance is rewarded according to worth—"as much as he has earned".

With damages there are statutory time limits within which claims must be brought. For a simple contract this is six years; on a deed it is twelve years. Time runs from the cause of action arising or when the plaintiff ought reasonably to have realised it had arisen (Limitation Act 1980).

With equitable remedies there is less time for, as we have noted, "delay defeats equity" (if in doubt *see* Chapter 2).

THE CONSUMER AND THE LAW

The law often reflects the balance between competing interests, whether they are public or private. In the area of consumer protection on the one hand there is the sanctity of freedom of contract and the right of tradesmen and retailers to get the best deal they can with the consuming public. On the other hand there is the need to protect the public from, e.g. defective products, unfair advertising and agreements which are too heavily biased in favour of the retailer.

Certain types of transactions are entered into by consumers every day—for example, the housewife visiting the supermarket to buy the weekly groceries, the handyman who visits the DIY shop or car accessory shop, or the schoolboy who visits the sweet shop for a bar of chocolate. They all enter into contracts for the sale and supply of goods and, from a practical point of view, this is probably the most important type of contract. The basis of the contract is that money changes hands in return for the goods.

However, consumers may wish to acquire goods but do not have the immediate finance to pay for them. In recent years hire-purchase and other forms of credit buying have been an important feature of many consumer transactions. This is particularly true of the purchase of more expensive and long-lasting products. It is not unusual for a married couple, setting up home for the first time, to buy a suite of furniture, carpets, washing machine and other things on some form of credit terms. Similarly, cars, vans and trucks either for domestic or commercial use are often the subject matter of a credit-leasing arrangement.

Because of the importance of these two forms of consumer transaction (i.e. sale of goods and credit purchase), it is not surprising that these are two of the main areas where the law has sought to afford the consumer extra protection, particularly in the form of statutory protection. This chapter examines these two areas. We will look at some points of criminal consumer law in Chapter 14.

CONSUMER LAW: CONTRACTS FOR THE SALE OF GOODS

These contracts contain express and implied conditions and warranties which are referred to as the terms of the contract. They set out the rights and obligations of the parties under the contract. So, for example, express terms are usually included in the contract by the parties themselves, whereas implied terms are often implied into the contract by statute, e.g. Sale of Goods Act 1979.

The distinction between conditions and warranties was discussed by the House of Lords in *Wickman Machine Tools Ltd.* v. *Schuler A.-G.* (1974). It was emphasised that only the courts could decide which particular category was appropriate for any particular part of a contract; parties cannot make the decision themselves.

Conditions

These are important contractual terms and a breach of them may enable the injured party to treat the contract as at an end. Often this means that the goods are returned to the seller and the buyer gets his money back. For example, on the sale of a car S says to B that the car is 1750cc and was made in 1980; if either of these statements is untrue there is a breach of a condition.

Warranties

These are less important contractual terms and, in the event of a breach the buyer may be able to claim damages, e.g. the difference in value between what the buyer contracted for and what he actually got. For example, on the sale of the same car S says to B that it has been serviced in the last three months. If this statement is untrue there is a breach of warranty.

The retailer may attempt, in the contract, to exclude liability for breach of conditions or warranties whether express or implied. Because this would cause hardship to the consumer who may have no choice but to accept such an exclusion if he wishes to purchase the goods, protection has been given by both the common law and statute. This prevents the seller including in contracts clauses which are very unfair to the consumer.

In *Karsales (Harrow) Ltd.* v. *Wallis* (1956) the buyer saw a Buick car in exeellent condition and he entered into a hire purchase agreement to buy it. A week later the "car" was delivered outside his house. It had, in fact, been towed there; the tyres had been changed, the cylinder head was off and all the valves were burnt out. The car would not go. The contract contained a comprehensive exclusion of liability clause in favour of the seller (to the effect that he would not be liable for any defects howsoever caused). It was held by the Court of Appeal that the seller could not rely on the exclusion clause in the contract. The fact was that the buyer had agreed to buy a car and the sellers had agreed to sell him one. What was eventually delivered was not a car at all and there was such a fundamental breach of the contract that no exclusion clause could cover it.

CONSUMER LAW: THE SALE OF GOODS ACT 1979

The law relating to contracts for the sale of goods has now been consolidated in the Sale of Goods Act 1979. The Act deals mainly with rules governing the parties' obligations to each other and the transfer of the ownership of the goods. Contracts of sale are usually made without the need for any formal requirements, e.g. cash sale of goods in shops or food and drink sold in a restaurant.

The contract of sale is defined as

a contract whereby the seller transfers or agrees to transfer the property in the goods to the buyer for a money consideration called the price.

This covers:
(*a*) a sale—where ownership of the goods passes immediately to the buyer when he tenders the price (e.g. most transactions in shops);
(*b*) an agreement to sell—where the parties agree that ownership is to pass in the future.

With certain exceptions the parties are free to make whatever sort of contract they wish. The obligations under the contract are largely a matter for the parties themselves to decide. In the absence of such express agreement the Act implies certain obligations.

SELLER'S OBLIGATIONS UNDER THE SALE OF GOODS ACT 1979

Title

Section 12(1) of the 1979 Act states there is

an implied condition on the part of the seller that in the case of a sale, he has a right to sell the goods, and in the case of an agreement to sell, he will have such a right at the time when the property is to pass.

So if the seller has no right to sell the goods because; e.g. if they are stolen he is in breach of this condition under the Act. In *Rowland* v. *Divall* (1923) a buyer who was sold a stolen car was held entitled to recover the full price from the seller when it had to be returned to its rightful owner.

Description

Section 13(1) states that

where there is a contract for the sale of goods by description there is an implied condition that the goods shall correspond with that description.

This applies to goods that are ordered from catalogues and brochures and to descriptions on the packaging of articles. There is a breach, for example, if the box refers to a blue double-size electric blanket, but when it's opened it contains a pink single-size blanket. In

Beale v. *Taylor* (1967) a car was advertised as a white Herald Convertible 1961. It was purchased but the buyer later discovered that while the description fitted the rear end of the car it did not apply to the front. The seller was held to be in breach of the term implied by s.13.

Quality or Fitness

If it is a private sale and the individuals are not contracting in the course of business then the Act implies no conditions on quality or fitness. For example, a washing machine advertised in a local newspaper by a private seller and bought by a private buyer. This means that the maxim *caveat emptor* (let the buyer beware) applies, and it is up to the buyer to ask all the relevant questions to ensure that the goods work and will do the job he wants.

If, however, it is a business sale (e.g. between a retailer and a private individual, or between two retailers) then there is an implied condition as to quality and fitness for purpose.

Section 14(2) states that

> where the seller sells goods in the course of a business there is an implied condition that the goods supplied under the contract are of merchantable quality.

"Merchantable quality" means, according to s.14(6) the goods are:

> as fit for the purpose or purposes for which goods of that kind are commonly bought as it is reasonable to expect having regard to any description applied to them, the price (if relevant) and all the other relevant circumstances.

However, the condition relating to merchantable quality does not apply, where, before the contract is made according to s.14(2):

(*a*) the seller draws the buyer's attention to a defect; or

(*b*) the buyer examines the goods and the defect is such as his examination ought to reveal.

The quality of goods which a buyer is entitled to expect varies with all the circumstances. However, second-hand goods or goods bought in a sale must still comply with this condition though obviously they may be of lower quality than new or full-price goods.

In addition s.14(3) states

> where the seller sells goods in the course of business and the buyer, expressly or by implication, makes known... to the seller... any particular purpose for which the goods are being bought, there is

an implied condition that the goods supplied are reasonably fit for the purpose, whether or not that is a purpose for which such goods are commonly supplied, except where the circumstances show that the buyer does not rely, or that it is unreasonable for him to rely, on the skill or judgement of the seller.

Therefore if the buyer expressly or impliedly makes known to the seller the purpose for which he requires the goods the seller will be in breach of the section if he fails to supply goods that will fulfil that purpose. The more the buyer relies on the seller's skill and expertise the greater is the seller's responsibility.

However, in *Griffiths* v. *Peter Conway Ltd.* (1939) the plaintiff bought a new tweed coat from the defendant. After wearing it for a while she developed a skin irritation, so she sued the defendant for breach of s.14(3). It was held that the garment was fit for its purpose for normal wear and as she had not made known to the seller that she had a sensitive skin and asked him to recommend a suitable coat, she was not able to sue.

Sample

Section 15 of the Act states that if goods are sold by sample there are these implied conditions:

(*a*) the bulk of the goods will correspond with the sample in quality;

(*b*) the buyer will have a reasonable opportunity of comparing the bulk with the sample;

(*c*) the goods will be free from any defect rendering them unmerchantable which would not be apparent on a reasonable examination of the sample.

This section applies, for example, to wallpaper or curtain material which is often ordered after looking at a retailer's pattern books.

In *Godley* v. *Perry* (1960) a boy was injured by a defective catapult purchased in a retail shop. The catapults had been bought by the retailer after being shown samples. It was held that the boy has a claim for breach of s.14(2) and (3) and the retailer had a claim against the wholesaler for breach of s.15(2)(*c*).

In *Ashington Piggeries* v. *Christopher Hill* (1972) the defendants asked the plaintiffs to manufacture food for pork farmers. The plaintiffs made it clear they knew nothing about pork breeding, but did suggest a variation in the compounds used. One consignment contained contaminated herring meal which caused serious losses on pork farmers. The defendants refused to pay for the meal and the plaintiffs sued for payment. The defendants counterclaimed for breach of contract. It was held by the House of Lords: (i) there was a breach of the implied condition of s.14 that the goods were reasonably fit for their purpose, the buyer having relied on the skill and judgment of the sellers; (ii) the sellers were also in breach of the implied condition that the goods were of merchantable quality.

It should be noted that the Unfair Contract Terms Act 1977, s.6, prevents the seller excluding his liability under the Sale of Goods Act 1979, ss.12–15, in any consumer sale. We saw this earlier in this chapter, when discussing exclusion clauses.

THE PASSING OF RISK AND OWNERSHIP UNDER THE SALE OF GOODS ACT 1979

Risk

In a contract for the sale of goods it is important to know when the property in the goods passes from the seller to the buyer. With the passing of property often goes the passing of the risk of, e.g. the goods being destroyed or damaged. This means that with expensive items, the buyer would be well advised to insure against such a loss occurring. Generally, if the contract refers to a specific item (e.g. a particular car in a retailer's showroom) the property passes as soon as the contract is made. If, however, modifications have to be made to the goods the property passes only when this has been done and the buyer has been notified to this effect.

If the buyer takes goods on approval the property only passes to the buyer when he signifies to the seller his intention to keep the goods. If goods have not been set aside or specifically assigned to the buyer then property only passes to the buyer when this process has been completed.

Ownership

If goods are sold by a seller who has no right to sell them, then he cannot give the buyer a good title to these goods. This is because the law states that no one can give what he does not have (*nemo dat quod non habet*). The strict application of this rule can therefore cause hardship to innocent buyers who purchase goods in good faith from sellers who may have no right to sell them. It is for this reason that a number of exceptions to the rule have developed where the innocent buyer will obtain a good title as against the true owner.

(*a*) Estoppel. If the owner knows his goods are being sold by a seller without good title he will be prevented (estopped) from later denying the seller's right to sell.

(*b*) Mercantile agent. If an owner deposits goods with a mercantile agent, whose ordinary business is to buy and sell goods, and the agent sells to an innocent buyer, the buyer obtains a good title.

(*c*) Seller or buyer in possession. If a seller is allowed to retain possession of goods after a sale, and if he sells to a third party the third party obtains a good title. Likewise, if a buyer obtains possession of goods before he has paid for them, and if he sells them, the third party obtains a good title.

(*d*) Seller with a voidable title. A sale by a seller with a voidable title (i.e. one which is valid until avoided) will give the buyer a good title provided that the title had not been avoided at the time of sale, and the buyer did not know of the defect in the title.

(*e*) Market overt. Market overt refers to shops in the City of London and market stalls in a regularly constituted market on market days during the hours between sunrise and sunset. Any sales in such markets give the buyer a good title if he purchased the goods for value and without notice of any defect in the seller's title.

(*f*) Motor vehicles subject to a hire-purchase agreement. A private buyer (not a motor trader) buying a motor vehicle which is subject to a hire-purchase agreement will obtain a good title to the vehicle if he had no knowledge of the agreement.

THE RIGHTS OF THE BUYER AND SELLER UNDER THE SALE OF GOODS ACT 1979

Once a contract for the sale of goods has been made the seller is under an obligation to deliver the goods. This can mean actual delivery or the buyer can be handed the means of access to the goods, e.g. the keys to a warehouse where the goods are stored. If the seller refuses to deliver the goods the buyer can:

(*a*) sue for damages for any loss incurred by him arising out of the refusal; or

(*b*) obtain an order for specific performance.

If the seller delivers the wrong goods then the buyer can accept or reject them as he sees fit.

If in turn the buyer refuses to accept delivery of the correct goods then he can be sued for damages. If the ownership of the goods has passed to the buyer and he refuses to pay then he can be sued for the price of the goods.

An unpaid seller may not have parted with possession of the goods when he learns of the buyer's refusal to pay the contract price. In this situation the seller has:

(*a*) a lien for the price. This means the seller can retain possession of the goods until he is paid;

(*b*) a right of stoppage in transit. This means that if the goods are in the process of being delivered to the buyer the seller can stop them and retain possession until paid.

The Sale of Goods Act 1979, s.19, allows a seller to "reserve the right of disposal" of the goods. This could enable him to recover possession of goods even if they have been delivered to the buyer if he has not been paid. However since the *Romalpa* Case (1976) it has been possible by including an appropriately worded clause in the contract of sale, for the seller to recover any goods still in the buyer's possession and the proceeds of any sales of the goods that have taken place. It meant that the property in the goods was not to pass to the buyer until the seller had been paid. The goods could be sold on but the second buyer was to regard the proceeds of sale as belonging to the unpaid seller.

BUYING GOODS ON CREDIT

There are many ways in which a consumer can obtain credit. He may seek a loan or overdraft facilities from his bank, large stores may have their own credit arrangements or he may use his credit card, e.g. Barclaycard and Access. Or he may enter into a credit arrangement that takes one of the three following forms.

Hire-purchase

This is a contract of hire which gives the hirer an option to purchase the goods at the end of the period of hire. During the hiring the purchase price plus interest is paid by instalments. The hirer has no right to sell the goods to a third party before all instalments have been paid. Therefore, the third party obtains no title to the goods except under Part III of the Hire-Purchase Act 1964 where the hirer sells a motor car to an innocent private purchaser.

Suppose, for example, that A wishes to buy a car from a garage. He asks for credit and completes a proposal form supplied by a finance company. The garage offers to sell the car to the finance company. If the finance company accepts both transactions it will buy the car from the garage and also enter into a contract with A to supply the car on instalment credit terms.

Credit Sale

This is a contract for the sale of goods which means that in return for the price the seller promises to transfer to the buyer the property (i.e. the ownership) in the goods. The buyer will be entitled to take possession (i.e. delivery of the goods) immediately. The ownership will usually transfer to the buyer at or before the time he takes delivery. Therefore, if the buyer sells the goods he will be selling his own goods and the person buying them will have a good title (i.e. ownership) to them.

Conditional Sale

This is also a contract for the sale of goods where the buyer takes possession immediately. However, the property (i.e. the ownership) in the goods does not transfer to the buyer until a condition has been fulfilled. This condition is usually that the buyer must complete the payment of all instalments under the agreement. Therefore, although the buyer obtains possession of the goods, until he has paid all the instalments the property (i.e. the ownership) of the goods remains with the seller. This means, in most cases, that a good title cannot be obtained by a third party if the goods are sold by the buyer prior to this date, except under Part III of the Hire-Purchase Act 1964, which as we have seen, concerns motor vehicles sold to private individuals.

THE CONSUMER CREDIT ACT 1974

All consumer credit agreements have now been brought within one statute, the Consumer Credit Act 1974. The aim of the statute is to provide reasonable protection for consumers. This aim is achieved in several ways:

(*a*) it regulates the formation, terms and enforcement of credit agreements;

(*b*) anyone engaged in the consumer credit business must be licensed to carry on the business;

(*c*) an advertisement for credit must show the true cost of the credit;

(*d*) restrictions are placed on door-to-door selling on credit; e.g. salesmen selling double-glazing on credit need to be licensed;

(*e*) it creates new criminal offences, e.g. trading without the necessary licence;

(*f*) it makes it impossible to contract out of the provisions of the Act.

The Act applies to "consumer credit agreements". This is defined in s.8 as credit agreements made between an individual (the "debtor") and any other person (the "creditor") by which the creditor provides the debtor with credit not exceeding £5,000. The term "individual" includes partnerships and unincorporated bodies but not companies.

Credit agreements include hire-purchase agreements, conditional sale agreements, credit sale agreements, credit card agreements, loan agreements, bank overdraft agreements, shop budget credit accounts, trading check and trading voucher agreements. In the Act these are all referred to as "regulated agreements" and they must comply with the provisions of the Act. Not included within the definition are ordinary hire agreements where the hirer never becomes the owner of the goods, e.g. television rentals. Hire agreements are, however, covered by certain provisions of the Act.

Making a regulated agreement

This is made like any other form of contract. It is usually in writing, often using a standard form provided by the creditor. Certain formal requirements must be complied with to ensure that the debtor (customer) is aware of the nature and full cost of the transaction and that he has a copy of the final written agreement. These formalities are:

(a) information on:
 (i)   the total charge for credit;
 (ii) the true annual percentage rate of charge;
 (iii) the price for which goods could be bought for cash;
(b) provision of a full and detailed written agreement covering all the terms of the agreement;
(c) signature of the agreement by the debtor and credit or should only take place when the agreement has been completely filled in;
(d) the debtor must receive a copy of the agreement.

In the event of failure to comply with these formalities the creditor will not be able to enforce the agreement without seeking an enforcement order from the court; the county court is the usual place for these cases, High Court applications being rare.

Cancellation of a Regulated Agreement

This covers mainly agreements made as a result of door-to-door salesmanship or agreements signed away from the creditor's business premises, e.g. in the debtor's own home. To exercise his right of cancellation the debtor must send a written notice to this effect to the creditor within five days of receiving his copy of the agreement.

The effect of cancellation is that the transaction is without effect and the debtor is entitled to the return of any deposit or the return of any goods traded in part-exchange. In return the debtor must either return the goods or make them available for collection by the creditor.

Liability of the creditor

In a hire purchase agreement it is the creditor (i.e. usually a finance house) and not the dealer (e.g. the garage who sold the car) who will be liable if there is a breach of any of the conditions and warranties implied by the Supply of Goods (Implied Terms) Act 1973. Any attempt to exclude liability for such breaches would be ineffective.

These terms closely resemble those implied into contracts for the sale of goods by the 1979 Act. With credit sales and conditional sales the liability for breach of contract and misrepresentation is shared between the finance house and the dealer, under the Consumer Credit Act 1974, ss.56, 75—provided that the finance house and the dealer had a "business link" (e.g. Access and a shop with an "Access Accepted here" sign in the window).

Termination of Regulated Agreements

If the debtor is in breach of the agreement, e.g. through failure to pay instalments, then the creditor may wish to terminate the agreement. To do this, under s.87 of the Act he must first serve a default notice setting out:

(*a*) the amount required to bring payments up-to-date;

(*b*) the time by which payments must be made (subject to a minimum of seven days);

(*c*) the consequences of failure to comply with the notice;

(*d*) the provision of the agreement under which the agreement can be terminated;

(*e*) the fact that if the breach is remedied the agreement will not be terminated.

If the notice is not complied with the creditor can exercise his right to terminate the agreement. The consequences of termination are:

(a) the creditor may be able to recover possession of the goods unless it is a hire-purchase agreement and the debtor has already paid a third of the total price of the goods. Here the goods should not be taken without an order from the county court. They are called "protected goods";

(*b*) the creditor may be able to claim further sums of money from the debtor. These may be either damages or an amount stipulated in the agreement which is payable on termination.

Recovery of goods by the creditor

If an agreement is terminated the creditor is entitled to recover possession of the goods. However,

(*a*) the creditor cannot, without the debtor's permission, or an order from the county court, enter premises to repossess the property;

(*b*) if the goods are "protected goods" then unless the debtor is prepared to hand them over a court order is again necessary to repossess them.

It is always open to the court on the application for a possession order by the creditor to make a "time order" giving the debtor more time to pay.

Money claim by the creditor

In addition to claiming recovery of the goods the creditor may also be entitled to:

(*a*) damages for repudiation of the contract by the debtor which aim to put the creditor in the position he would have been in if the contract had been completed;

(*b*) the arrears in instalments plus any damages for the debtor's failure to take reasonable care of the goods;

(*c*) a minimum payment stipulated in the contract provided it is not excessive in the light of the circumstances of the case.

Powers of the court

The court may make the following orders:

(*a*) a time order giving the debtor extra time to pay;

(*b*) a return order ordering the debtor to return the goods to the creditor;

(*c*) a transfer order allowing the debtor to return part of the goods and allowing him to keep the other part.

Debtor's right of termination

Section 99 gives a debtor under a regulated hire-purchase or conditional sale agreement a statutory right of termination. He should give notice, in writing, of his intention to terminate, usually to the creditor. When the debtor has exercised his right of termination he has to return goods which are not protected goods. He must also pay:

(*a*) any loss caused by his failure to take reasonable care of the goods; plus

(*b*) all arrears due; plus

(*c*) a sum sufficient to bring his payments up to half of the total price.

Chapter 14

The Criminal Law

INTRODUCTION

In Chapter one we considered the nature of the criminal law, when comparing it with the civil law. In Chapter four we considered the classification and range of criminal offences, when dealing with the jurisdiction of the various criminal courts. In Chapter seven we examined the way in which a criminal trial is dealt with in those courts. In Chapters nine and ten we considered the criminal capacity of such persons as children, the mentally disordered and corporations (legal persons). In this chapter we are to examine a little of the substance of the criminal law itself.

CRIMINAL LAW: DEFINITION OF CRIME

There are many definitions to be found in the books and cases. All have their uses and drawbacks, it all rather depends upon the points the writer wishes to extract from the definition he is framing. As a general definition, Professor Card offers:

> A crime or offence is an illegal act, omission or event, whether or not it is also a tort, a breach of contract or a breach of trust, the principal consequence of which is that the offender, if he is detected and the police decide to prosecute, is prosecuted by or in the name of the State, and if he is found guilty is liable to be punished whether or not he is also ordered to compensate his victim.

This brings out the "public" nature of crimes, the usual agency of enforcement and the main point of the proceedings, to punish offenders. There are other agencies of enforcement, such as trading standards officers, and there are other purposes to criminal proceedings, like deterrence.

CLASSIFYING CRIMES

There are various ways in which crimes can be classified:

(a) As between offences created by Acts of Parliament and those common law offences developed by the judges over the years. Most crimes are statutory. They might be new crimes—like the failure to wear a seat belt when required. This was created by means of the Motor Vehicles (Wearing of Seat Belts) Regulations 1982, which were made under the Road Traffic Act 1972. (We examined such lawmaking powers in Chapter three, when considering delegated legislation.) If they are not new crimes, they might be the result of a reworking of the common law, or a consolidation of earlier statute law. Such crimes are to be found in the Theft Act 1968 (which will be discussed later in this chapter). The classification might be between statutory crimes like these and common law crimes, such as murder, the basic definition of which has not changed for centuries; Sir Edward Coke wrote, in 1644:

> Murder is when a man unlawfully killeth... any reasonable creature in rerum natura (in being) under the King's peace with malice forethought (intent to kill or to cause grievous bodily harm), either expressed by the party, or implied by law, so as the party wounded, or hurt, etc. die of the wound, or hurt, etc. within a year and a day after the same.

Murder, too, will be seen in more detail later in this chapter.

(b) It is possible to classify crimes into "arrestable" and "non-arrestable" offences. Before 1967 the split was between "felonies", which, generally, were serious crimes, and "misdemeanours", which were not. However, the distinctions became blurred and this new classification was made possible by the Criminal Law Act 1967. Under this Act certain offences are classified as "arrestable" in that an arrest can be made without a warrant (a written authority from a magistrate to a policeman to arrest an individual). So the distinction lies between these "arrestable" offences and all those others for which no general power exists and for which a warrant is required if an arrest is to be made.

The 1967 Acts says, in s.2(1).

> The powers of summary arrest conferred by the following subsections shall apply to offences for which the sentence is fixed by law or for which a person (not previously convicted) may under or by virtue of any enactment be sentenced to imprisonment for a term of five years... and to attempts to commit any such offence... "arrestable offence" means any such offence or attempt.

An example of an offence for which the sentence is fixed by law is murder (for which the penalty is life imprisonment). Offences carrying five years' imprisonment or more include theft (10 years), burglary (14 years), robbery (life), blackmail (14 years), unlawful wounding (5 years)—but it must be remembered that these are maxima. The courts have to be impressed before the maximum sentence is awarded. Nevertheless, they are (with many others) all arrestable offences because the accused could be sentenced to five years' (or more) imprisonment. More will be added later in the chapter about the precise allocation of powers of arrest amongst individuals within society.

(c) It is possible to classify by mode of trial. Indeed we did so when dealing with the jurisdiction of those courts which deal with criminal trials at first instance—the magistrates' and the Crown Courts.

CRIMINAL LIABILITY: THE ELEMENTS OF A CRIME

The general rule is: *actus non facit reum nisi mens sit rea,* which means that an act is not wicked in itself, it is not wicked unless the mind too is wicked. That is, each crime requires a (prohibited act), something not supposed to be acceptable, and generally "not done" (e.g. appropriating property belonging to another), and the requisite intention (e.g. appropriating dishonestly and with the intention of permanently depriving the true owner of it). This means that both *actus reus* and *mens rea* must usually be present before a crime can be said to have been committed. For example, in the crime of theft, the Theft Act 1968 says:

A person is guilty of theft if he dishonestly appropriates property belonging to another with the intention of permanently depriving the other of it; and "thief" and "steal" shall be construed accordingly.

Can you pick out the *actus reus* (what you are not supposed to do) and the two parts of the *mens rea* (wicked state of mind) within this offence?

An *actus reus* could, of course, consist of an omission to act when a duty to act existed, e.g. to stop at a red traffic light.

The *mens rea* requirement, particularly within a statutory offence, is often signalled by words such as "maliciously, knowingly, wilfully, permitting, suffering, etc." It could consist of a particular intention (e.g. the "intention permanently to deprive") or it might be sufficient that the accused was "reckless" (e.g. speeding along the high street, with no intention to knock over anyone in particular, but not caring either). If the accused intended to commit an offence, then the reason why (the motive) is not usually relevant. Many of the defences we are to consider later in this chapter for a variety of reasons amount to little more than a reasoned argument of lack of *mens rea*. Thus they amount, if they are successful, to a variety of ways to show that the prosecution has not established the basic requirements of the offence charged.

STRICT LIABILITY OFFENCES

Whilst most crimes require both *actus reus* and *mens rea*, there are some offences which require no *mens rea* at all. That is, just doing the prohibited act is enough. This is called an offence of "strict liability" or an "absolute offence".

The courts have a working rule, a presumption, that unless a statute expressly states that a strict liability offence has been created, then it has not. This was seen in *Sweet* v. *Parsley* (1970) where Miss Sweet's conviction for being concerned in the management of premises which were used for the purpose of smoking cannabis (contrary to the Dangerous Drugs Act 1965, s.5) was quashed on the basis that she had no knowledge of these circumstances. She only visited to collect the rent. Lord Reid said:

> Our first duty is to consider the words of the Act; if they show a clear intention to create an absolute offence, that is an end of the matter. But such cases are very rare. Sometimes the words of the section which creates a particular offence make it clear that mens rea is required in one form or another. Such cases are quite frequent. But in a very large number of cases there is no clear indication either way. In such cases there has for centuries been a presumption that Parliament did not intend to make criminals of persons who were in no way blameworthy in what they did. That means that, whenever a section is silent as to mens rea, there is a presumption that, in order to give effect to the will of Parliament, we must read in words appropriate to require mens rea.

There are absolute offences created from time to time. The justifications seem to vary. Either, the offences are so petty that lengthy submissions about *mens rea* would waste the court's time (e.g. many motoring and parking offences), or, and much more importantly, the offence might be so socially dangerous that the law should outlaw the activity alone. It should not be concerned with the accused's intention. For example, the requirement that someone owning a firearm should also be licensed to do so. The Firearms Act 1968, s.1, makes this provision.

Sometimes this "hard line" can work what might seem to some to be injustice. In *R.* v. *Howells* (1977), for instance, the accused had bought a gun in a pub for £115, believing it to be an antique. In s.58(2) of the 1968 Act an ornament such as this would not need a licence; but it was a modern copy, not an antique. Therefore Howells needed a licence, despite his (honest) belief that he did not. Browne LJ said:

> This subsection relates to facts and not beliefs... This court has reached the decision that section 1 should be construed strictly. First, the wording would, on the face of it, so indicate. Secondly, the danger to the community resulting from the possession of lethal firearms is obviously so great that an absolute prohibition must have been the intention of Parliament when considered in conjunction with the words of the section. Thirdly, to allow a defence of honest and reasonable belief that the firearm was an antique and therefore excluded would be likely to defeat the clear intention of the Act.

DEFENCES TO CRIME

An accused might seek to undermine the prosecution by disputing an element of the offence charged. For example, he might claim that his taking of the property he is accused of stealing was not dishonest—"He said I could borrow it any time"—thus defeating an accusation of theft, because dishonesty is an essential ingredient of the offence.

On the other hand, the accused might raise a defence of a more general nature; one which is available in answer to many different criminal charges.

insanity

We examined this defence earlier (in Chapter 9) when dealing with the criminal responsibility of the mentally disordered. We noted then that the defence is based upon the famous "M'Naghten Rules"

In *R.* v. *Kemp* (1957) the accused hit his wife with a mallet. He was suffering from arteriosclerosis (hardening of the arteries) which restricted the flow of blood to his brain, so that he did not know what he was doing when he hit her. The "Rules" mention "a defect of reason from disease of the mind". The accused's illness was held to fall within this category because it was capable of affecting the mind. Kemp was found "guilty but insane". These days (since the Criminal Procedure (Insanity) Act 1964) the verdict would be "not guilty by reason of insanity", but the accused would be hospitalised just the same. We also noted the statutory defence of "diminished responsibility" in Chapter 9. It is only available against a charge of murder, and if it is successfully raised it only reduces the conviction from murder to manslaughter.

automatism

If the accused had no mental contact with the activities that his body has been up to then he might be classed as an "automaton" for the purpose of criminal liability. If his plea of automatism involves a disease of the mind then the M'Naghten Rules apply—it is regarded as a plea of insanity. This was recently confirmed in *R.* v. *Sullivan* (1983), where the accused attacked his victim during an epileptic fit. However, if there is no disease of the mind, if the action resulted from, say, a blow on the head (concussion), then the defence can lead to an acquittal. It relies upon the act having been involuntary. Sir Matthew Hale, a great seventeenth century lawyer, wrote:

> If there be an actual forcing of a man, as if A by force take the arm of B and the weapon in his hand, and therewith stabs C whereof he dies, this is murder in A, and B is not guilty.

Here, of course, B's act was involuntary. In a similar way, if while driving you are attacked by a swarm of bees, then your subsequent and doubtlessly frantic movements could not truly be said to be voluntary, and the consequent wreckage could be held not to have been your fault. On the other hand, if you cause damage with your car because you have fallen asleep at the wheel it might easily be regarded as having been your fault. You must have felt drowsy. You ought to have pulled over. The court held just this in *Kay* v. *Butterworth* (1945).

intoxication

Intoxication is a state of mind which can be achieved by various means: drink, drugs, etc. Voluntary or self-induced intoxication is no defence to a criminal charge in itself. However, if the intoxication gives rise to a "disease of the mind", then the M'Naghten Rules might apply. Furthermore, if the offence requires a specific intent (e.g. murder, criminal damage, theft, robbery, burglary, handling stolen goods) and if the accused was intoxicated at the time, then that state of mind will be taken into account by the court when assessing whether the necessary intention existed in him.

In *DPP* v. *Majewski* (1976) the appellant was involved in a brawl outside a public house and also assaulted police officers. In his defence he claimed he had been taking drugs and these had mixed with alcohol and he had no recollection of what had happened. The House of Lords held that unless the offence was one that required proof of specific or ulterior intent it was no defence that, by reason of self-induced intoxication, the appellant did not intend to do the act which constituted the offence.

It is clear that drink taken for "dutch courage", the ability to steel oneself to an act which would otherwise not be done, cannot be a defence. In *Attorney-General for Northern Ireland* v. *Gallagher*

(1961) the accused had decided to kill his wife. Lord Denning said:

> He bought a knife for the purpose and a bottle of whisky—either to give himself dutch courage to do the deed or to drown his conscience after it. He did in fact carry out his intention. He killed his wife with the knife and drank much of the whisky before or after he killed her . . . this case differs from all others in the books in that the respondent, whilst sane and sober, before he took to the drink, had already made up his mind to kill his wife. This seems to me to be far worse—and far more deserving of condemnation— than the case of a man who, before getting drunk, has no intention to kill, but afterwards in his cups, whilst drunk, kills another by an act which he would not dream of doing when sober. Yet, by the law of England, in this latter case his drunkenness is no defence even though it has distorted his reason and his will-power. So why should it be a defence in the present case?

Sir Matthew Hale also wrote about drunkenness:

> This vice both deprive men of the use of reason, and puts many men into a perfect, but temporary phrenzy . . . by the laws of England such a person shall have no privilege by this voluntary contracted madness, but shall have the same judgment as if he were in his right senses.

necessity

This defence might arise where the accused admits the allegedly criminal act, but claims that he did it when defending himself or his property, or in order to prevent the commission of a crime of violence against someone else.

There is very little case law on the point. The Criminal Law Act 1967 provides an excuse for the use of reasonable force in the prevention of crime or in making an arrest. Obviously the use of force on another would usually, without this "lawful excuse", be a crime. The Act says:

> s.3(1) A person may use such force as is reasonable in the circumstances in the prevention of crime, or in effecting or assisting in the lawful arrest of offenders or suspected offenders or of persons unlawfully at large.

Another occasion upon which the defence might arise is when the accused has committed an allegedly criminal act, but he has done so simply to prevent harm to himself or to another or to property— where the act prevented would not have been a crime had it happened. (Thus the reaction is not the "prevention of crime" within the 1967 Act.) It is thought that a general defence of necessity does exist in circumstances like this, but there is little evidence upon which to base such thought.

There is only one directly relevant English case, and the defence failed there. It was *R. v. Dudley and Stephens* (1884). The two accused with a cabin boy had been shipwrecked from a yacht called "Mignonette". They had been adrift in an open boat for 20 days. They had not eaten for eight days. So they ate the cabin boy. They were rescued four days later. The jury at their trial for murder thought that they would not have survived to be rescued had they not killed the boy, but the two were convicted and sentenced to death. Later their sentences were commuted to six months imprisonment. Professor Williams wrote:

> The decision cannot be considered as final authority for the proposition that in no circumstances, whatever is at stake, can life be deliberately taken.

mistake

Where the prosecution have to prove intention, recklessness or guilty knowledge in the accused as part of the alleged offence, then a mistake could be pleaded as a defence by him where it resulted in him lacking that requirement. The mistake need not be reasonable. In *D.P.P.* v. *Morgan* (1976), for example, it was held that an unreasonable but honestly held belief that a woman was consenting would be a defence to rape. Consent must be lacking, it was, but the accused was mistaken about it. The jury (or the magistrates) must be satisfied about the error. The 1976 decision was given statutory form in the Sexual Offences (Amendment) Act 1976.

If the accused is mistaken about a more general state of affairs rather than the circumstances within a single event, then his mistake will need to be reasonable if it is to excuse criminal liability. For example, in *R. v. Tolson* (1889), Mrs Tolson was charged with bigamy. Her husband had deserted her in 1881. In 1887 she went through a ceremony of marriage with another man. She honestly, reasonably but mistakenly believed that her first husband had been drowned at sea. The ship he was supposed to have been aboard, bound for America, had gone down with all hands. Had she waited just under a year the presumption of death after seven years' inexplicable absence would have protected her. As it was, the court was convinced of her good faith, and the reasonable grounds of her mistake. Her convictions was quashed on appeal.

duress

Where the accused is charged with having committed any crime except (probably) murder and (possibly) some kinds of treason, but the allegedly criminal act was committed whilst under duress, then the accused has a defence.

The threat under which he felt forced to act must have been of death or serious bodily harm. The accused must have been left no third alternative. That is, he must have been faced with either committing the allegedly criminal act or not doing so and facing the horrible consequences. So in *R. v. Hudson and Taylor* (1971) two girls were charged with perjury. They had been the principal prosecution witnesses in a "wounding" trial. The accused there was called Wright. The girls failed to identify him. He was acquitted. When tried for perjury they explained that several large men, including one called Farrell who had a reputation for violence, had approached them before the trial and promised to "cut them up" if they testified against Wright. Anxious to avoid being filleted they acceded to the request. They were convicted of perjury, but the verdict was quashed on appeal. It was thought that the defence of duress ought to be available to those who had no real choice. There had been a choice of seeking police protection here, but its potential effectiveness in all the circumstances had to be taken into account. It was an issue which ought to have been left to the jury. It had not been. The appeal was allowed.

PARTICULAR CRIMES

Theft

Having considered the broader aspects of criminal liability, we must now focus a little closer on some particular offences. Theft is defined in the Theft Act 1968, s.1(1), as follows:

> A person is guilty of theft if he dishonestly appropriates property belonging to another with the intention of permanently depriving the other of it; and "thief" and "steal" shall be construed accordingly.

We met this definition earlier in this chapter. The section continues:

> (2) It is immaterial whether the appropriation is made with a view to gain, or is made for the thief's own benefit.
> (3) The five following sections of this Act shall have effect as regards the interpretation and operation of this section (and, except as otherwise provided by this Act, shall apply only for purposes of this section).

Sections 2–6 are designed as aids to the interpretation of s.1, which contains the basic offence of theft. Section 2 expands the notion of dishonesty. It provides three "excuses" for the accused. That is, there are three possible reasons set out (the accused may think of more!) in the Act which, if believed by the jury or the magistrates (for dishonesty is a matter of fact for them to decide) will mean that the appropriation was not dishonest and theft had, therefore, not been committed.

Section 2 says:

(1) A person's appropriation of property belonging to another is not to be regarded as dishonest—

(a) if he appropriates the property in the belief that he has in law the right to deprive the other of it, on behalf of himself or of a third person; or

(b) if he appropriates the property in the belief that he would have the other's consent if the other knew of the appropriation and the circumstances of it; or

(c) (except where the property came to him as trustee or personal representative) if he appropriates the property in the belief that the person to whom the property belongs cannot be discovered by taking reasonable steps.

So, if he believes he has (a) a legal right to it (he thinks it is his bike), or (b) that the owner would not mind or (c) he finds it and cannot trace the owner, he is not dishonest, and therefore not a thief (if the jury believe his story).

However, saying that you will pay when challenged is not good enough; s.2 continues:

(2) A person's appropriation of property belonging to another may be dishonest notwithstanding that he is willing to pay for the property.

The *actus reus* of theft consists of appropriation, which means assuming the rights of an owner (selling, destroying etc.). Section 3 of the Act says:

(1) Any assumptions by a person of the rights of an owner amounts to an appropriation, and this includes, where he has come by the property (innocently or not) without stealing it, any later assumption of a right to it by keeping or dealing with it as owner.

The goods taken must be "property", but this will not usually include land; "property" does include money and "things in action".

There are proprietary interests which can only be protected by taking legal action. They cannot be seen, touched or carried away, but they do have value e.g. copyright, patents, shares. The Act says:

4(1) "Property" includes money and all other property, real or personal, including things in action and other intangible property.

(2) A person cannot steal land, or things forming part of land and severed from it by him or by his directions, except in the following cases, that is to say—

(*a*) when he is a trustee or personal representative, or is authorised by power of attorney, or as liquidator of a company, or otherwise, to sell or dispose of land belonging to another, and he appropriates the land or anything forming part of it by dealing with it in breach of the confidence reposed in him; or

(*b*) when he is not in possession of the land and appropriates anything forming part of the land by severing it or causing it to be severed, or after it has been severed; or

(*c*) when, being in possession of the land under a tenancy, he appropriates the whole or part of any fixture or structure let to be used with the land.

Wild flowers, fruit and animals are not "property" for this purpose, although there may be other offences committed by picking certain wild flowers. It is not theft, however, unless the "appropriation" is done for commercial purposes:

4(3) A person who picks mushrooms growing wild on any land, or who picks flowers, fruit or foliage from a plant growing wild on any land, does not (although not in possession of the land) steal what he picks, unless he does it for reward or for sale or other commercial purpose.

For purpose of this subsection "mushrooms" includes any fungus, and "plant" includes any shrub or tree.

(4) Wild creatures, tamed or untamed, shall be regarded as property; but a person cannot steal a wild creature not tamed nor ordinarily kept in captivity, or the carcass of any creature, unless either it has been reduced in possession by or on behalf of another person and possession of it has not been lost or abandoned, or another person is in course of reducing it into possession.

This "property" must "belong to another". It is sufficient that the other person has possession, control or any proprietary right or interest. So property can be stolen from anyone in possession or control, not just the owner.

If you "profit" by another's mistake (e.g. by being overcharged in the supermarket) you ought not to keep the cash; because the Act says, in s.5(4):

Where a person gets property by another's mistake, and is under an obligation to make restoration (in whole or in part) of the property or its proceeds or of the value thereof, then to the extent of that obligation the property or proceeds shall be regarded (as against him) as belonging to the person entitled to restoration, an intention not to make restoration shall be regarded accordingly as an intention to deprive that person of the property or proceeds.

Finally, the accused must "intend permanently to deprive" another of the property. This means that he intends to treat the property as his own, to dispose of as he chooses (selling it on, lending, destroying); the Theft Act 1968, s.6(1) says this:

A person appropriating property belonging to another without meaning the other permanently to lose the thing itself is nevertheless to be regarded as having the intention of permanently depriving the other of it if his intention is to treat the thing as his own to dispose of regardless of the other's rights; and a borrowing or lending of it may amount to so treating it if but only if, the borrowing or lending is for a period and in circumstances making it equivalent to an outright taking or disposal.

This is important in cases such as the extended "borrowing" of property which "uses it up"—like a "multiple-journey" bus ticket. I "borrow" it from you and give it back after so long (or so many journeys) that it has lost its value and despite the fact that you have it back in your hand, my activities amount to theft.

Robbery

Robbery is defined within the Theft Act 1968. Ten years' imprisonment is the maximum for theft, but it can be life for robbery, because s.8(1) says:

A person is guilty of robbery if he steals, and immediately before or at the time of doing so, and in order to do so, he uses force on any person or puts or seeks to put any person in fear of being then and there subjected to force.

All the elements of theft must be proved ("if he steals") and the force must be directed towards "the person", rather than the property being stolen, and this must be directly connected with the theft.

Burglary

Burglary is committed by trespassers. It is not "breaking and entering", neither is it confined to stealing.

The 1968 Act, s.9, says:

(1) A person is guilty of burglary if—
(a) he enters any building or part of a building as a trespasser and

with intent to commit any such offence as is mentioned in subsection (2) below; or

(b) having entered any building or part of a building as a trespasser he steals or attempts to steal anything in the building or that part of it or inflicts or attempts to inflict on any person therein any grievous bodily harm.

(2) The offences referred to in subsection (1)(a) above are offences of stealing anything in the building or part of a building in question, or inflicting on any person therein any grievous bodily harm or raping any woman therein, and of doing unlawful damage to the building or anything therein.

There is an aggravated form of burglary within the 1968 Act. Whilst 14 years' jail is the maximum for burglary, life can be given for the more serious offence; by s.10(1):

A person is guilty of aggravated burglary if he commits any burglary and at the time has with him any firearm or imitation firearm, any weapon of offence, or any explosive.

Taking motor vehicles and pedal cycles without authority

The Theft Act 1968 also contains offences short of stealing. Sometimes they are called "joy riding":

12(1) Subject to subsections (5) and (6) below, a person shall be guilty of an offence if, without having the consent of the owner or other lawful authority, he takes any conveyance for his own or another's use or, knowing that any conveyance has been taken without such authority, drives it or allows himself to be carried in or on it.

(2) A person guilty of an offence under subsection (1) above shall on conviction on indictment be liable to imprisonment for a term not exceeding three years.

. . .

(5) Subsection (1) above shall not apply in relation to pedal cycles; but, subject to subsection (6) below, a person who, without having the consent of the owner or other lawful authority, takes a pedal cycle for his own or another's use, or rides a pedal cycle knowing it to have been taken without such authority, shall on summary conviction be liable to a fine not exceeding level three on the standard scale.

(6) A person does not commit an offence under this section by anything done in the belief that he has lawful authority to do it or that he would have the owner's consent if the owner knew of his doing it and the circumstances of it.

Earlier in this chapter we considered the classification of crimes as between arrestable and non-arrestable offences. One of the qualities which can make an offence arrestable, as we saw, was that the statute creating it stipulated that it should be so, despite the sentence available to the court being less than that generally found with such offences. Section 12(1) contains arrestable offences; s.12(3) says so:

> Offences under subsection (1) above and attempts to commit them shall be deemed for all purposes to be arrestable offences within the meaning of section 2 of the Criminal Law Act 1967.

Offences involving deception in the Theft Acts

There are two sections in the 1968 Act which are directly concerned with gains by deception. There was a further Theft Act in 1978 which created three new offences out of one small part of one of the sections in the earlier Act s.16(2)(*a*), which it repealed and replaced.

The first of these sections in the 1968 Act, s.15(1), is concerned with the offence of obtaining property by deception:

> A person who by any deception dishonestly obtains property belonging to another, with the intention of permanently depriving the other of it, shall on conviction on indictment be liable to imprisonment for a term not exceeding ten years.

The Act goes on to explain what it meant by "deception", in s.15(4):

> For purposes of this section "deception" means any deception (whether deliberate or reckless) by words or conduct as to fact or as to law, including a deception as to the present intentions of the person using the deception or any other person.

An old favourite of a case on deception by conduct is *R*. v. *Barnard* (1837). It is still authoritative. The accused went into a shop in Oxford wearing academic dress, a cap and gown. He was not a member of the university, but the shopkeeper was fooled. He sold the accused goods on credit. The accused was convicted of the offence which this section of the 1968 Act replaced. The words of a judge in the case, Bolland B, are often quoted:

> If nothing had passed in words, I should have laid down that the fact of the prisoner's appearing in the cap and gown would have been pregnant evidence from which a jury should infer that he pretended he was a member of the university.

The other section in the 1968 Act involves obtaining what is called a "pecuniary advantage" by deception. Fortunately, s.16 of the Act explains:

(1) A person who by any deception dishonestly obtains for himself or another any pecuniary advantage shall on conviction on indictment be liable to imprisonment for a term not exceeding five years.

(2) The cases in which a pecuniary advantage within the meaning of this section is to be regarded as obtained for a person are cases where—

[(a) any debt or charge for which he makes himself liable or is or may become liable (including one not legally enforceable) is reduced or in whole or in part evaded or deferred; or]

(b) he is allowed to borrow by way of overdraft, or to take out any policy of insurance or annuity contract, or obtains an improvement of the terms on which he is allowed to do so; or

(c) he is given the opportunity to earn remuneration or greater remuneration in an office or employment, or to win money by betting.

(3) For purposes of this section "deception" has the same meaning as in section 15 of this Act.

Section 16(2)(a) is placed in brackets here because it was repealed and replaced by the three new offences in the Theft Act 1978. The wording as it stood had given rise to uncertainty. It was referred to as "a judicial nightmare".

The new offences are called obtaining services by deception, evasion of liability by deception and making off without payment. The 1978 Act says:

1(1) A person who by any deception dishonestly obtains services from another shall be guilty of an offence.

2(1) . . . where a person by any deception—

(a) dishonestly secures the remission of the whole or part of any existing liability to make a payment, whether his own liability or another's; or

(b) with intent to make permanent default in whole or in part on any existing liability to make a payment, or with intent to let another do so, dishonestly induces the creditor or any person claiming payment on his behalf of the creditor to wait for payment (whether or not the due date for payment is deferred) or to forgo payment; or (*c*) dishonestly obtains any exemption from or statement of liability to make a payment;

he shall be guilty of an offence.

Consider also s.3(1), which says:

A person who, knowing that payment on the spot for any goods supplied or service done is required or expected from him, dishonestly makes off without having paid as required or expected and with intent to avoid payment of the amount due shall be guilty of an offence.

So if I trick you into thinking I will pay you for painting the outside of my house I have obtained services by deception (s.1); if I use your non-transferrable membership card to get into the ground to watch a home fixture, I have dishonestly obtained exemption (s.2(1)(*c*)); if I run off with my "three number 42's" from the local Chinese "take-away", I have made off (s.3).

Blackmail

Blackmail is the stuff the movies thrive on. It has a wonderful definition in the 1968 Act; it is "an unwarranted demand with menaces", as can be seen from the statutory provisions:

21(1) A person is guilty of blackmail if, with a view to gain for himself or another or with intent to cause loss to another, he makes any unwarranted demand with menaces; and for this purpose a demand with menaces is unwarranted unless the person making it does so in belief—
(*a*) that he has reasonable grounds for making the demand; and
(*b*) that the use of menaces is a proper means of reinforcing the demand.
(2) The nature of the act or omission demanded is immaterial, and it is also immaterial whether the menaces relate to action to be taken by the person making the demand.
(3) A person guilty of blackmail shall on conviction on indictment be liable to imprisonment for a term not exceeding fourteen years.

Handling

If the accused receives stolen goods or assists in their retention, removal, disposal or realisation, he is accused of handling within the 1968 Act. Colloquially referred to as "fencing" or "receiving", it is interesting to note that it carries a heavier maximum sentence than theft itself, 14 years. The Act defines the offence; in s.22(1):

A person handles stolen goods if (otherwise than in the course of stealing) knowing or believing them to be stolen goods he dishonestly receives the goods or dishonestly undertakes or assists in their retention, removal, disposal or realisation by or for the benefit of another person, or if he arranges to do so.

Murder

We met Coke's classic definition of murder earlier in this chapter:

Murder is when a man unlawfully killeth... any reasonable creature *in rerum natura* (in being) under the King's peace with malice forethought (intent to kill or to cause grievous bodily harm), either expressed by the party, or implied by law, so as the party wounded, or hurt, etc. die of the wound, or hurt, etc. within a year and a day after the same.

From this definition there are five points to note:

(*a*) "a reasonable creature" is a human, rather than a dog or a dolphin;

(*b*) *In rerum natura* or "in being" means alive rather than, for example, unborn. There is a crime called child destruction (created by the Infant Life (Preservation) Act 1929) which is designed to protect the life of the unborn but, as they say, viable child. No conviction can be brought upon an accused who acted in good faith in order to preserve the life of the mother. Otherwise, after 28 weeks of pregnancy the child is presumed capable of being born alive. This offence overlaps, of course, with abortion—the intentional procuring of a miscarriage. There are grounds upon which an abortion can be lawful, under the Abortion Act 1967;

(*c*) "Under the King's peace"—not an enemy in wartime;

(*d*) "malice forethought"—as has been added in parentheses, this amounts to the *mens rea* for murder. The intent to kill is required, or at least the intent to cause really serious bodily harm (grievous bodily harm). In *R*. v. *Errington* (1838), for example, the accused covered a man in straw, threw hot cinders over it, and killed him. Despite the lack of evidence of intent to kill, the accused was charged with murder. There was evidence that the accused intended to cause serious bodily injury;

(*e*) "within a year and a day"—this is just a matter of causation, of establishing that it was the accused's activity which caused the death.

Since the Murder (Abolition of Death Penalty) Act 1965, the fixed penalty for murder is life imprisonment. The judge will often add his recommendations about minimum periods of servitude. This seems illogical, but the prisoner is unlikely to be given any hope of release on any basis before the expiry of this period of time.

Manslaughter

This is killing a human too, but this time without the malice aforethought required for murder. Furthermore, as we saw in Chapter 9, and earlier in this chapter, the success of a defence of diminished responsibility to a murder charge will result in a conviction for manslaughter.

Where a defence of provocation is accepted by a jury in a murder trial, their verdict will be manslaughter. The Homicide Act 1957, s.3, says:

> Where on a charge of murder there is evidence on which the jury can find that the person charged was provoked (whether by things done or by things said or by both together) to lose his self control, the question whether the provocation was enough to make a reasonable man do as he did shall be left to be determined by the jury; and in determining that question the jury shall take into account everything both done and said according to the effect which, in their opinion, it would have on a reasonable man.

A conviction for manslaughter is also the appropriate result of a trial for murder where a suicide pact (an agreement where all agreed have the urge to die), leaves a survivor who was instrumental in the death of another party to the agreement, and himself had a "settled intention of dying in pursuance of the pact" (1957 Act, s.4). Since the Suicide Act 1961, suicide itself is no longer a crime, but it is an offence to aid, abet, counsel or procure the suicide of another.

Killing as the result of an unlawful and dangerous act is unlikely to amount to murder, but it is tried as manslaughter. The dangerousness of the act is measured by the standards of a reasonable man. Would he agree that pushing supermarket trolleys off multi-storey car parks at night in virtually deserted city centres amounts to an unlawful and dangerous act? Killing through gross negligence is manslaughter too, like the signalman who forgets to close the gates. This criminal negligence must amount to a wanton disregard for others. It is more than inadvertence.

If a woman kills her baby who is less than one year old because of post-natal depression or some related cause, then the charge will probably be infanticide. If it is murder, the jury can return a verdict of infanticide—it is thus a kind of defence. Infanticide has the same extremely broad sentencing freedom as manslaughter.

Assaults and woundings

An assault comprises any intentional or reckless activity which has the effect of inducing in another the fear of immediate and unlawful personal violence.

Assault and battery are often mentioned together. A battery is the actual application of force to another. Thus, you could assault without battery, if you miss with the punch; and you could batter without assault, if you attack from behind. They are different things. Nevertheless, in criminal law contexts, the word assault is often used to include a battery.

There are some assaults which are justifiable, although for this to be so only reasonable force (in all the circumstances of the case) must have been used. They include: assault in the furtherance of legal duties, like making lawful arrests (discussed later in this chapter), the use of lawful correction, like a father smacking his son, self-defence, the defence of one's husband or wife, child or someone else who is dear to one, and the defence of property.

There are various kinds of assault. The basic offence is a common law crime—but statutes have created variations on the theme:

(*a*) *Common assault.* This is a crime under the Offences against the Person Act 1861, s.42. The individuals involved in this type of offence sometimes initiate the criminal proceedings. The police are only concerned to prevent a breach of the peace, so they will intervene.

(*b*) *Aggravated assault.* Under s.43 of the 1861 Act a common assault becomes more serious if violence is used upon a boy under 14 or any female.

(*c*) *Actual bodily harm.* Under s.47 of the 1861 Act, there is an offence where the assault interferes with the health and comfort of the victim, but falls short of grievous bodily harm.

(*d*) *Assault intending to resist arrest* is an offence under s.33 of the 1861 Act.

(*e*) *Unlawful and malicious wounding or infliction of grievous bodily harm* is an offence under s.20 of the 1861 Act, whether or not an instrument is used.

(*f*) *Grievous bodily harm* with intent under s.18 of the 1861 Act. It is an offence unlawfully and maliciously to wound, or cause grievous bodily harm to that person or to prevent or resist the lawful arrest or detention of any person.

(*g*) *Assaults on the police.* Here the Police Act 1964, s.51, applies. It creates a variety of possibilities including assault, wilful resistance and obstruction of a constable in the execution of his duty. Of more serious consequence than the assault itself is wounding the victim.

Terminology

In order to avoid doubt and confusion, we ought to look at the terminology used in these offences:

(*a*) for a "wound" the skin needs to be broken. A bruise alone will not do;

(*b*) "grievous bodily harm" means really serious bodily harm;

(*c*) "maliciously" here means either an intention to do what was done, or recklessness about it, so that the accused must have foreseen that the harm might be done, but he went ahead anyway, not caring about it. Recklessness also includes deliberately refusing to consider a risk which might well exist ("shutting one's eyes to the risk" is a commonly used expression).

Criminal damage

This is a collection of crimes against property. The law is mainly found in the Criminal Damage Act 1971. "Property" for this purpose is defined in s.10 of the 1971 Act. It includes all property of a tangible nature, whether real or personal, including money and tamed wild animals. It does not include wild flowers, fruit and fungi.

There are three main offences: destroying or damaging property, threatening to destroy or damage it and possessing anything with the intention of destroying or damaging property. The Act says:

1 (1) A person who without lawful excuse destroys or damages any property belonging to another intending to destroy or damage any such property or being reckless as to whether any such property would be destroyed or damaged shall be guilty of an offence.

(2) A person who without lawful excuse destroys or damages any property, whether belonging to himself or another—

(*a*) intending to destroy or damage any property or being reckless as to whether any property would be destroyed or damaged, and

(*b*) intending by the destruction or damage to endanger the life of another or being reckless as to whether the life of another would be thereby endangered

shall be guilty of an offence.

(3) An offence committed under this section by destroying or damaging property by fire shall be charged as arson.

2 A person who without lawful excuse makes to another a threat, intending that the other would fear it would be carried out:

(*a*) to destroy or damage any property belonging to that other or a third person, or

(*b*) to destroy or damage his own property in a way which he knows is likely to endanger the life of that other or a third person,
shall be guilty of an offence.

3 A person who has anything in his custody or under his control intending without lawful excuse to use it or cause or permit another to use it:

(*a*) to destroy or damage any property belonging to some other person, or

(*b*) to destroy or damage his own or the user's property in a way he knows is likely to endanger the life of some other person, shall be guilty of an offence.

CONSUMERS AND THE CRIMINAL LAW

Since the nineteenth century the criminal law has attempted to protect consumers by imposing sanctions for the breach of statutory obligations placed upon manufacturers and retailers. These obligations cover a wide range of activities, from maintaining high standards of public safety and hygiene to ensuring that weighing and measuring equipment for the sale of goods (e.g. petrol pumps), is accurate. Liability for these offences is usually strict, with no need to prove *mens rea* before the accused can be convicted. Prosecutions are normally brought by public officials, e.g. environmental health officers or trading standards officers, employed by local authorities. These prosecutions often arise from routine checks carried out by the officers or from complaints from consumers. Although the outcome of a successful prosecution is usually a fine, the criminal court may award compensation to the consumer for any personal injury, loss or damage resulting from the offence (Powers of Criminal Courts Act 1973, s.35). It should also be borne in mind that consumer protection may be afforded by the criminal law in an indirect way e.g. imposing sanctions under the Theft Act 1968 for deception practised on a consumer. The following four sections deal with statutes that are of particular importance in protecting the consumer.

The Trade Descriptions Acts 1968 and 1972

It is an offence under the 1968 Act for any person, in the course of trade or business:

(*a*) to apply a false trade description to goods (s.1); or

(*b*) to supply, or offer to supply, goods with such a description (s.1); or

(*c*) to give a false indication as to the price of goods (s.11); or

(*d*) knowingly or recklessly to make a false statement as to the provision of any services, accommodation or facilities (s.14). (This offence, unlike the others, is not an offence of strict liability.)

Under the 1972 Act it is an offence if, in the course of trade or business, a person supplies or offers to supply goods manufactured outside the UK which have a name or mark likely to be taken as a UK name or mark.

For the avoidance of doubt, we will look a little more closely at some of this terminology.

False trade description

A trade description is an indication of any of the following:

(*a*) quantity, size or gauge;

(*b*) method of manufacture, production etc.;

(*c*) composition;

(*d*) fitness for purpose, strength, performance, behaviour or accuracy;

(*e*) physical characteristics not included above;

(*f*) testing and the results thereof;

(*g*) approval by any person or conformity with an approved type;

(*h*) place or date of manufacture, production etc.;

(*i*) person by whom manufactured, produced etc.;

(*j*) other history, including previous ownership or use.

The description must be "false to a material degree". This means that it must have been capable of inducing the sale or supply of the goods. The meaning to be attributed to the description is essentially decided by considering its likely effect on the ordinary man, e.g. a "beautiful" car has been held to indicate both its appearance and its running order.

The indication of the above matters may be either direct or indirect, and by any means. Thus oral representations, advertisements, mileometer readings, etc. are all capable of being trade descriptions.

Sale or supply

The offence under s.1 of the 1968 Act is committed either by applying the false trade description of goods, or supplying, or offering to supply, goods to which such a description has been applied. Thus, if a manufacturer applies a label describing his sweaters as "all wool" and this is untrue, both he and the retailer who sells these sweaters still bearing this label commit an offence. Even if the sweaters were not sold but merely displayed in the retailer's shop there would be liability, as exposing goods for supply is deemed by the Act to be an "offer" to supply (s.6); it is not an invitation to treat as in the law of contract (*see* Chapter 13).

False indications as to price

Section 11 creates three offences relating to the pricing of goods where the supplier in commercial transactions falsely indicates that the price:

(*a*) equals or is less than the recommended price;

(*b*) is less than the price at which he previously offered the goods; or

(*c*) is less than the price actually charged.

In order to secure a conviction under (*b*) the prosecution will have to show that the goods have not been displayed for sale at the higher price for a continuous period of at least 28 days during the preceding six months. As the Act does not require the higher priced offer to have been made at the same shop, there will be no offence if it has been made at only one of many branch stores of a large retail chain.

This section does not cover certain other misleading trade practices in relation to pricing. For example, it does not prevent a trader comparing his price with the goods' value, the price charged "elsewhere" or by another specified person. (The first two are now crimes by virtue of the Price Marking (Bargain Offers) Order 1979, made under the Prices Act 1974.)

False statements as to services

There can be no liability under the Act of 1968, s.14 unless, at the time the statement was made, it was false and the defendant knew it, or was reckless whether it was false. Therefore a holiday brochure published at a time when the services advertised do not exist is an offence, as is confirmation of an airline reservation when no seat was available owing to the airline's overbooking policy (this actually happened in *Taylor* v. *British Airways Board* (1976)).

The section does not apply to promises about future services only.

Defences

A person will have a defence to a charge under ss.1 and 11 if he indicates by a disclaimer that the consumer should place no reliance on the trade description, e.g. a notice stating that the reading on a car's mileometer should not be taken as indicating its true mileage. It is also a defence to a charge of supplying goods with a false trade description for the defendant to show that he did not know, and could not with reasonable diligence have ascertained, that the goods did not conform to the description or that the description had been applied to them. As regards s.14 a trader will have a defence if he neither possessed the required knowledge nor was reckless at the time of the alleged offence.

In addition to these defences there is a defence of general application contained in s.24. Under this section the trader can defend himself if *he* can prove that the offence was caused by:

(*a*) his mistake; or

(*b*) reliance on information supplied to him; or

(*c*) the act or default of another person; or

(*d*) an accident; or

(*e*) some other cause beyond his control, AND in any event that he took all reasonable precautions and exercised all due diligence to avoid the commission of the offence by himself or any person under his control.

The Unsolicited Goods and Services Act 1971

We met this statute in Chapter 13, when considering the rules about communication of acceptance in the formation of contracts. This statute is designed to prevent inertia selling, i.e. unordered goods sent to the consumer with the implication that he is expected to pay for them. The Act provides that six months after such receipt the goods are deemed to belong unconditionally to the recipient. If the recipient does not want to wait six months, he may send a written notice to the sender asking him to remove the goods. If 30 days elapse and the goods are not removed, they belong to the recipient.

The Act also contains criminal sanctions which are confined to persons acting in the course of a trade or business. It is an offence for such persons to demand payment for unsolicited goods without reasonably believing in a right to payment. In such cases it is also an offence:

(*a*) to assert a right to payment; or

(*b*) to threaten legal proceedings; or

(*c*) to place, or threaten to place, the consumer's name on a default list; or

(*d*) to invoke, or threaten to invoke, any other collection procedure.

The Fair Trading Act 1973

This Act created the post of Director General of Fair Trading and gave him wide powers to prevent, by way of statutory order, undesirable consumer trade practices. Any breach of such an order will be a crime and the approach under the Act to both liability and defences is very similar to that contained in the Trade Descriptions Act 1968 (above).

The Director is also required to perform a number of other functions, including, for example, the administration of the licensing system created by the Consumer Credit Act 1974.

The Consumer Safety Act 1978

This Act empowers the Secretary of State to make regulations concerning the safe design, construction, manufacture, assembly and packaging of products. Its aim is to try to ensure that consumer products are designed and built to high safety standards e.g. that electrical appliances do not electrocute consumers.

The marketing of unsafe products may be prevented by the Secretary of State issuing:

(*a*) a prohibition order, which is a general ban on all traders from supplying specified unsafe goods;

(*b*) a prohibition notice, which is a particular ban relating only to the trader upon whom it is served;

(*c*) a notice to warn, which applies to the particular trader served and, unlike the above, concerns goods which he has already supplied. The notice can require the trader to publish a warning about unsafe products, e.g. an advertisement warning purchasers of a particular make of car that it has defective brakes which should be checked by the dealer.

Contravention of safety regulations, a prohibition order or notice, and a notice to warn is a crime.

This Act is unusual among the criminal statutes giving consumer protection, in that it confers a specific civil remedy on an injured party. Thus he may bring an action for damages against a trader who has infringed a safety regulation or a prohibition order. There is no need to prove negligence and the right of action cannot be excluded by any exemption clause.

CRIMINAL LAW ARREST

An arrest is the taking or restraining of a person, depriving him of his liberty, so that he is available to answer an accusation of crime. We met the definition of arrestable offences earlier in this chapter, when classifying crimes as between them and non-arrestable offences. To recap, the Criminal Law Act 1967 says that

an arrestable offence is one for which the sentence is fixed by law, or for which a person (not previously convicted) may under or by virtue of any enactment be sentenced to imprisonment for a term of five years, and attempts to commit any such offence.

To these must be added those which are arrestable because the statute which created them says so. We noted that this was the case with the crime of taking a motor vehicle without authority within the Theft Act 1968, s.12.

The power to make an arrest is also conferred by the 1967 Act. It is very important to distinguish the powers that everybody ("any person") has from those which are only conferred on the police ("a constable"). People such as store detectives have no special powers to arrest those they suspect. The Act says that

Any person may arrest without warrant:

(*a*) Any person who is, or whom he with reasonable cause suspects to be in the act of committing an arrestable offence; and

(*b*) where an arrestable offence has been committed, any person who is, or whom he with reasonable cause suspects to be, guilty of the offence.

In addition to the above powers a constable may arrest without warrant:

(*a*) when he, with reasonable cause, suspects that an arrestable offence has been committed and he, with reasonable cause suspects any person to be guilty of it;

(*b*) any person who is, or whom he, with reasonable cause suspects to be, about to commit an arrestable offence.

For the purpose of arresting a person under any power as above, a constable may enter (if need be by force) and search any place where that person is, or where the constable with reasonable cause suspects him to be.

In order to give an idea of the sort of offences which come within the category of arrestable offences, here is a list of a few of them:

abduction of women by force (Sexual Offences Act 1956);
abstracting electricity (Theft Act 1968);
aiding and abetting the suicide of another (Suicide Act 1961);
assault occasioning actual bodily harm (Offences against the Person Act 1861);
blackmail (Theft Act 1968);
burglary (Theft Act 1968);
criminal damage (Criminal Damage Act 1971);
criminal deception (Theft Act 1968);
criminal use and possession of firearms (Firearms Act 1968);
death by reckless driving (Road Traffic Act 1972);
false accounting (Theft Act 1968);
forgery (Forgery and Counterfeiting Act 1981);
handling stolen goods (Theft Act 1968);
indecent assault on any female under 13 (Sexual Offences Act 1956);
indecent assault on any male (Sexual Offences Act 1956);
living on the earnings of prostitution (Sexual Offences Act 1956);
manslaughter (common law);
murder (common law);
perjury (Perjury Act 1911);
rape (Sexual Offences Act 1956);

robbery (Theft Act 1968);
taking a conveyance without authority (Theft Act 1968);
theft (Theft Act 1968);
unlawful sexual intercourse with any female under 13 (Sexual Offences Act 1956);
woundings (Offences against the Person Act 1861).

Apart from these statutory powers, there is a power at common law for anyone to arrest anyone found committing a breach of the peace, or to prevent an immediate renewal of a breach of the peace.

Bail

Once a person has been deprived of his liberty, the question arises whether he should be detained. He may be released on bail before trial (*see* Chapter 7) or before committal for trial (*see* Chapter 4), by the police or by the magistrates or by the Crown Court.

"Bail" used to mean the security put up by a third party (called a surety) to ensure that the accused turned up at the court. However, under the Bail Act 1976, bail is now granted direct to a person under arrest or in custody and who is to be released for the time being. He is then under a duty to present himself when required. Should security be required from someone else, it is called a recognisance.

Under the Magistrates' Courts Act 1980, if the accused was arrested under a warrant issued by a magistrate, bail will be granted by the police only if the warrant is "endorsed for bail" (sometimes called "backed for" bail). Conditions can be attached (e.g. the provision of sureties). If he was arrested without warrant (e.g. for an arrestable offence) then the police can grant bail. The accused must then turn up at the court when required. If the offence is not serious and the accused cannot be brought before a magistrates' court as soon as practicable and normally at least within 24 hours, he ought to be granted bail. The police might require one or more sureties; since they cannot order this, any case where this is wanted must be brought to the magistrates.

Once before the magistrates, the accused could be released on bail if the hearing is adjourned, or if he is committed for trial or sentence (but release on bail pending sentence at the Crown Court is exceptionally rare). The prosecution can object to bail being granted. If the defendant is refused bail he can apply for it to a High Court judge or to the Crown Court.

The Bail Act 1976 has created a presumption in favour of bail. It should be granted. Naturally, there are instances where it will not be appropriate. If the offence charged is imprisonable, bail may be refused if the court believes that the accused, if released, would fail to appear as required, or might commit another offence, or intimidate witnesses, or that he ought to be detained for his own protection or welfare, or if the court requires reports about him which can only be prepared if he is in custody. If the offence is not imprisonable the grounds for refusal are much narrower. Bail will be granted unless the court believes the accused will not show up at court.

A defendant who has been granted bail but fails to turn up at the court when required to do so may have committed the offence of "absconding". He can therefore expect to be immediately arrested and tried for both offences!

Sureties may be required—and the court can decide upon both their financial resources and suitability. There is an offence committed by anyone who agrees to indemnify a surety: that is, a person who agrees to pay the surety back for any loss he might sustain in losing the recognisance (money) he put up to secure the grant of bail to the accused.

Chapter 15

Family Law

MARRIAGE

Getting engaged

"Will you marry me?" said the lovelorn lad; "Yes", she said. It is an agreement, but it is not a contract. Neither can sue the other for breach of promise of marriage—not since the Law Reform (Miscellaneous Provisions) Act 1970, s.1(1), which provides:

> an agreement between two persons to marry one another shall not under the law of England and Wales have effect as a contract giving rise to legal rights and no action shall lie in England and Wales for breach of such an agreement, whatever the law applicable to the agreement.

Of course, the problems may not end there. The couple might have started buying essentials for the home (e.g. sheets, microwave oven) and there remains the question of the ring. Property issues should be solved informally when the couple split up. If the engagement was formal, however, it might be that a certain formality is appropriate. The law provides the same mechanisms as are used between a husband and wife to ascertain the rights over individual items of property. The ring stays with the lady, unless it was given conditionally on the wedding (which is not likely and would be very difficult to prove). It is a rebuttable presumption that an engagement ring was an absolute gift.

Just living together

Apart from whatever moral standpoint which might seem appropriate to the couple and those close to them, the law distinguishes between married and unmarried couples living together. For example, the man is under no duty to support his girlfriend, only his wife—unless they have children, then he has to support them all.

Children born to unmarried parents are, of course, illegitimate. This affects the issue of custody if the couple split up. If they were married the court will choose the more appropriate parent; usually the mother but neither has a better right to custody before the order is made. With illegitimate children the mother has the basic right to custody and the father would need to apply to a court for custody or access. Illegitimate children cannot inherit from relatives, other than their parents, within the intestacy rules. The unmarried woman cannot inherit from her man either under those rules, although she could claim from his estate as a dependant.

Unless the house is in joint names, or the woman has materially contributed towards it (or if it is protected under the Rent Acts), she has no right to remain in a house owned or rented by her man. The wife is far better protected. Finally, many social security benefits are not available to the unmarried (e.g. widows' benefits), but supplementary benefit or family income supplement can be claimed.

Generally, though, the law is moving towards a recognition that people choose not to marry and yet achieve very stable relationships. The distinctions are fading.

The requirements

The classic definition of marriage is that of Lord Penzance (in *Hyde* v. *Hyde* (1866)):

> I conceive that marriage as understood in Christendom, may ... be defined as the voluntary union for life of one man and one woman to the exclusion of all others.

So marriage in England is monogamous (one spouse only), and it is intended by both parties, at the time it takes place, to last for life. Anything else is not recognised as a marriage, if it is made in England. We considered the concept of domicile in Chapter 9. Broadly; it involves the link of an individual with a particular legal system. Nobody domiciled in England can make a valid marriage anywhere, unless it meet Lord Penzance's definition.

Furthermore the parties to the marriage must have the necessary legal capacity. Age is crucial. Before 1929 a boy could marry at 14, a girl at 12, but the Age of Marriage Act 1929 raised the age to 16 for both. Between the ages of 16 and 18 everybody (except a widow or widower) requires consent to marry. Often it is stated that parental consent is needed, and if refused a court can give it. However, it may not be so simple (one may perhaps not have any parents!). The person whose consent is required can be found by examining the Marriage Act 1949, Sched. 2:

CONSENT REQUIRED TO THE MARRIAGE OF AN INFANT BY COMMON LICENCE
OR SUPERINTENDENT REGISTRAR'S CERTIFICATE
I. WHERE THE INFANT IS LEGITIMATE

Circumstances	Person or Persons whose consent is required
1. Where both parents are living:	
(a) if the parents are living together;	Both parents.
(b) if the parents are divorced or separated by order of any court or by agreement;	The parent to whom the custody of the infant is committed by order of the court or by the agreement, or, if the custody of the infant is so committed to one parent during part of the year and to the other parent during the rest of the year, both parents.
(c) if one parent has been deserted by the other;	The parent who has been deserted.
(d) if both parents have been deprived of custody of infant by order of any court.	The person to whose custody the infant is committed by order of the court.
2. Where one parent is dead:	The surviving parent.
(a) if there is no other guardian;	The surviving parent and the guardian if acting jointly or the surviving parent or the guardian if the parent or guardian is the sole guardian of the infant.
(b) if a guardian has been appointed by the deceased parent (or by the court under the Guardianship of Minors Act 1971, s.3).	
3. Where both parents are dead.	The guardian or guardians appointed by the deceased parents or by the court under the Guardianship of Minors Act 1971, ss. 3 or 5.

II. WHERE THE INFANT IS ILLEGITIMATE

Circumstances	Person whose consent is required
If the mother of the infant is alive.	The mother, or if she has by order of any court been deprived of the custody of the infant, the person to whom the custody of the infant has been committed by order of the court.

If the mother of the infant is dead.	The guardian appointed by the mother.

If the consent is refused then the court can be approached. The usual court is the magistrates', although the High Court and county courts also have jurisdiction. The parties attend at the magistrates' domestic court. The public are excluded, the powers of the press are restricted. There are three justices usually and there should be a man and a woman deciding the case. Everybody involved is given notice of the hearing. There is a case that says there is no appeal, but it is probably no longer a reliable authority.

It may be an exaggeration to describe parental consent as a requirement for marriage, because the absence of it does not invalidate the marriage. The parties are married—but there must have been fraud of some kind (forged documents etc.) so they can expect trouble.

Apart from considerations of age, there is a requirement for a valid marriage that the parties are not too closely related to each other already. This could be a relationship by blood or marriage. The restrictions are called the prohibited degrees of kindred and affinity. A marriage within the prohibited degrees is void. They are set out in the Marriage Act 1949, Sched. 1. There is a list of those people a man cannot marry and beside it one restricting women:

PROHIBITED DEGREES OF RELATIONSHIP

Mother (adoptive mother or former adoptive mother);	Father (adoptive father or former adoptive father);
Daughter (adoptive daughter or former adoptive daughter);	Son (adoptive son or former adoptive son);
Father's mother;	Father's father;
Mother's mother;	Mother's father;
Son's daughter;	Son's son;
Daughter's daughter;	Daughter's son;
Sister;	Brother;
Wife's mother;	Husband's father;
Wife's daughter;	Husband's son;
Father's wife;	Mother's husband;
Son's wife;	Daughter's husband;
Father's father's wife;	Father's mother's husband;
Mother's father's wife;	Mother's mother's husband;
Wife's father's mother;	Husband's father's father;
Wife's mother's mother;	Husband's mother's father;
Wife's son's daughter;	Husband's son's son;
Wife's daughter's daughter;	Husband's daughter's son;

Son's son's wife;	Son's daughter's husband;
Daughter's son's wife;	Daughter's daughter's husband;
Father's sister;	Father's brother;
Mother's sister;	Mother's brother;
Brother's daughter;	Brother's son;
Sister's daughter.	Sister's son.

It is a fairly obvious requirement of the parties to a marriage that they are not already married to someone else. If either is already married then the second marriage is void and the crime of bigamy may have been committed (contrary to the Offences against the Person Act 1861, s.57). The maximum punishment is seven years' imprisonment. However, if the alleged bigamist believed in good faith, and on reasonable grounds, that his first marriage had been dissolved, or annulled, or that his first wife was dead, but he was wrong, this belief might constitute a good defence. In *R.* v. *Tolson* (1889) Mrs Tolson was deserted by her husband in 1881 and she believed he was drowned. She re-married in 1887. Even though her first husband re-appeared it was held that she was not guilty of bigamy since she had reasonable grounds for believing he was dead.

If his wife had been continuously absent for seven years, and if he had no cause to believe that she was still alive, then an application could be made to the court for a decree called a presumption of death and dissolution of marriage (under the Matrimonial Causes Act 1973, s.19). With one of these the second marriage would be valid, even if the first wife did turn up, and bigamy would not have been committed.

The formalities

The precise arrangements will depend upon whether the couples are to be married in accordance with the rites of the Church of England, or on the authority of a superintendent registrar's certificate.

FORMALITIES

Church of England weddings

Before the ceremony of marriage one possible course is for banns to be read in the church which is the usual place of worship of the parties. This is done three times, and consists of an announcement of the forthcoming wedding and an instruction to the congregation that if any of them knows of a cause or just impediment to the marriage "ye are to declare it".

If banns are not read, a common licence could be issued by or on behalf of a bishop. The couple swear that no impediment exists. They can then marry in a church or chapel in the area either of them has lived in for the previous 15 days.

A further option is for a superintendent registrar's certificate to be issued, allowing (subject to the agreement of the clergy) the marriage in either party's local church. The residence requirement is only seven days, but before the certificate is issued, there must be a notice of marriage written into a book which is open to public inspection, and left there for 21 days. Again, the parties make a solemn declaration about lack of impediment.

The final possibility is the special licence which is issued by or on behalf of the Archbishop of Canterbury. If granted, a wedding can take place immediately and anywhere. This power comes from the Ecclesiastical Licences Act 1533.

The ceremony itself is laid down in the Book of Common Prayer or in the Alternative Services Book. Two witnesses must be present, apart from the clergyman.

Weddings with a superintendent registrar's certificate

If it is not to be a Church of England wedding, the parties need a certificate. Notice must be given to the local superintendent registrar, and the solemn declaration of no impediment is made. With a certificate the couple can be married in a registered building (i.e. registered as suitable by the Registrar General) by a registrar or another authorised person (usually the appropriate minister of the chosen religion). A solemn declaration of no impediment must be included in the ceremony somewhere.

Alternatively, with a certificate, the wedding could take place in a register office (office of the superintendent registrar). Weddings in registered buildings and register offices must have at least two witnesses and take place between 8 am and 6 pm. The doors must be left open while the ceremony is conducted.

A certificate will also permit a wedding in accordance with the customs of the Society of Friends (Quakers) or those of the Jewish faith. These can be behind closed doors, at any time and without witnesses.

Where the circumstances are extraordinary (e.g. deathbed marriages), the Registrar General can issue a licence for a wedding somewhere other than a registered building or a register office.

VOID AND VOIDABLE MARRIAGES

A void marriage is one which never happened. There was such a serious defect in the circumstances that the marriage never took effect. In a sense, therefore, it is not a variety of marriage at all. There is no need to ask a court for a decree of nullity, although if the circumstances are disputed, then the court will settle the matter.

The Matrimonial Causes Act 1973, s.11, sets out the defects which are regarded as sufficiently serious to render the marriage void—to prevent it happening at all:

A marriage celebrated after 31st July 1971 shall be void on the following grounds only, that is to say—

(*a*) that it is not a valid marriage under the provisions of the Marriages Acts 1949 to 1970 (that is to say where—
  (i) the parties are within the prohibited degrees of relationship;
  (ii) the parties have intermarried in disregard of certain requirements as to the formation of marriage);

(*b*) that at the time of the marriage either party was already lawfully married;

(*c*) that the parties are not respectively male and female;

(*d*) in the case of a polygamous marriage entered into outside England and Wales, that either party was at the time of the marriage domiciled in England and Wales.

We have examined these points already in this chapter.

A voidable marriage, on the other hand, is valid. It will remain so until it is annulled by a court at the request of one (or both) of the parties. Such a request must be based on one (or more) particular grounds. It is not a divorce. It is a request for annullment. The 1973 Act lists these grounds as well in s.12:

A marriage celebrated after 31st July 1971 shall be voidable on the following grounds only, that is to say—

(*a*) that the marriage has not been consummated owing to the incapacity of either party to consummate it;

(*b*) that the marriage has not been consummated owing to the wilful refusal of the respondent to consummate it;

(*c*) that either party to the marriage did not validly consent to it, whether in consequence of duress, mistake, unsoundness of mind or otherwise;

(*d*) that at the time of the marriage either party, though capable of giving a valid consent, was suffering (whether continuously or intermittently) from mental disorder within the meaning of the Mental Health Act 1983 of such a kind or to such an extent as to be unfitted for marriage;

(*e*) that at the time of the marriage the respondent was suffering from venereal disease in a communicable form;

(*f*) that at the time of the marriage the respondent was pregnant by some person other than the petitioner.

These grounds are fairly self-explanatory. Cases (*a*) and (*b*) mean that sexual intercourse has not taken place because one or other party cannot or will not participate. Case (*c*) involves duress of some kind that amounts to fear for your life, your limbs or your liberty; any mistake relied on must be fundamental (e.g. about the nature of the ceremony or its implications) not just about a person's bank balance or job prospects, and unsoundness of mind might be illness or incapacity through drink or drugs. In connection with case (d) it will be recalled that we considered marriage and the mentally disordered in Chapter 9. Cases (e) and (f) speak for themselves.

Applications for decrees of nullity are heard by the courts which deal with divorce petitions. The procedure is similar, and the powers with regard to ordering for financial provision are the same.

MARRIED COUPLES: DUTIES TOWARDS EACH OTHER

Cohabitation

Married couples vary, of course, but broadly getting married gives both people the "right" to each other's company. This includes a sexual aspect to their relationship, but there is no way of enforcing the rights involved in cohabitation—which are referred to as "consortium". The loss of consortium might amount to desertion, and therefore trigger off other rights. We will consider them later in this chapter.

Maintenance

According to the common law a man is bound to maintain his wife, but she is not bound to maintain him. His duty lapses if she deserts him, or the marriage is dissolved or annulled. Her adultery used to be a bar to maintenance, but (since the Domestic Proceedings and Magistrates' Court Act 1978) it is now treated as "conduct to be taken into consideration by the court" if she applies for an order for maintenance. Fortunately, legislation (the Matrimonial Causes Act 1973) now imposes a duty on the wife to maintain her husband where the circumstances require it.

The magistrates' courts have the jurisdiction to order that maintenance be paid. (We will examine this later in this chapter.) Payments ordered after the couple have formally split up are also called maintenance. Until it was abolished in 1970, the wife had the power to pledge her husband's credit with traders for necessaries—food, clothing, medical and legal expenses etc. There survives still a common household agency presumption—that she can pledge his credit for household necessities—but the husband can revoke this by telling the tradesmen concerned.

Legal relationships

It is possible for the couple to enter into legal relationships, e.g. to make a binding contract—although the courts presume against it. Either partner can institute criminal proceedings against the other. They can sue each other in tort but may be stopped from going past the opening stages of the case if the court thinks the action cannot be justified. Rights in succession law will be examined in Chapter 16.

MARRIED COUPLES: DUTIES TOWARDS THE CHILDREN

The duty to educate

This extends from the age of 5 to 16. The duty is imposed upon parents, guardians and anyone else "in possession" of the child. The child must receive efficient full time education, suitable to his age, ability and aptitude—so schools are not essential provided the duty can be satisfied at home. If the local authority is not satisfied it may make an attendance order. Ignoring it is a crime, and the "custodians" of the child may be brought before the local magistrates. Furthermore, there is a duty to ensure regular attendance at school. Prolonged, repeated and unjustified absences show breach of the duty, which is also an offence. If the local authority cannot obtain compliance from the custodians the child will be taken into the authority's care (by use of care proceedings at the magistrates' court), and the parental powers pass to the local authority. (Note also that the local authority has the power to make a resolution vesting all parental rights in itself with regard to a particular child in certain circumstances.)

The duty to maintain

This is the duty to provide adequate food, clothing and shelter, if necessary by means of social security benefits. Neglect is a criminal offence, and can also lead to care proceedings. Parents in difficulty can request that the local authority take the child into care. There may be a requirement of financial contribution—but it will not exceed the boarding-out allowance paid to foster parents, no matter what the true costs may be.

The magistrates have the power to order that payments be made to maintain children, regardless of whether they are also considering the question of custody, or of affiliation (naming the father of an illegitimate child).

The duty to protect

This varies with the age of the child. The criminal law provides that it is an offence to do the following: (a) leave a child under 12 in a room with an unguarded fire (if death or serious injury results);

(*b*) allow a child under 16 to train for dangerous performances;

(*c*) give intoxicating liquid to a child under five;

(*d*) be found drunk in a public place whilst in charge of a child under seven;

(*e*) be involved in the seduction or prostitution of a daughter under 16; or

(*f*) leave a child with a baby-sitter who is too young or with an unregistered child-minder.

There are many others.

As far as the civil (i.e. non-criminal) law is concerned, it is possible for a child to sue his parents for compensation if he is injured through their neglect.

Of course, if the local authority is not satisfied with the treatment of a child, care proceedings can be instituted.

ENDING THE MARRIAGE: OR NOT

Marriages do not always continue "till death doth them part". If the marriage was voidable (seen earlier in this chapter) and the right to avoid has been exercised, it is over. If the couple want to split up but not formally end the marriage, a separation, or maintenance agreement can be made, or a matrimonial order, or a petition can be brought for judicial separation. If the parties are to be freed to remarry, divorce is necessary.

Separation agreements

The couple may agree to live apart so that they are free from the duty to cohabit. The point of a formal agreement is to settle the issues of property ownership, custody of the children, access to them for the other party and some provision for maintenance. A maintenance agreement is made where both parties have not agreed to separate but one wishes to leave the other. If a separation agreement is made, then desertion cannot be the ground selected for a later divorce. Often separation agreements are put into a deed—the most formal of legal transactions. This is done to provide concrete evidence of the terms of the agreement.

Matrimonial orders

These are available from the magistrates' courts and many county courts (those which have been designated divorce county courts by the Lord Chancellor).

A matrimonial order can be obtained on one of four grounds specified in the Domestic Proceedings and Magistrates' Courts Act 1978. These are that the party complained of (usually the husband):

(*a*) has failed to provide reasonable maintenance for the applicant; or

(*b*) has failed to provide or make a proper contribution towards reasonable maintenance for any child of the family; or

(*c*) has behaved in such a way that the applicant cannot reasonably be expected to live with him (called the respondent); or

(*d*) has deserted the applicant.

Orders can be made for periodic payments or lump sums (which are subject to a £500 upper limit).

Judicial separation

This order can be obtained from the Family Division of the High Court, or, in undefended cases, from a divorce county court. An important distinction between applying for judicial separation and petitioning for divorce, is that a petition for judicial separation may be made at any time after the marriage, whereas a divorce petition usually has to wait for three years from the date of the marriage. These orders are quite rare. Their main purpose is to provide for parties who do not agree with divorce but who need to separate and to settle their affairs as well as the division of the matrimonial property and/or obtain a larger provision for maintenance and resettlement of larger (capital) sums that could be obtained from the magistrates. Of course, the marriage survives a judicial separation. The parties cannot remarry without a divorce. Indeed, there may be religious reasons why a divorce cannot be petitioned for, but equally good reasons why the parties should be allowed to split up. Judicial separation can also pave the way for a divorce once the three year initial prohibition on divorce petitions has expired.

In order to obtain a judicial separation the applicant will need to establish one of the following: adultery, unreasonable behaviour, desertion for at least two years; living apart for at least two years and the other party's consent, or living apart for five years (even if one party refuses consent). These are the same factors which influence the court into granting a divorce, but an important difference is that the court need not be satisfied of the irretrievable breakdown of the marriage, as it must be before a divorce can be granted.

The judicial separation will not be granted until the court is satisfied with the arrangements for the welfare of the children. The same powers exist for financial provision as for divorce. The order can be rescinded if the couple get back together.

Divorce

A petition for divorce cannot be presented within the first three years of marriage unless there is evidence to satisfy the court of exceptional hardship suffered by the petitioner or the exceptional depravity of the other party (the respondent). These cases are not common, but include sexual perversion, prostitution or other unreasonable behaviour which causes grave injury to health or perhaps danger to life itself. Anyway, the judge would need to be satisfied about the arrangements for the welfare of any children involved, and of the lack of hope of reconciliation—because this "three year rule" is designed to give the marriage a chance to work.

If the petitioner cannot obtain a divorce on this basis then an application for judicial separation could be made, where there is no "three year rule".

Divorce: the only ground
Since the Divorce Reform Act 1969 came into force on 1st January 1971, there has been only one ground for divorce: irretrievable breakdown of marriage. There are five facts, "proof of any of which could satisfy the court that the marriage has broken down irretrievably" (but even if one or more of them can be proved the court, weighing the evidence as a whole, might find that it has not). These five facts are to be found in the consolidating statute, the Matrimonial Causes Act 1973:

(1) A petition for divorce may be presented to the court by either party to a marriage on the ground that the marriage has broken down irretrievably.

(2) The court hearing a petition for divorce shall not hold the marriage to have broken down irretrievably unless the petitioner satifies the court of one or more of the following facts, that is to say—

(*a*) that the respondent has committed adultery and the petitioner finds it intolerable to live with the respondent;

(*b*) that the respondent has behaved in such a way that the petitioner cannot reasonably be expected to live with the respondent;

(*c*) that the respondent has deserted the petitioner for a continuous period of at least two years immediately preceding the presentation of the petition;

(*d*) that the parties to the marriage have lived apart for a continuous period of at least two years immediately preceding the presentation of the petition (hereafter in this Act referred to as "two years' separation") and the respondent consents to a decree being granted;

(*e*) that the parties to the marriage have lived apart for a continuous period of at least five years immediately preceding the presentation of the petition (hereafter in this Act referred to as "five years' separation").

(3) On a petition for divorce it shall be the duty of the court to inquire, so far as it reasonably can, into the facts alleged by the petitioner and into any facts alleged by the respondent.

(4) If the court is satisfied on the evidence of any such fact as is mentioned in subsection (2) above, then, unless it is satisfied on all the evidence that the marriage has not broken down irretrievably, it shall grant a decree of divorce.

IRRETRIEVABLE BREAKDOWN: THE "FIVE FACTS"

Adultery

This is voluntary sexual intercourse between someone who is married and someone of the opposite sex other than the marriage partner. A raped woman has not committed adultery, but a man who committed rape has. Curiously, it is not required that the fact of adultery should make it intolerable for the innocent party to carry on living together with the one who has committed adultery (*Cleary* v. *Cleary* (1974)). If the "other person" can be named he or she should (normally) be made a party to the proceedings (the co-respondent).

Unreasonable behaviour

Each case is examined on its merits, but the behaviour must have been such as to cause the marriage to break down. Supporting evidence from friends, doctors, psychiatrists and so on would help establish that the petitioner cannot reasonably be expected to carry on living with the respondent.

Desertion

This is one partner leaving, against the wishes of the other. It must have lasted at least two years before the petition is filed at the court. The deserted partner can petition without the other partner's consent. The two years must be continuous but, illogically, it can be interrupted by up to six months together although these months do not count towards the 24. (This applies to the "living apart" rules too.)

Living apart for two years

Both must agree to the divorce for the petition to be successful. They could live under the same roof, but separately (e.g. by not sharing meals).

Living apart for five years

There is no need for both parties to agree, but the respondent could oppose the petition on the basis that the divorce would cause grave financial or other hardship.

Associated matters

The court will also wish to consider the issues of custody of and access to the children, the division of matrimonial property and the important question of the provision of maintenance for the spouse and the children.

When the court is satisfied that the marriage has irretrievably broken down a decree *nisi* will usually be awarded. When all the other considerations have been settled, the petitioner can apply for the decree to be made absolute by filling in the appropriate form. This can be done at any time after six weeks from the grant of the decree *nisi*. Of course, the application need not be made. The parties could get back together. The decree *nisi* could be rescinded. It is only when the decree is made absolute that the marriage is dissolved. Only then are the parties free to marry. If they go through a ceremony of marriage before the decree is made absolute it would probably amount to the criminal offence of bigamy, which we have already considered.

MAINTENANCE

This could be applied for by itself, as we have already noted in this chapter, or together with ("ancillary to") proceedings for divorce, nullity or judicial separation.

Totally separately, under the Domestic Proceedings and Magistrates' Courts Act 1978 there is a mutual duty on each party to a marriage to maintain the other and any children of the family.

The court can order periodical payments, secured periodical payments (this is where a capital sum is invested, and can be made available if maintenance payments do not appear). A lump sum can be ordered. It could be paid in instalments. It could be a "spouse order" or a "child order" (a "spouse order" lapses on remarriage). There is no limit to the number of orders the court can make.

In assessing the financial provision that is to be ordered, all the circumstances have to be taken into account. These will include (*see* the Matrimonial Causes Act 1973, s.24): the income, earning capacity and property of each of the marriage partners, and their own needs, obligations and responsibilities, the financial needs of the children (especially education), the standard of living of the family before the provision arose, the income, earning capacity and property of the children, any physical or mental disabilities in either partner or the children, the contribution that was made towards the welfare of the family by each partner, their ages, the duration of the marriage, and so on. Of course, the court must not reduce the means of the respondent below subsistence level. If one partner has agreed to pay a specific amount by way of maintenance, a "consent order" can be made to seal it. If the partners have been apart for three months or more and regular payments have been made, these could be embodied in a "consent order", but such an order would lapse if they re-unite.

When the court makes an order for financial provision it sometimes uses the so-called one-third rule. That is, the gross income of the partners is assessed and one-third becomes payable as maintenance: this was decided in *Wachtel* v. *Wachtel* (1973), and later cases contain detailed variations to deal with special problems.

Where the circumstances of the parties change (sickness, redundancy, pools win) the order can be varied by the court.

If the money is not forthcoming, steps can be taken to enforce the order much in the same way as judgments debts are enforced generally. We considered this at the end of Chapter 6. Probably the most useful method is the attachment of earnings order under which the money is deducted by the employer and paid into court.

If the reason for non-payment is seen as "wilful refusal" or "culpable neglect" the court can actually imprison the recalcitrant party—but only for a maximum of six weeks. This will not discharge any liability to pay, including the arrears to the date of imprisonment. However, unless the court directs otherwise, arrears will not accrue while the jail sentence is being served.

Chapter 16

The Law of Succession

ARE WILLS NECESSARY?

The answer is yes, if you want any direct control over how your property is to be distributed after your death. If there is no will the property will go to others according to the intestacy rules—which means that your awful aunt might get the stereo. Actually, a will can only direct your property if it is left unchallenged by those who depended upon you. A carefully drawn will can minimise tax liability. A solicitor should be instructed when a will is drawn up. It costs between about £8 and £20. The Green Form scheme for legal advice and assistance, which we met in Chapter 8, covers the making of wills.

The most common errors in home-made wills—perhaps written out on one of the forms available from stationers for about 50p—are that not all the property of the person making the will (the testator) is disposed of, and so he dies partly intestate, or gifts are made to witnesses or the spouses of witnesses, who therefore cannot take (although the will remains valid), or the will is altered, and the alterations are not witnessed and are therefore invalid. Further errors include gifts being made without taking into account the effect of a beneficiary dying before the testator, or the testator remarrying, or the testator not taking into account all those who could claim to be dependent upon him, and they later demand that provisions be made from the estate when the will is revealed. A will has no effect until the testator dies.

MAKING A WILL

The testator must be an adult, over 18, unless he is in the forces and on active service. He must know what he is about, as Cockburn CJ said (in *Banks* v. *Goodfellow* (1870)):

As to the testator's capacity, he must, in the language of the law, have a sound and disposing mind and memory. In other words, he ought to be capable of making his will with an understanding of the nature of the business in which he is engaged, a recollection of the property he means to dispose of, of the persons who are the objects of his bounty, and the manner in which it is to be distributed between them. It is not necessary that he should view his will with the eye of a lawyer, and comprehend its provisions in their legal form. It is sufficient if he has such a mind and memory as will enable him to understand the elements of which it is composed, and the disposition of his property in its simple forms.

The formalities required and essential for validity were significantly changed by the Administration of Justice Act 1982 which contains a wide variety of unrelated changes all listed in a single statute. Section 17 repeals and replaces the Wills Act 1837, s.9, and sets the formalities for making a will. The new version of the section largely repeats them, but it is no longer necessary for a will to be signed "at the foot or end thereof".

Now a will is valid if:

(a) it is in writing; and

(b) it is signed by the testator, or by someone else in his presence and by his direction—so that it appears that the testator intended by his signature to give effect to the will; and

(c) this signature is made or acknowledged by the testator in the presence of two or more witnesses present at the same time; and

(d) each witness either attests and signs the will or acknowledges his signature in the presence of the testator (but not necessarily in the presence of any other witness).

It must therefore:

(a) be written down somewhere, usually as a formal document (although in a case called *In the goods of Barnes* (1926), it was written on an egg shell);

(b) be signed; the testator must make a mark, and anything will do as long as it is intended as a signature. The cases include the following examples: a rubber stamp (*Re Jenkins* (1863)), an engraved seal (*In the goods of Emerson* (1882)), and a thumb print (*Re Finn* (1935));

(c) be witnessed by two or more witnesses who are present at the same time as the will is signed (or the signature is acknowledged by the testator). The witnesses need to see the signature, not the will. There is no need for them to read it. Anyone who understands what he is doing and can see can be a witness; there is no age qualification. If a beneficiary is a witness the attestation is valid but the gift fails. Furthermore if there is a gift to the spouse of a witness, that gift fails too (Wills Act 1837, s.15); this restriction on taking a benefit is limited, however, to the minimum number of witnesses, namely two. If there are more than two, and if the third and later witnesses (or their spouses) are beneficiaries then the gifts to them are unaffected (Wills Act 1968, s.1). There must be two witnesses who are not beneficiaries for any further witness who is a beneficiary to keep the gift;

(*d*) be signed by the witnesses who must sign in the presence of the testator. He need not actually watch. It is enough if he could have watched had he wanted to.

Privileged wills

Some wills can be valid without this formal, strict procedure. They are called privileged wills. They arise usually where the testator is in great danger (and therefore feels he ought to make a will quickly). The Wills Act 1837, s.11, says:

> Provided always, that any soldier being in actual military service, or any mariner or seaman being at sea, may dispose of his personal estate as he might have done before the making of this Act.

The privilege was extended to airmen by the Wills (Soldiers and Sailors) Act 1918. A famous example concerned a belligerent airman (*Re Wingham* (1949)), where a RAF trainee pilot put what he referred to as his "will" onto paper—but it was not witnessed, so it would not be accepted as valid unless, as a trainee, he was on active military service. Denning LJ (as he then was) gave a lucid explanation of the privilege:

> The plain meaning of the statutes is that any soldier, sailor or airman is entitled to the privilege, if he is actually serving with the Armed Forces in connexion with military operations which are or have been taking place or are believed to be imminent. It does not, of course, include officers on half-pay or men on the reserve, or the territorials, when not called up for service. They are not actually serving. Nor does it include members of the forces serving in this country, or on routine garrison duty overseas, in time of peace, when military operations are not imminent. They are actually serving, but are not in actual "military" service, because no military operations are afoot. It does, however, include all our men serving—or called up for service—in the wars; and women too, for that matter. It includes not only those actively engaged with the enemy but all who are training to fight him. It also includes those members of the Forces who, under stress of war, both work at their jobs and man the defences, such as the Home Guard. It includes not only the fighting men but also those who serve in the forces, doctors, nurses, chaplains, WRNS, ATS, and so forth. It includes them all, whether they are in the field or in

barracks, in billets or sleeping at home. It includes them although they may be captured by the enemy or interned by neutrals. It includes them not only in time of war but also when war is imminent. After hostilities are ended, it may still include them, as, for instance, when they garrison the countries which we occupy, or when they are engaged in military operations overseas. In all these cases they are plainly "in actual military service". Doubtful cases may arise in peacetime when a soldier is in, or is about to be sent to, a disturbed area or an isolated post, where he may be involved in military operations. As to these cases, all I say is that, in case of doubt, the serving soldier should be given the benefit of the privilege.

So a privileged will can be oral or written; it could lack a signature or witnesses or witnesses' signatures. Provided the testator intended to make a will, it is valid.

CHANGING A WILL

If the will is altered before it is executed (signed and witnessed) then it will be valid in its altered form. Where the alterations are made later, the 1837 Act, s.21, provides that the alteration has no effect unless either "the words or effect of the will before such alteration shall not be apparent", or the alteration is executed in the same manner as the will itself. As to this point of trying to see what the will said before it was altered, magnifying glasses have been used (*In the goods of Ibbetson* (1839)); the paper has even been held up to the light with a crossing out (obliteration) surrounded with brown paper (*Ffinch* v. *Combe* (1894)). Alterations on the will must be formally executed. A later document which amends a will must be formally executed too; it is called a codicil.

REVOKING A WILL

A will can be revoked. There are four ways.

Formal method

By a document which is formally executed in the way the will was executed. In fact most wills begin with a revocation clause:

> I hereby revoke all former wills and testamentary instruments made by me and declare this to be my last will.

There is a doctrine with the extraordinary name of dependant relative revocation. It means, broadly, conditional revocation, so that if you revoke your will formally, intending to make another one, or thinking that the rules of intestacy will meet your requirements, and you do not actually make the new will, or the rules do not have that effect (and if there is enough evidence of all this), then the revocation is not effective. The will survives.

Where a later will is made without a revocation clause then the two are read together, and to the extent (perhaps total) that they conflict the later one prevails.

Informal method

Privileged wills can be made informally, and they can also be revoked informally. They last even if the testator leaves the services (and loses his privileged position to make another one informally—so he could revoke informally but he would have to satisfy the usual requirements to replace it).

By destruction

The Wills Act 1837, s.20, says:

> No will or codicil, or any part thereof, shall be revoked otherwise than as aforesaid, or by another will or codicil, executed in manner hereinbefore required, or by some writing declaring an intention to revoke the same, and executed in the manner in which a will is herein before required to be executed, or by the burning, tearing, or otherwise destroying the same by the testator, or by some person in his presence and by his direction, with the intention of revoking the same.

Here we are concerned with "burning, tearing or otherwise destroying... with the intention of revoking" (called *animus revocandi*). Just writing "cancelled" is not enough. Tearing off a part of the sheet will usually leave the rest effective. If the testator cannot physically manage to destroy the will, it may be done by someone else, but it must be done in his presence and by his direction. The intention is very important. A mentally disordered testator may make a will during a lucid interval but not revoke it when his illness returns. If the will is lost there is a presumption (rebuttable with appropriate evidence) that it was destroyed *animo revocandi*.

By marriage

This is automatic revocation. A marriage revokes a will unless it was made with that particular marriage in mind (none other) and the intention that the marriage should not revoke the will. In *Pilot* v. *Gainfort* (1931), for example, the testator named a woman (Diana

Featherstone Pilot) and referred to her as his wife, although he did not marry her for three years. The will survived the marriage. The law is now to be found in the Wills Act 1837, s.18 (as substituted by the Administration of Justice Act 1982, s.18).

PROVIDING FOR DEPENDANTS

Relatives are usually provided for in the will, if there is one. If not, they are provided for by the operation of the rules of intestacy (of which, details later).

Where either the will or the intestacy rules do not make "reasonable financial provision" for dependants, however, they can apply to the court for such provision out of the estate. This right is provided by the Inheritance (Provision for Family and Dependants) Act 1975. Section 1 (1) of the Act says:

Where after the commencement of this Act a person dies domiciled in England and Wales and is survived by any of the following persons:

(*a*) the wife or husband of the deceased;

(*b*) a former wife or former husband of the deceased who has not remarried;

(*c*) a child of the deceased;

(*d*) any person (not being a child of the deceased) who, in the case of any marriage to which the deceased was at any time a party, was treated by the deceased as a child of the family in relation to that marriage;

(*e*) any person (not being a person included in the foregoing paragraphs of this subsection) who immediately before the death of the deceased was being maintained, either wholly or partly, by the deceased;

that person may apply to the court for an order under section 2 of this Act on the ground that the disposition of the deceased's estate effected by his will or the law relating to intestacy, or the combination of his will and that law, is not such as to make reasonable financial provision for the applicant.

Incidentally, under s.1(1)(*c*) any child of the deceased can apply. Age, marital status and financial dependence upon the deceased are all irrelevant to the right to apply, but an adult who is quite able to support himself is not likely to sway the sympathy of the court much.

This "reasonable financial provision" means maintenance—enough to live on, unless the applicant happens to be the surviving spouse, where it means more than just maintenance. The court could, for example, add a lump sum.

The powers of the court are wide and flexible. It may order periodical payments from the estate, lump sums, transfers of property, settlement of property so that the applicant can take the benefit, use of estate property so as to acquire other property for the applicant, and so on. It can make an interim payment too, if the applicant is in sufficient need. It can even order someone else to pay the applicant, if it appears that property was distributed before the death with the aim of avoiding making appropriate provision.

Naturally, the court will take into account all the surrounding circumstances. According to the Inheritance (Provision for Family and Dependants) Act 1975, s.3, these will include: the applicant's financial needs (including education) and his current and potential assets, the needs and resources of other applicants, those of the beneficiaries under the will, the obligations and responsibilities that the deceased owed the applicant, other applicants and the beneficiaries, the size of the net estate, the mental and physical health of the applicants and beneficiaries, and so on. If the applicant is a surviving or former spouse (not remarried) then the age, the length of the marriage and the contribution of the applicant to the deceased's family will be relevant. A rough guide might be the financial provision that would have been ordered had the spouse and deceased been parted by divorce rather than the "grim reaper".

If the applicant falls within s.1(1)(d), the court will consider whether the deceased had taken on the obligation to maintain, on what basis, for how long, whether he knew the child was not his and anyone else's responsibilities towards that child. Similar considerations of assumed responsibility will be taken into account with applicants within s.1(1)(e).

There is a time limit of six months from the date that the estate is made the responsibility of personal representatives within which applications should be made. (There is a power to entertain late applications.)

The application should be made to the county court if the net estate does not exceed £30,000. Otherwise, the High Court should be approached.

INTESTACY

If the deceased left no will, he died intestate. If he left a will but failed to dispose of all his property, he died partially intestate. There are intestacy rules which provide for the distribution of property not disposed of by will.

The intestacy rules apply to the distribution of the net estate; that is, the property which is left when the personal representatives (administrators in this case) have paid the funeral, testamentary and administration expenses, together with all the deceased's debts and liabilities.

The rules speak of "spouses" and "issue". A "spouse" is a husband or wife, not someone with whom the deceased was living (cohabitor, "common law wife") nor a divorced husband or wife. "Issue" includes children, grandchildren and subsequent direct descendants. Adopted children and illegitimate children are included, as is a child conceived but not born when the deceased died.

The distribution of the net estate depends upon who the deceased leaves behind him. There are five main situations:

(*a*) *Surviving spouse and issue.* Here the spouse takes all the personal chattels absolutely (furniture, jewellery, books, pictures, etc., but nothing which is used for business purposes), plus £40,000 plus a life interest in half of whatever is left. Usually this means the interest on half of the remaining money. The issue take the other half of the remainder of the net estate (i.e. after the personal chattels and the lump sum have been subtracted).

(*b*) *Surviving spouse but no issue.* The spouse takes the personal chattels plus £85,000 plus half of the balance absolutely. The other half goes to the parents of the deceased (not step-parents or mother/father-in-law). If no parents are alive then any brothers and sisters take the other half of the balance, if they are at least 18 (or 16 or 17 and married). If no brothers or sisters are alive but their issue survive and are 18 (or 16 or 17 and married) then they take the other half.

(*c*) *Surviving spouse but no issue nor any of the relatives mentioned in (b) above.* The spouse takes the whole net estate absolutely.

(*d*) *No surviving spouse but surviving issue.* Here the net estate passes entirely to the relatives who survive. This is the order of preference—once a survivor is found nobody lower in the order takes anything. The order is this: first, parents, then brothers and sisters, then brothers and sisters "of the half-blood", then grandparents, then uncles and aunts, then uncles and aunts "of the half-blood". If nobody here survives, the property is called *bona vacantia*—and will go to the Crown.

Where anyone under 18 receives property upon the operation of the intestacy rules, it is held in trust for them until they reach that age.

PERSONAL REPRESENTATIVES

When someone dies the people who clear up his affairs are called his personal representatives (PRs). Their precise duties depend upon the circumstances they have been left in. There are, broadly, four stages in dealing with the estate: obtaining the right to act as PRs, assessing the value of the estate, obtaining probate and distributing the estate.

Obtaining the right to act

PRs will be either executors or administrators. An executor is named as such in the will. If there is no will, or if there is one but nobody is named (or someone is named but refuses to act) then the PRs will be administrators.

Executors apply for a grant of probate. Administrators apply for a grant of letters of administration—any will which dealt with only part of the estate is submitted for probate. Sometimes a will fails to mention executors; in this case a grant of letters of administration "with the will annexed" is sought. An administrator can be anyone who has an interest in the estate. It is usually the next of kin, perhaps with professional help from a solicitor.

A grant of probate or letters of administration is not necessary for a "small estate"—where the deceased left just cash and personal effects and the relatives are agreed on how they should be shared, and/or the deceased left only a small amount in certain saving schemes (like building societies, or National Savings) where they may get the money out without undue formality. However there is no obligation to pay out in the absence of probate or letters of administration. Any assets which are jointly owned by the deceased and his surviving spouse (house, furniture, video cassette recorder) will pass automatically to the spouse.

If you hear that somebody is applying for probate or letters of administration whom you believe might not be suitable then you can object to the grant by informing the local probate office. You will then be given the chance to voice your objections before any grant will be made. Such an application is called a *caveat*.

An application for probate or letters of administration is made at the Personal Application Department of the local Probate Registry. Forms have to be filled in, details obtained. A death certificate is necessary, and a copy of the will, if there is one.

Assessing the estate

The PRs need to search out details of the deceased's assets in order to fill in the forms supplied by the registry—savings certificates, premium bonds, stocks and shares, unit trusts, accounts at the bank, building society, Trustee Savings Bank, insurance policies, household and personal goods, money due from an employer, occupational pension, land and other similar property, business interests, unclaimed social security benefits, tax rebates and all the debts owed to the deceased.

As against these assets, the PRs must calculate the deceased's liabilities. These might include: rates owed, rent or mortgage payments, telephone bills, fuel bills, credit card accounts, overdrafts, hire purchase or other credit deals, personal loans, income tax. The PRs should check for other debts by advertising for unknown creditors in the local paper and in the *London Gazette*. Usually two months must be allowed for creditors to come forward. There are other debts which must be taken into account: the funeral expenses (but not a tombstone), probate fees, capital transfer tax (if any), any solicitor's bill and other expenses incurred by the PRs (phone calls, travel to the Probate Registry, etc.).

If the debts exceed the assets there is a prescribed order for payment. The funeral testamentary and administration expenses are paid first, then the order of priority is similar to that used when the assets of a bankrupt are divided.

Obtaining probate

With all the details to hand the forms can be filled in. These, the death certificate and the will (where there is one) are taken or sent to the local Probate Registry. Naturally, there are fees to pay—for personal application and probate fees. Documents are prepared by the Registry called the Executor's Oath and the Inland Revenue Affidavit. They must be signed by the PRs. They also swear on oath.

The grant of probate is sent on later, with a copy of the will. The original is kept at Somerset House in London.

Distributing the estate

Now that the PRs have the grant they can call in all the deceased's assets. They will open an account into which to pour them. They then drain off enough to pay the deceased's debts and liabilities.

Then the estate can be distributed in accordance with either the will or the intestacy rules, as appropriate. The PRs should then prepare a full account of what was done with the assets of the estate, the deceased's debts, the funeral expenses, the administration expenses, the legacies given out (with signed receipts from the lucky recipients). All the papers should be filed away safely—for twelve years.

Chapter 17

The Worker and the Law

THE CONTRACT OF EMPLOYMENT

This contract provides the basis of the rights, duties and liabilities of the parties to it—the employer and employee. There is still considerable freedom of contract. The framework remains that of common law contract rules (as was seen in Chapter 13), but Parliament intervenes increasingly in the labour law field, and there are certain statutes which will require our attention. The contract we are to examine is that for a full time employee rather than an independent contractor (we considered this very important distinction in Chapter 12 when dealing with vicarious liability).

There are no formal requirements for the contract of employment. It could be oral, by conduct, partly written or entirely written. The written contract is to be preferred because its provisions will be readily available for reference. A term that is written in the contract cannot be negatived by evidence of what happens in practice. Furthermore, it will be easier to bring about changes if the contract is written (e.g. reduce overtime, restrict the choice of holiday dates, introduce a shift system).

Whether the contract is written, partly written or just oral, the employee has a right to written particulars of it, and this within the first 13 weeks of his employment. The details required in the written statement are provided by one of the major statutes in this field, the Employment Protection (Consolidation) Act 1978:

1(1) Not later than thirteen weeks after the beginning of an employee's period of employment with an employer, the employer shall give to the employee a written statement in accordance with the following provisions of this section.
(2) An employer shall in a statement under this section—
(a) identify the parties;
(b) specify the date when the employment began;
(c) state whether any employment with a previous employer

counts as part of the employee's continuous period of employment, and, if so, specify the date when the continuous period of employment began.

(3) A statement under this section shall contain the following particulars of the terms of employment as at a specified date not more than one week before the statement is given, that is to say—

(*a*) the scale or rate of remuneration, or the method of calculating remuneration,

(*b*) the intervals at which remuneration is paid (that is, whether weekly or monthly or by some other period),

(*c*) any terms and conditions relating to hours of work (including any terms and conditions relating to normal working hours),

(*d*) any terms and conditions relating to—

(i) entitlement to holidays, including public holidays, and holiday pay (the particulars given being sufficient to enable the employee's entitlement, including any entitlement to accrued holiday pay on the termination of employment, to be precisely calculated),

(ii) incapacity for work due to sickness or injury, including any provisions for sick pay,

(iii) pensions and pension schemes;

(*e*) the length of notice which the employee is obliged to give and entitled to receive to determine his contract of employment; and

(*f*) the title of the job which the employee is employed to do . . .

(4) Subject to subsection (5) every statement given to an employee under this section shall include a note—

(*a*) specifying any disciplinary rules applicable to the employee or referring to a document which is reasonably accessible to the employee and which specifies such rules;

(*b*) specifying, by description or otherwise—

(i) a person to whom the employee can apply if he is dissatisfied with any disciplinary decision relating to him; and

(ii) a person to whom the employee can apply for the purpose of seeking redress of any grievance relating to his employment, and the manner in which any such applications should be made;

(*c*) where there are further steps consequent upon any such application, explaining those steps or referring to a document which is reasonably accessible to the employee and which explains them.

The idea behind all these requirements, and others which require employers to produce written documents (itemised pay statements, reasons for dismissal, safety policy) is simply to let the employee know where he stands.

Most of the details required in the written particulars would be included if the contract were written. Things like lay-offs, guaranteed weeks, pension schemes, holidays, sick pay, and so on, are not prescribed by law. They are to be agreed. The employer must say what they are, but the law makes no particular demands about time and/or money at times like these. They might well have been settled by negotiation with a trade union—but they should appear in the written contracts made with individuals. Where a statute does make a detailed requirement, such as a minimum period of notice, it can always be varied upwards in the contract, by agreement.

The contract will also contain implied terms. We noted how terms can be implied into contracts in Chapter 13. The courts might imply a term in a particular case if it is needed for the contract to make business sense. In *Stevenson* v. *Teeside Bridge and Engineering* (1971) a construction engineer's contract was held to contain an implied term that he would move his place of work as each job was completed. Alternatively, the term could be implied because of the effect of a particular rule of law, statute or common law. We will examine this effect from each side in turn, as implied duties.

THE DUTIES OF THE EMPLOYER

There are a number of duties required of employers both at common law and under a variety of statutes.

To treat the employee with respect

Until 1875 it was a criminal offence for a servant not to do his work. There were about 10,000 prosecutions brought every year. The courts now regard oppressive conduct as amounting to constructive dismissal. This means that the employer is in breach of the contract. The employee is free to leave and sue for damages. In *Cox* v. *Phillips Industries Ltd.* (1976), the plaintiff was moved from one job to another. He was not given any precise responsibilities or duties. He became depressed and eventually fell ill. The employers were held to have acted in breach of contract in their neglect of him, and he was awarded £500 damages.

Furthermore, the employer must not unlawfully discriminate amongst his employees on the grounds of sex or race. The Race Relations Act 1976 and the Sex Discrimination Act 1975 are written in the same way: first the idea of discrimination is explained, then that discrimination which is unlawful is stated, then the exceptions, when an employer is able to discriminate. For example, the 1976 Act states:

1(1) A person discriminates against another in any circumstances relevant for the purposes of any provision of this Act if—

(*a*) on racial grounds he treats that other less favourably than he treats or would treat other persons; or

(*b*) he applies to that other a requirement or condition which he applies or would apply equally to persons not of the same racial group as that other but—

(i) which is such that the proportion of persons of the same racial group as that other who can comply with it is considerably smaller than the proportion of persons not of that racial group who can comply with it; and

(ii) which he cannot show to be justifiable irrespective of the colour, race, nationality, or ethnic or national origins of the person to whom it is applied; and

(iii) which is to the detriment of that other because he cannot comply with it.

Later on the same Act says:

3(1) In this Act, unless the context otherwise requires—"racial grounds" means any of the following grounds, namely colour, race, nationality or ethnic or national origins;

"racial group" means any group of persons defined by reference to colour, race, nationality or ethnic or national origins, and references to a person's racial group refer to any racial group into which he falls.

4(1) It is unlawful for a person, in relation to employment by him at an establishment in Great Britain, to discriminate against another—

(*a*) in the arrangements he makes for the purpose of determining who should be offered that employment; or

(*b*) in the terms on which he offers him that employment; or

(*c*) by refusing or deliberately omitting to offer him that employment.

(2) It is unlawful for a person, in the case of a person employed by him at an establishment in Great Britain, to discriminate against that employee—

(*a*) in the terms of employment which he affords him; or

(*b*) in the way he affords him access to opportunities for promotion, transfer or training, or to any other benefits, facilities or services, or by refusing or deliberately omitting to afford him access to them; or

(*c*) by dismissing him, or subjecting him to any other detriment.

5(1) In relation to racial discrimination—

(*a*) section 4(1) (*a*) or (*c*) does not apply to any employment where being of a particular racial group is a genuine occupational qualification for the job; and

(*b*) section 4(2)(*b*) does not apply to opportunities for promotion or transfer to, or training for, such employment.

(2) Being of a particular racial group is a genuine occupational qualification for a job only where—

(*a*) the job involves participation in a dramatic performance or other entertainment in a capacity for which a person of that racial group is required for reasons of authenticity; or

(*b*) the job involves participation as an artist's or photographic model in the production of a work of art, visual image or sequence of visual images for which a person of that racial group is required for reasons of authenticity; or

(*c*) the job involves working in a place where food or drink is (for payment or not) provided to and consumed by members of the public or a section of the public in a particular setting for which, in that job, a person of that racial group is required for reasons of authenticity; or

(*d*) the holder of the job provides persons of that racial group with personal services promoting their welfare, and those services can most effectively be provided by a person of that racial group.

It is worth adding that this "acceptable" discrimination becomes unlawful if the employer already has enough employees within the racial group in question, whom it would be reasonable to put on those duties.

A complainant can take his grievance to an industrial tribunal (*see* Chapter 4). There are other employees who are entitled to "respect" in specific ways because of statutory additions to the general common law requirement of respect: e.g. the disabled, trade union members, pregnant women, rehabilitated offenders.

However, this duty of respect does not extend to an obligation to provide references. There is no duty to provide a reference; indeed, it may be ill advised to do so in some cases. If it is derogatory a defamation action might follow. If it is full of undeserved praise then the party relying on it could sue (we considered these tortious aspects in Chapter 12). Furthermore, if it recommends an ex-employee who was dismissed as incapable, then an industrial tribunal might well find the dismissal to have been unfair.

To provide work

This is not usually implied into the contract of employment, although it seems that the duty may exist where not working loses the employee his reputation (e.g. an actor, as in *Clayton* v. *Oliver* (1930)), or, if not working reduces income because it deprives the employee of his commission or piece work rate or shift allowance. It probably also exists in apprenticeship contracts.

To remunerate

This is a basic common law duty on the employer. Failure to pay wages amounts to breach of contract. Action can be taken in the courts in the usual way.

If the industry in which the unpaid employee works has a Wages Council the employee can ask the wages inspector from the Department of Employment to act on his behalf and recover the payments due.

The failure also probably amounts to a constructive dismissal of the employee (unless it is very temporary—a brief cash-flow problem, perhaps). The lack of work does not cancel the duty to pay, provided that the employee is ready and willing to work. However, some contracts provide for the lack of work on a guaranteed payments scheme. After having worked for an employer for four weeks, the Employment Protection (Consolidation) Act 1978 ss.12–18, give the employee a right to guarantee payments. However, they will not be paid in certain prescribed circumstances; these include where the lack of work is due to a trade dispute, or if he refuses suitable alternative work.

There are other statutory rights to payment. They include circumstances where the employee is suspended on certain specified medical grounds (1978 Act, s.19), or where the employee is entitled to maternity pay (1978 Act, s.33), or performing duties as a trade union official, or a safety representative, or where the employee has been declared redundant and is seeking work elsewhere, or is pregnant and attending for ante-natal care. Time off is allowed (with pay if the contract provides for it) for public duties such as serving as a magistrate, a school governor or on a jury.

To indemnify

This includes refunding employees expenses, incurred within the course of employment together with answering to third parties for the authorised activities of employees.

To take reasonable care of the employee

In *Smith* v. *Austin Lifts* (1959), Lord Simmonds stressed that the law should avoid "any tendency to treat the relationship between employer and skilled workman as equivalent to that of nurse and imbecile child". However, there is both a common law and a statutory duty upon the employer to take reasonable care. The injured employee would bring his action, not for breach of contract (despite the fact that the courts are quite prepared to regard these duties as part of the contract) but either for the tort of negligence or for breach of statutory duty, or both together.

The Employers' Liability (Compulsory Insurance) Act 1969 requires that employers insure against employees' claims for personal injuries.

There is a general duty at common law upon an employer to take care of his employees. This is a personal duty owed to employees individually. So whilst a general safety policy may be acceptable generally, if there are individuals at risk because, perhaps, they cannot read warning signs, or they cannot read the language in which the signs are written, or they are disabled, then a greater duty is owed towards these individuals. *Paris* v. *Stepney Borough Council* (1951) (which we considered in Chapter 12) concerned a one-eyed workman who ought to have been particularly carefully looked after.

This general duty of care can be regarded from three aspects:

(*a*) *A duty to provide safe equipment and premises.* The case of *Davie* v. *New Merton Board Mills* (1959) involved a workman who was injured by a broken tool which his employer had provided. The employer escaped liability because he had used a reputable supplier. This will no longer suffice. The Employers Liability (Defective Equipment) Act 1969 imposes strict liability for the quality of equipment provided.

(*b*) *A duty to provide competent staff.* So, in *Hudson* v. *Ridge* (1957), a persistent practical joker who injured a colleague ought to have been sacked. The employer was held liable for the injury.

(*c*) *A duty to provide a safe system of work.* There have been cases like *Wilsons and Clyde Coal* v. *English* (1938), where the lack of adequate safety precautions in a coal mine was held to amount to a breach of the duty owed by the employer. However, as we saw in Chapter 12, the problem involved in bringing an action in negligence is that the plaintiff must prove fault. Thus, if the nature of the employee's injury was not reasonably foreseeable then this action will fail. Nevertheless, many of the statutory duties are strict; that is, there is no need to prove fault, just failure to meet the statutory requirements. For example, in the Factories Act 1961, s.14(1), it says

Every dangerous part of any machinery . . . shall be securely fenced unless it is in such a position or of such construction as to be as safe to every person employed or working on the premises as it would be if securely fenced.

Salmond LJ said, in *Millard* v. *Sierck Tubes* (1969), where an employee's hand was dragged into an inadequately fenced drill:

> Foreseeability of injury is of very considerable importance when the issue is: "was there a dangerous part of machinery?" Once the two questions: "is the machine dangerous?" and "is there a duty to fence it?" have been answered in the affirmative, foreseeability is no longer relevant. If it is then proved that the plaintiff has suffered an injury by some part of his body coming into contact with the machinery and that this would not have occurred if the defendants had complied with their clear statutory duty, the defendants are liable.

We have met the Unfair Contract Terms Act 1977 on several occasions already. We have noted that it provides in s.2(1):

> A person cannot by reference to any contract term or to a notice given to persons generally or to particular persons exclude or restrict his liability for death or personal injury resulting from negligence.

This obviously applies to warning notices in the workplace and exclusion clauses in contracts of employment.

Under the Health and Safety Etc. at Work Act 1974

The 1974 Act creates no civil law liability. Breach of the requirements of the Act and regulations made under it amounts to a criminal offence. The Act contains these provisions in s.2:

> 2(1) It shall be the duty of every employer to ensure, so far as is reasonably practicable, the health, safety and welfare at work of all his employees.
> (2) Without prejudice to the generality of the above, the matters to which that duty extends include in particular:
> (a) the provision and maintenance of plant and systems of work that are, so far as is reasonably practicable, safe and without risks to health;
> (b) arrangements for ensuring, so far as is reasonably practicable, safety and absence of risks to health in connection with the use, handling, storage and transport of articles and substances;
> (c) the provision of such information, instructions, training and supervision as is necessary to ensure, so far as is reasonably practicable, the health and safety at work of his employees;
> (d) so far as is reasonably practicable as regards any place of

work under the employer's control, the maintenance of it in a condition that is safe and without risks to health and the provision and maintenance of means of access to and egress from it that are safe and without such risks;

(e) the provision and maintenance of a working environment for his employees that is, so far as is reasonably practicable, safe, without risks to health and adequate as regards facilities and arrangements for their welfare at work.

(3) Except in such cases as may be prescribed, it shall be the duty of every employer to prepare and as often as may be appropriate revise a written statement of this general policy with respect to the health and safety at work of his employees and the organisation and arrangements for the time being in force for carrying out that policy and to bring the statement and any revision of it to the notice of all his employees.

THE DUTIES OF THE EMPLOYEE

This is the other side of the coin. The law imposes a variety of duties on the employee. They all stem, directly or indirectly, from the nature of the relationship which exists between the employer and employee. It is a relationship of trust. It follows that persistent lateness, theft of the employer's property, go-slows, sit-ins, and similar behaviour are breaches of this trust and consequently breaches of contract. It is part of the contract of employment that the employee will work carefully and competently in the interests of his employer. The employee must obey all lawful orders (i.e. those which are within the contract and also within the general law). An obvious breach of duty is the employee taking bribes. He must not allow personal interests to conflict with those of his employer. Any "secret profit" taken will amount to a breach of contract and can be claimed by the employer. Any activity which might affect the employer's business in a serious way (e.g. setting up in competition) amounts to breach of contract. Any betrayal of trade or company secrets also is breach of contract.

TERMINATING THE CONTRACT OF EMPLOYMENT

Notice

The contract might be for a fixed term, or it might have been made to achieve a particular task. After the time or the task it ends. Most contracts of employment are open-ended, with provision for termination by notice. The length of the notice is contractual, the parties agree on a suitable period. The Employment Protection (Consolidation) Act 1978 provides:

49(1) The notice required to be given by an employer to terminate the contract of employment of a person who has been continuously employed for four weeks or more—

(a) shall be not less than one week's notice if his period of continuous employment is less than two years;

(b) shall be not less than one week's notice for each year of continuous employment if his period of continuous employment is two years or more but less than twelve years; and

(c) shall be not less than twelve weeks' notice if his period of continuous employment is twelve years or more.

(2) The notice required to be given by an employee who has been continuously employed for four weeks or more to terminate his contract of employment shall be not less than one week.

Thus, if the contract sets a period of notice for either side, that will be enforced. If there is no period stated, then reasonable notice must be given. However, the notice cannot fall below the statutory minimum unless the right to dismiss without notice exists. This is not common. In any event, the fear of being taken to an industrial tribunal might well induce the employer to give the proper notice. Nevertheless, the traditional grounds for this summary dismissal are:

(a) wilful, serious, repeated disobedience;

(b) infidelity (selling trade secrets, perhaps);

(c) incompetence (e.g. lies about qualifications);

(d) gross negligence;

(e) strikes;

(f) other serious misconduct.

The employee should give a week's notice—unless the employer's conduct is seriously in breach of the contract. This is called, as we have already noted, constructive dismissal.

Redundancy

Where an employee is dismissed, and the dismissal is, as the 1978 Act puts it (in s.81(2)):

attributable wholly or mainly to—

(a) the fact that his employer has ceased, or intends to cease, to carry on the business for the purposes of which the employee was employed by him, or has ceased, or intends to cease, to carry on that business in the place where the employee was so employed, or

(b) the fact that the requirements of that business, for employees to carry out work of a particular kind, or for employees to carry out work of a particular kind in the place where he was so employed, have ceased or diminished or are expected to cease or diminish.

—then the employee, provided he has worked for the employer for the qualifying period, will be paid a redundancy payment.

There are a number of employees who are excluded, and employees who refuse to take on suitable alternative work add themselves to that number.

Unfair dismissal

If the employee has worked for the qualifying period, then despite having been given proper notice he may still be able to claim, before an industrial tribunal, that he has been unfairly dismissed. This is not breach of contract. It is an argument created by statute and based on the idea that an employer must always act reasonably in dismissing employees, despite the position in contract law. So if the employer had less than the full facts, if the situation did not warrant dismissal, if there were mitigating circumstances, if the disciplinary rules and procedures had not been made clear to the employee, if the employee had been given no chance to put his side of the case, if he had been given no opportunity to mend his ways nor been given specific warnings (e.g. one oral and two written warnings), if the actual manner of dismissal was not in accordance with agreed procedures or relevant codes of practice, then the tribunal might well regard the employer's action as having been unreasonable in the particular circumstances of the case in question.

There are certain dismissals which are always unfair. These include dismissal because of union membership, following improper selection for redundancy or on the grounds of pregnancy, where the employee is still ready, willing and able to work.

Where the industrial tribunal is satisfied that the dismissal was unfair it has the power to order re-engagement, reinstatement or a substantial sum by way of compensation.

Chapter 18

Social Security

THE RANGE OF BENEFITS

There are about 60 different cash benefits available to those who qualify. In this chapter we will glance at them—and the necessary qualifications.

There are three main types of benefit:

(*a*) *National Insurance benefits.* These are the benefits where the qualifications are based upon your contribution record into the National Insurance scheme. There is no means test. You do not have to be poor, but your record of contributions must be adequate.

(*b*) *Means tested benefits.* In these cases you do have to be poor, but there is no need for a National Insurance contribution record.

(*c*) *Non-contributory benefits.* In these cases special qualifications apply—your National Insurance contribution record is not relevant, you do not need to be poor, and they are not means-tested benefits.

These three types of benefit are not representative of the situations in which a claim might be necessary. It is easier to see the overall system (which is actually a jumbled assortment of benefits, not a system) by examining the different circumstances which might give rise to a claim. The actual figures for qualification for benefit, and of the benefit (if granted) vary from time to time. So, to avoid disappointment, they will be omitted. The current figures are readily available from agencies such as the Citizens' Advice Bureaux.

BENEFITS FOR THOSE SHORT OF MONEY

Family income supplement

People who are in work but getting very low wages can claim FIS. The work must be full-time, but the self-employed can claim. This is a means-tested benefit.

Supplementary Benefit

Those who are 16 or over and out of work might qualify. It is means-tested. Small amounts of savings and part-time work might not disqualify the claimant; it depends upon the difference between what you need (there are set scales) and what income you have coming in.

Free NHS Dental Treatment

Those on FIS or SB (i.e. supplementary benefit) qualify. So do pregnant women, women who have had a baby within the last year, children under 16 and those under 19, and in full-time education. These people have an automatic right to free treatment. Others might qualify too, if they satisfy the means test.

Free NHS glasses

Those on FIS or SB qualify. So do children under 16, and those under 19, and in full-time education. These qualify automatically. Other claimants are means-tested.

Free NHS prescriptions

Those on FIS or SB qualify. So do pregnant women, children under 16, those over pension age (60 for women, 65 for men), women who have had a baby within the last year, war pensioners (those injured in war obtain free prescriptions to treat the injury—their "pensioned disablement"), and those who suffer from particular, specified medical conditions. Other claimants are means-tested.

Prescriptions can also be bought with "season tickets". They are available to anyone who does not qualify for free prescriptions. Those who need treatment often can save money this way.

Free milk and vitamins

Families on FIS or SB, which contain pregnant women or nursing mothers or children under five qualify. So do some disabled children and other children in day nurseries. Other claimants are means-tested.

Rent rebates and allowances, and rate rebates

Rent rebates are allowed to council tenants, rent allowances to those of private landlords. Tenants of either kind and owner occupiers can claim rate debates. These are all means-tested.

BENEFITS FOR PREGNANT WOMEN

Maternity grant

This is non-contributory. Pregnant women and those who have just had children qualify. They should apply between 14 weeks before expected delivery and 12 weeks afterwards.

Maternity allowance

This is a National Insurance benefit. The pregnant woman's contribution record must be adequate in the relevant tax year. Her husband's contributions do not count.

Maternity leave with pay

This is non-contributory. Broadly speaking, the claimant must have worked for the same employer for at least two years. The employer pays and reclaims from the Department of Employment.

Free prescriptions, dental treatment, milk and vitamins

These have already been discussed.

BENEFITS FOR THOSE WITH CHILDREN

Child Benefit

A parent or anyone else who is responsible for a child under 16, or a young person who is under 19 and in full time education will qualify. This is a non-contributory benefit.

Guardian's allowance

Those who take an orphan child into the family and qualify for child benefit will qualify here. It is a non-contributory benefit.

Free prescriptions, dental treatment and glasses

Those under 16, and those under 19, in full time education qualify, as we noted above.

BENEFITS FOR SINGLE PARENTS

One parent benefit

Parents who are widowed, divorced, separated or single qualify. This is a non-contributory benefit.

Child's special allowance

This is designed to replace the maintenance payment for the single parent whose former spouse has died. It cannot be claimed with one parent allowance, nor if the claimant remarries. It is a National

Insurance benefit, paid on the contribution record of the late husband.

Other benefits

Special consideration is given to single parents in the calculations for tax liability, FIS and SB.

THOSE AT SCHOOL OR COLLEGE

Free school meals

Children of families on FIS or SB qualify automatically. Some local authorities provide free school meals to others. These are means-tested.

Free school milk, fares to school, educational maintenance allowances, school uniform and clothing grants

Many (but not all) local authorities are prepared to provide these benefits. Where provided they are means-tested.

Student grants and allowances

Mandatory grants are the grants which local authorities must provide for some courses (usually at degree level or the equivalent). Other courses may attract discretionary grants. Over and above a minimal award, where they are provided these benefits are means-tested.

NHS charges

Free glasses, dental treatment and prescriptions are provided for those under 16 (*see* above).

PEOPLE OUT OF WORK

Unemployment benefit

This is a National Insurance benefit, based on your contribution record. The claimant must be fit and able to work. It is paid only for a year.

Redundancy payments

Claimants qualify by working for the same employer for at least two years. Nobody over retirement age qualifies. This is a non-contributory benefit. The employer pays, and reclaims part of it from the Redundancy Fund.

Job search and employment transfer allowances, employment rehabilitation, youth training allowances.

These are all non-contributory benefits paid to those who are having difficulties as a result of unemployment.

THOSE WHO ARE ILL

Sickness benefit

This is a National Insurance benefit, paid on the contribution record. Those who are not working through illness qualify.

Invalidity benefit

This is a longer-term version of sickness benefit. It is paid after six months of sickness benefit. It is also a National Insurance benefit.

Non-contributory invalidity pension

This is a smaller amount of money, paid to those whose National Insurance contribution records is inadequate for invalidity benefit.

Patients' travelling expenses to hospital

Those on FIS or SB and war pensioners qualify. Other claimants are means-tested.

PEOPLE INJURED AT WORK

Industrial injury benefit

This is a non-contributory benefit paid to those injured at work.

Industrial Disablement benefit

This is a longer-term version of industrial injury benefit. There are various allowances added to a basic figure. They vary with the extent of the disablement. This is a non-contributory benefit.

Industrial Death Benefit

This is a non-contributory benefit paid to the widow and dependants of those who die from an accident at work, or industrial disease.

THOSE INJURED IN WAR OR IN THE ARMED FORCES

War Disablement pension

This is a non-contributory benefit paid to those in the armed forces who were injured in the First World War or after September 1939.

War Widows or dependants' pension

Generally non-contributory, this is paid to the dependants of those who die in the armed forces.

THOSE INJURED BY CRIME

The Criminal Injuries Compensation Board makes payments to those injured in crimes of violence, or their dependants if death results. It is non-contributory.

THE DISABLED AND HANDICAPPED

Attendance allowance

Non-contributory, this is paid to those who need a lot of looking after.

Invalid care allowance

Also non-contributory, this is paid to those who are not at work because they are looking after someone who is disabled or handicapped.

Mobility allowance

Non-contributory, this is paid to those who are unable to walk.

Assistance with fares to work

Non-contributory, this is paid to those who are unable to use public transport.

Other benefits

Further to the above, there is an enormous range of benefits, services and facilities available to the disabled and handicapped. Some are non-contributory, others means-tested. They extend over housing, meals, holidays, laundry and a wealth of other needs and activities.

THOSE WHO ARE RETIRED

Retirement pension

A National Insurance benefit, this is paid to men over 65 and women over 60. There is no need to give up work completely but if a substantial amount of work is done the DHSS may review the case and can withdraw the pension. The benefit depends upon one's contribution record. Widows are paid on their late husbands' records. Married women can qualify on their husbands' records, although the money will be less. There is an extra pension paid to those over 80, and a supplementary pension to those who have less income than needs calculated (on the same sort of basis as SB).

THOSE IN NEED OF LEGAL AID, OR ADVICE AND ASSISTANCE

We examined this in Chapter 8.

WIDOWS

Widow's allowance

This is a National Insurance benefit paid to widows of men who were receiving a retirement pension. The late husband's record is used.

Widowed mother's allowance

Another National Insurance benefit, this is calculated on the late husband's record, and paid to widows with children under 19.

Widow's pension

Calculated as above, and paid to widows, over 40, often when widowed mother's allowance ends because the children reach 19.

Death grant

A National Insurance benefit (currently £30), paid usually to the next of kin. It is designed to go towards funeral expenses. It does, but not far.

Widow's retirement pension

This is similar to widow's pension but has fewer restrictions about the widow's earnings.

Chapter 19

Aspects of Housing Law

A CLASSIFICATION OF PROPERTY

Property in English law can be divided up (classified) firstly into real property (sometimes called reality) and personal property (or personalty). Real property is freehold land. To be in "freehold possession of land" is an approximation in terminology to owning it in such a way as not to have any hindrances upon you in selling it, or leaving it in your will.

All property that is not realty is personal property. This can be subdivided into chattels real and chattels personal. Chattels real is the term given to leasehold land; chattels personal comprise all other personal property.

To complete the classification, chattels personal can be subdivided. The subdivision is into choses in action and choses in possession. A chose in action is a proprietary interest which can be protected only by taking legal action. This property has no physical existence and yet it might have considerable value. Copyright, for example, has no physical existence (it is incorporeal property), and the only way a copyright owner can assert his ownership formally is by taking legal action. Such property is, therefore, referred to as a chose (or thing) in action. Any other property (e.g. books, pens, bikes) is a "chose in possession". Ownership can be asserted without the need to take legal action. You can go and take it back.

In this chapter we are concerned with the types of property interest in land: freehold and leasehold (real property and chattels real). Freeholders and leaseholders are commonly referred to as "owners". The intended meaning may be clear, but the term is technically slightly inaccurate. A freehold estate falls short of the outright ownership possible with choses in possession. A leasehold interest is a temporary thing—a week to 999 years! A 99-year lease is quite common on a flat for instance. After it has run its time, and perhaps been assigned (this being loosely referred to as sold) to several people during that time, the interest will revert to the freeholder (or his successor) who granted the lease in the first place.

THE DUTIES OF FREEHOLDERS AND LEASEHOLDERS

The law requires many things of those who own their own homes.

Local rates

The local authority raises some of its money by levying rates from householders occupying properties within its area. Valuation of houses, flats, etc. is done by a department of the Inland Revenue. This is called the rateable value. The money payable is calculated by multiplying this rateable value by a figure which is set yearly by the local authority. For example, a house in Cornwall may happen to be situated in the area governed by Caradon District Council. The local "rate in £" is 116.00p for 1982–83; the rateable value of the house is 169. The liability is £196.04.

Water rates

These are paid to the local water board—in the Cornish house it will be due to South West Water. The liability is calculated in the same way. Their "rate in £" is multiplied by the rateable value.

Duties towards others

These vary. Some lie within the law of tort such as nuisance and occupiers' liability (*see* Chapter 12). Others are contained within byelaws or the general law—pets, fences, trees, bonfires, parties, trees, nude sunbathing, the use of hosepipes in reasonable summer weather and a host of others.

AFFORDING TO BE A FREEHOLDER OR LEASEHOLDER: MORTGAGES

A mortgage of land is an arrangement whereby a borrower (called the mortgagor) supplies security for money advanced to him by a lender (called the mortgagee). This mortgage gives the mortgagee rights over the land used as security whereby he can recover his money if the mortgagor fails to repay him. These rights include taking possession, sale of the property, the appointment of a receiver (who may use the land so as to make a profit which can be paid to the mortgagee), and foreclosure (termination of the arrangement). In practice, mortgagees are reluctant to exercise these rights. They will usually agree to reduce the required repayment and extend the terms (i.e. the number of years the arrangement is to continue).

  A prospective purchaser usually approaches a building society for the money. If it is prepared to deal with him he will have a choice of arrangements, usually between a repayment mortgage and an endowment mortgage. The better choice depends upon the applicant's individual circumstances. The difference is, broadly, that the repayment mortgage is paid off over a period of years (perhaps 25) in such a way that each payment comprises an element of interest (which attracts tax relief) and an element of the capital sum lent. On the other hand, an endowment mortgage involves two payments: the one to the building society is just to meet the interest liability; the other is to an insurance company, under a policy which matures when the capital sum falls due (again, perhaps in 25 years), and when it matures it yields at least that capital sum. Usually the opportunity to extend the term can be given only to payments on a repayment mortgage.

RENTING A HOUSE

In 1900 85 per cent of homes were rented; in 1980 the figure had fallen to 45 per cent, but it was still a substantial proportion. Of rented homes, about 33 per cent are in the private sector (i.e. involving private landlords), and 67 per cent are in the public sector (mostly local authority landlords, although there is a significant number of housing associations in operation too).

The relationship between a landlord and tenant will be governed by statute. The most important Acts are the Rent Act 1977 and the Housing Act 1980, but there are many others. Indeed the law of landlord and tenant is a minefield of statute and case law. We can look at only the broadest of outlines here.

RENTING IN THE PRIVATE SECTOR

The Rent Act 1977 is designed to protect the tenant. He can be removed only in specified circumstances. The rent he must pay can be fixed by a rent officer.

In order to obtain the full protection of the 1977 Act the contract must be for a letting and not a licence (which is an arrangement which grants permission to occupy rather than setting up a landlord and tenant relationship). The letting must comprise a separate dwelling of living rooms—away from the landlord. Very expensive lettings are also outside the full protection of the 1977 Act.

Other rental agreements carry protection, but to a lesser extent. These include:

(*a*) rental agreements which include payment for services—beyond just a place to stay,

(*b*) licence agreements which include exclusive possession—away from the landlord (the courts will examine such agreements closely to see whether they are in fact lettings and not licences, and therefore fully protected);

(*c*) agreements involving a resident landlord.

There are further agreements which fall outside the protection of the 1977 Act altogether. These include:

(a) licences that do not incorporate exclusive possession;

(b) holiday lettings (although the courts are vigilant in spotting inner city "holiday camps");

(c) student lettings;

(d) board and lodging (not necessarily "digs" but including at least one meal);

(e) public houses—where the "tenant" lives "over the shop".

THE PRIVATE SECTOR: THE CONTENT OF PROTECTION

(a) *Security of tenure.* A tenancy for a fixed period ends at the period's expiry. Any other tenancy ends with notice to quit. A weekly or monthly tenancy requires 28 days' notice in writing, set to expire on a day when rent is due.

When the tenancy ends the tenant might leave the premises. He might not. He can be removed only by a court order for possession. (He is now a statutory tenant.) The landlord applies to the county court for possession. The court must grant it if the landlord wants the property back for his own occupation, or for that of a relative who previously lived there, or if the property is a "retirement" home and the landlord has retired.

In most cases the tenant must be told in advance that these events might happen. This is especially true with the relatively new idea of a shorthold tenancy (which was created by the Housing Act 1980), where property can be let for up to five years, and be available thereafter to the landlord, provided the prescribed notice has been issued.

Apart from these mandatory grounds, there are also grounds upon which the court has the discretion to grant an order for possession: that the landlord wants the property and can provide a suitable alternative, that the tenant has been a nuisance to other tenants, or has fallen into arrears with his rent, or has neglected the property, or sublet it, or has himself given notice and now refuses to go where the landlord has arranged to re-let, and (in certain circumstances) where the landlord requires the property for his own occupation or that of his close family. An order, if made on discretionary grounds, can always be suspended.

With the agreements carrying less than full protection (but not those without protection), the county court can, since the Housing Act 1980, postpone a possession order for three months. Such a rental agreement in called a restricted contract. Still the landlord must go to court for a possession order before eviction can be carried out.

(b) *Fixing the rent*. Where the protection is full either party can approach the rent officer and have a fair rent fixed despite what might have been agreed between them when the tenancy began. The rent is fixed for at least two years. It is registered. The register should be inspected to check levels nearby before making applications. From the rent officer's decision there lies an appeal route to a rent assessment committee.

A tenancy carrying some but not full protection (i.e. a restricted tenancy, created under the Housing Act 1980), can still have the rent fixed, but there is no automatic security of tenure.

(c) *Harrassment*. Harrassment of a tenant by his landlord is a criminal offence under the Criminal Law Act 1977 and the Protection from Eviction Act 1977. It might consist of cutting off services (gas, electricity, water), excessive noise or just general aggravation.

THE PUBLIC SECTOR: THE CONTENT OF PROTECTION

About 30 per cent of all homes are rented from the public sector (67 per cent of rented homes). Despite an increasing number of local authority tenants who are seeking to exercise their right to buy, the vast majority still choose to pay rent.

Such tenancies fall outside the protection of the Rent Act 1977, but the Housing Act 1980 has provided something very similar for them: they are called secure tenancies. The local authority will need a possession order before it can evict. Broadly, the same grounds apply as in the private sector (considered above). There are additional grounds. These include:

(a) where the tenant lied his way into council accommodation (e.g. by giving false statements about his circumstances);

(b) where the tenant was housed in a particular unit as a temporary measure (e.g. pending repairs elsewhere);

(c) where the house is overcrowded or underpopulated (the council must achieve a proper use of its property);

(d) where the unit is "specialised" (e.g. for the elderly or handicapped) and the tenant is not qualified; or

(e) where the local authority proposes to demolish the site, and has found a suitable alternative.

In every case the court must be satisfied that the grant of the possession order would be reasonable in the circumstances.

An important difference between public and private sector housing is that the rent officer has no power to decide the level of local authority rents. It is a matter of politics and economics.

Appendix I

Bibliography

Armour, L. A. J. and Samuel, G. H., *Cases in Tort*, Macdonald & Evans

Baker, C. D., *Tort*, Sweet and Maxwell

Baker, N. L., *The Law and the Individual*, Macdonald & Evans

Cross, R. and Jones, P. A., *Introduction to Criminal Law*, Butterworths

Curzon, L. B., *Criminal Law*, Macdonald & Evans

Curzon, L. B., *The Law of Succession*, Macdonald & Evans

Davies, F. R., *Contract*, Sweet and Maxwell

Denham, P., *A Modern Introduction to Law*, Arnold

Diamond, A. L. and Borrie, G., *The Consumer Society and the Law*, Penguin

Dobson, A. P., *Sale of Goods and Consumer Credit*, Sweet and Maxwell

Drake, C. D., *Labour Law*, Sweet and Maxwell

Grant, Judge B. and Levin, J., *Family Law*, Sweet and Maxwell

Hamblin, C. and Wright, F. B., *Introduction to Commercial Law*, Sweet and Maxwell

James, P. S., *Introduction to English Law*, Butterworths

Leder, M. J., *Consumer Law*, Macdonald & Evans

Lister, R., *Welfare Benefits*, Sweet and Maxwell

Major, W. T., *The Law of Contract*, Macdonald & Evans

Major, W. T., *Cases in Contract Law*, Macdonald & Evans

Pace, P. J., *Family Law*, Macdonald & Evans

Price, J. P., *The English Legal System*, Macdonald & Evans

Redmond, P. W. D., *General Principles of English Law*, Macdonald & Evans

Seago, P., *Criminal Law*, Sweet and Maxwell

Tyas, J. G. M., *Law of Torts*, Sweet and Maxwell

Wright, M. and Carr, C. J., *Labour Law*, Macdonald & Evans

Appendix II

Examination Technique

The aim of this chapter is to point out some of the common mistakes, in the author's experience, made by examination candidates and to try to provide some useful hints on how to approach the examination day and the examination paper itself. All too often candidates' efforts are spoilt by paying insufficient attention to considering how to tackle the examination paper. They have obviously spent a considerable time learning the material outlined in the syllabus but then let themselves down by not presenting the information in the correct manner. It is hoped that this chapter will help to avoid such disappointment.

1. Common Mistakes made by Examination Candidates

(*a*) Failing to answer the right number of questions, either because they answer too few or too many questions. They do not check the rubric and so, e.g. fail to complete the required number of questions from different sections of the examination paper.

(*b*) Writing the conclusion to an answer before the main part of the answer has been completed. Or writing too short an answer so that no part or particular point is properly developed.

(*c*) Answering the question they hoped would be set rather than the question the examiner has actually set. It may be the right topic but the answer bears little relation to required approach for the particular question.

(*d*) Running out of time so that the paper is not completed or the last answer is very short and incomplete.

(*e*) Too much time spent on the first answer, sometimes over half the examination time has obviously been spent on this answer to the detriment of the other answers.

(*f*) Writing the question out which is a complete waste of time and earns no marks.

(*g*) Writing social or general answers rather than answers that have a mainly legal content. The social or general context in which the law operates can be dealt with but should not dominate the answer.

(*h*) Poor handwriting so the examiner cannot even read the answers.

2. The Examination itself

(*a*) Make sure you arrive in good time for the examination. If you arrive late and hot and bothered you have got to waste time settling yourself down.

(*b*) Make sure you have everything you need, pens, pencils, rulers, etc. If you need a lucky mascot take it with you!

(*c*) Make sure the desk is comfortable, i.e. not too close to a radiator or in hot sun. If it isn't level do something about it before the examination begins.

(*d*) Make sure you have the correct answer book and that you have filled in your name, examination number and centre number correctly.

(*e*) Read through the examination paper carefully and slowly at least twice before you decide which questions you are going to answer. Check the number of questions you need to answer.

(*f*) Select the questions you are going to answer and tick them on the examination paper. If you don't think you can do the required number at first, don't panic, just choose as your last question one you at least recognise and can attempt to answer.

(*g*) Use the first few minutes of the examination to make brief notes on each of the questions you are going to answer. This will be helpful to you if you are running short of time at the end of the examination and trying to write and think quickly. It should help you to get at least the main points of an answer down in a reasonable order.

(*h*) Plan how much time you can spend on each answer and try to keep to your time schedule. It is usual to spend about twenty-five minutes writing-time per answer. Be careful not to spend too much time writing your first answer.

(*i*) Write the answer to the question you know best first to calm your nerves and give yourself confidence. Make sure you answer the right number of questions by ticking them again on the paper as you complete them. If you are short of time write your last answer in a coherent note form making sure you bring out the important points relevant to the question.

(*j*) If possible leave yourself enough time at the end of the examination to check your answers quickly. If you have made notes and jottings that you don't want marked, cross them out.

(*k*) If you have used any supplementary answer sheets make sure your name is on them, number them and tie them into the main answer book.

3. Answering Examination Questions

(a) The most important principle is read the question carefully, each word is important. This should set you off on the right track.

(b) Note the plaintiff and defendant, who is to be advised about what? Identify the areas of law involved and pick out the main facts. Make a note of any likely defences and remedies.

(c) Try to write a short introductory paragraph. For example, a *short* history of the law in that area or something that sets the law in context.

(d) Structure your answer so that you work through in a logical way. State the principle of law involved at each step and try to support it either by reference to a decided case or an example. Make sure, e.g. that you have stated and explained all the elements of a tort or defined the appropriate area of contract or criminal law.

(e) Try to use accurate legal phrases and expressions, e.g.: discharge of duty: rescission of contract: void and voidable contracts.

(f) Use cases to illustrate your points of legal principle whenever possible. Try to put the name of the case, but if you cannot remember it don't worry. Indicate the case you mean by a *brief* reference to the facts. Concentrate on the legal principle involved in the case.

(g) The argument of the legal points involved is more important than the answer itself. Don't worry if you don't know the answer but make sure you have argued the point from both the plaintiff's and the defendant's point of view.

(h) Try to write a short concluding paragraph in which you sum up the main points and attempt to answer the question which you were being asked.

(i) Practise trying to write answers in the allotted time under examination conditions prior to the examination itself. Timing answers is vitally important and will help to improve your confidence as well as your technique. Try and obtain past examination papers to help you become familiar with the type of questions you are likely to face in the real examination.

(j) Try to be as up to date as possible in the law you include in your answers, e.g. watch the newspapers for new and relevant statutes and cases.

4. Answering Problem Questions

(a) The aim of a problem question is to encourage the candidate to explain the law and then apply it to a set of hypothetical facts to provide a legal answer.

(b) All too often candidates do not use the problem questions to display their knowledge, leave too much unsaid or do not expand a point. You should assume the examiner knows nothing of the topic.

(*c*) Method and reasoning are more important than the answer or conclusion reached. It is therefore very important to explain fully the steps by which the answer was arrived at.

(*d*) It is necessary to identify the relevant areas of law involved and the plaintiff and defendant. If the rubric states you are to advise a particular party then you will need to advise "for" and "against". Or the rubric may say "discuss" when you will need to be certain you have identified all potential plaintiffs and defendants and possible areas of law involved.

(*e*) Make sure you explain all legal points fully, e.g. the elements of a tort, or what constitutes acceptance in contract. Definitions are useful starting points. Try to support each element or legal point with authority, i.e. an appropriate case that illustrates the point involved.

(*f*) When quoting a case make sure it is identified either by names or facts and then concentrate on explaining the principle on which the decision is based.

(*g*) The most important part of an answer to a problem question is the application of the law to the hypothetical facts. Don't leave this until the end of the answer; try to apply the law to the appropriate facts as each stage of the answer is completed. For example if the problem is to do with negligence use the facts to illustrate; (i) why a duty of care is owed; (ii) what constitutes the breach; and (iii) what constitutes the damage that results.

(*h*) Work your way systematically and logically through the facts. For example don't refer to defences until you have established the appropriate tort or breach of contract. Make sure you are not advising someone to sue who has suffered no damage.

(*i*) If possible, try to round off your answer by drawing a conclusion.

5. Answering Essay Questions

(*a*) Read the essay question very carefully and make sure you know what you are being asked to discuss.

(*b*) Use an opening paragraph or introduction to set the scene for the approach you are going to take in the answer. It may be useful at this stage to identify the areas of law you will be referring to.

(*c*) Try to develop your answer logically. If possible deal with a point completely before moving on to the next; it always looks "bitty" if you have to come back to a point later in the answer.

(*d*) Use appropriate case law to illustrate the legal points you are making in your answer in exactly the same way as with the answers to problem questions.

(*e*) Try to include a quotation or comment from reading you have done which relates to the answer. If possible include your own comments and thoughts on the matter under discussion. Try to give as balanced a view as possible of any arguments which may be relevant. If there have been recent developments or new statutory provisions which may not be in the text books but which you know about, include a reference to them.

(*f*) Keep checking that your answer is relevant, that you are not straying off the point. Try not to lapse into "social" answers or too much generality; remember it is a law examination paper and requires legal answers.

(*g*) Before you write the conclusion read the question again. Use the last paragraph to bring together your main arguments and to emphasise the points which you feel answer the question most satisfactorily. Make sure you finish the answer in such a way that the examiner is in no doubt that you understand the question and have really tried to discuss the issues and come to an appropriate conclusion.

(*h*) If it is an essay question that requires a large amount of factual information make sure that you include as much explanation and detail as possible on each of the areas that you discuss. If you can remember most of the areas that you feel are relevant then try to state them in the introduction to the answer so that you create a check-list or structure for the rest of the answer. Cases, examples or section numbers of statutes will again be very important and should be used whenever possible.

Specimen Test Questions

1. What are the chief direct and indirect sources of English law? (OLE 1983)

2. Explain how the European Court of Human Rights is linked into the ordinary legal system. (OLE 1983)

3. How is the Court of Appeal organised? Discuss the work and powers of its divisions. (OLE 1983)

4. John has been convicted in the magistrates' court and wishes to appeal against sentence and conviction. Consider the avenues and grounds for appeal which may be open to him. (OLE 1983)

5. What acts are covered by "trespass to the person"? What defences may be open to someone who has been sued for this tort? (OLE 1983)

6. On what facts is it possible to obtain a divorce? Describe shortly the ways in which the courts handle the financial problems which arise on divorce. (OLE 1983)

7. (a) Bertram agrees to purchase Charles' house for £75,000. He signs a contract to this effect; but Charles, who has now received a higher offer, changes his mind and refuses to sign the contract. Discuss.

(b) David owes Eric £500, to be paid on 1st March 1983. On that date David has only £350. Eric agrees to accept this sum together with a bicycle worth £50 "in final settlement". Later Eric regrets this and claims another £100. Discuss. (OLE 1983)

8. Explain the rules governing the doctrine of consideration in the law of contract. (OLE 1983)

9. (a) What are the main requirements of a valid will?

(b) In what circumstances may disappointed dependants of the testator apply to the court for redress?

10. "The 'duty of care' is an essential element of the tort of negligence." Discuss. (OLE 1983)

11. (a) What is meant by delegated legislation? Illustrate your answer with examples.

(b) Why do we need delegated legislation?

(c) What controls are exercised by Parliament over delegated legislation? (AEB 1983)

12. (a) Describe the development of tribunals and explain two of the main areas of their work.

(b) What advantages do tribunals have over the courts? (AEB 1983)

13. Anna and John have just left school and are about to start work.

(a) Explain to John the legal rights of employees;

(b) Explain to Anna the legislation which particularly affects the employment of women. (AEB 1983)

14. Discuss the capacity of a minor in relation to (a) entering into a contract; (b) making a will; (c) getting married; and (d) committing a crime. (AEB 1983)

15. (a) Emily saw a sewing machine advertised by "Sewrite" in a newspaper for £100. She sent off a cheque for £100, but a week later received a letter and her cheque back. The letter said "Sorry, incorrect price stated in the advertisement, we can offer you the sewing machine for £125." Advise Emily.

(b) On 1st June Emily decided to buy the sewing machine and wrote to "Sewrite" accepting their offer to sell the sewing machine at £125. She posted her letter that evening. On 2nd June "Sewrite" wrote to Emily revoking their offer to sell; the letter arrived on 3rd June.

(i) Advise Emily.

(ii) How, if at all, would your advice be different if "Sewrite" had stated in their letter that acceptance must be by telephone? (AEB 1983)

16. Mark takes Peter's electric guitar without his permission. Mark feels certain Peter will not mind his using the guitar, but later Mark sells it for a very good price. When Peter is told of the sale he becomes extremely angry and punches Mark, breaking his nose.

(a) Explain whether any criminal offences has been committed by: (i) Mark; (ii) Peter.

(b) If criminal offences have been committed which courts would deal with them and why? (AEB 1983)

17. While eating a slice of bread from a loaf baked by Better Bakeries, Mary bites on a stone. The stone breaks her tooth and she suffers severe toothache for several days.

(a) In what tort can Mary sue and for what remedy?

(b) How can Mary obtain the help of a solicitor and financial help to bring her action?

(c) Describe any criminal action that can be taken against Better Bakeries. (AEB 1983)

18. Martin and Helen have been married for six years and have three children. After endless arguments, Helen leaves Martin, taking the three children with her to live with her mother.

(*a*) Explain to Helen:

    (i) whether she will be entitled to a divorce;

    (ii) the financial provision that could be made for her and the children if a divorce were granted.

(*b*) If Martin and Helen eventually obtain a decree nisi of divorce what would be the legal consequences if Martin married Rita? (AEB 1983)

19. The XYZ Union plan to march through London to the House of Commons. The march is to be followed by a rally in Hyde Park to demonstrate against the government. The rally is to be addressed by Harold, a well-known political agitator.

(*a*) Advise (i) the Union members, (ii) Harold on aspects of the law which you feel are appropriate.

Harold is eventually arrested for breach of the peace at the rally.

(*b*) Explain: (i) whether Harold is likely to obtain bail; (ii) the court which would deal with his offence. (AEB 1983)

20. (*a*) Explain the criminal jurisdiction of the magistrates' courts.

(*b*) Do you agree with the comment that magistrates are "judicial beasts of burden"? (AEB 1983)

21. (*a*) Explain what is meant by the ratio decidendi and obiter dicta of a case.

(*b*) Must the court always follow an apparently binding precedent? (AEB 1983)

22. (*a*) Explain how a civil case differs from a criminal case.

(*b*) Describe the procedure involved in bringing a civil case in *either* (i) the High Court; *or* (ii) the county court. (AEB 1983)

23. (*a*) What is "unemployment benefit" and when may it be claimed?

(*b*) What is "supplementary benefit" and when may it be claimed? (AEB 1983)

Index

292 INDEX

(1) Explain how civil case differs from Criminal Case

(2) How is the court of Appeal organised Discuss the work and power of it in civil cases.